Writing the Wrongs

Writing
the
Wrongs

*Eva Valesh and the
Rise of Labor Journalism*

ELIZABETH FAUE

CORNELL UNIVERSITY PRESS

Ithaca & London

First published 2002 by Cornell University Press

Printed in the United States of America

Library of Congress Cataloging-in-Publication Data
Faue, Elizabeth.
    Writing the wrongs : Eva Valesh and the rise of labor journalism/
Elizabeth Faue.
    p. cm.
    Includes bibliographical references and index.
    ISBN 0-8014-3461-0 (alk. paper)
    1. Valesh, Eva McDonald, 1866–1956. 2. Journalists—United States—
Biography. 3. Labor journalism—United States. I. Title.
    PN4874.V25 F38 2002
    070'.92331'092—dc21   2001006507

Cornell University Press strives to use environmentally responsible suppliers and materials to the fullest extent possible in the publishing of its books. Such materials include vegetable-based, low-VOC inks and acid-free papers that are recycled, totally chlorine-free, or partly composed of nonwood fibers. For further information, visit our website at www.cornellpress.cornell.edu.

Cloth printing   10 9 8 7 6 5 4 3 2 1

in memory of my mother, Yvonne,
whose gift of memory I share,
and for my father, Vincent,
who taught me about John Wayne movies,
war stories, and the difference between the two

Contents

ILLUSTRATIONS

Acknowledgments

Writing the life story of labor journalist Eva McDonald Valesh has required some patience not only on my part but also on the part of friends and family who, as often as not, were favored by or subjected to my telling tales. Along the way, I drew on their insight, affection, camaraderie, and intellect.

I have to begin by thanking Dolores (Lordie) Lautman, Eva's granddaughter, who shared her genealogical research and some of the photographs that grace this volume. It is rare to find someone so generous with her labor of love—and rarer still to find that someone has personal knowledge of one's own subject. I would be remiss if I did not also name the late Alice Finnerty, Eva's other granddaughter, and the late Mary Valesh, Eva's daughter-in-law. The record would be impoverished but for their generosity.

Among archivists, I want to thank the Minnesota Historical Society, especially for the labor and wisdom of Dallas Lindgren, Debbie Miller, and Ann Regan. I also thank John Stinson of the Manuscripts Division of the New York Public Library, James Huston at the Library of Congress, Kenneth Craven at the Humanities Research Center Library at the University of Texas, Peter Albert of the George Meany Archives, Kathryn Harris of the Illinois State Historical Society, Brian Shovers of the Montana Historical Society, John Brewer of the Capitol Historical Society, and Mary Marshall Clark of the Columbia University Oral History Research Office. During the final stages of any writing project, the encouragement and insight of editors become crucial to an author's well-being. I here need thank above all Sheri Englund and Candace Akins of Cornell University Press for making the book better and the process more enjoyable.

During the writing of this book, Paula Baker was an important source of both historical insight and scholarly criticism. We shared many evenings on the phone struggling over the meaning of politics and the quirkiness of life. Even when we disagreed, which was often enough, Paula helped to clarify things. Her chronic skepticism, on the other hand, frequently muddled the issues again. Long my advisor in life as well as in history, Sara Evans contributed to the project design, read the penultimate draft with critical insight, and wrote numerous letters of recommendation—a little-acknowledged but essential labor of academic life. Bonnie Smith helped make my time in New Brunswick much more pleasant with her company and plenty of cappuccino. Her critical ability, sense of humor, and appreciation for the art of writing enhanced the book as well. Since 1991, Nancy Isenberg and I have had a long conversation about feminist theory, women's history, and movies. She generously read my manuscript, and the final version is better for her insights. Susan Geiger and Janet Spector, feminist scholars with whom I studied, have continued to influence my work and my life by their example; I teach, write, and think better for knowing them.

Jeff Kolnick's letters kept me amused and consoled for more than a few years while I worked on this book. My reading of late-nineteenth-century politics owes much to our discussions. Mary Jo Maynes shared her own excellent study of working-class autobiography and helped me make crucial connections. Peter Rachleff read the penultimate draft and gave new insights into the questions I raised. Angel Kwolek-Folland read chapters of the book at a critical point. As usual, she taught me something about my own work. Mary Blewett sent me her work on the New Bedford strike and copies of relevant coverage from the New Bedford textile strike scrapbooks at Harvard.

Over the past few years, I have shared stories of Eva Valesh's life with seminars at the Hall Center for Economic and Social History of the University of Kansas; the Institute for Research on Women at Rutgers University; the Max Planck Institute for History in Göttingen; the University of Minnesota; the University of Vienna; Southwest State University in Marshall, Minnesota; and the University of Wisconsin–Eau Claire. Birgitta Bader-Zaar, Kathy Brown, John Bukowczyk, John Campbell, Claudia Clark, David Cohen, Laura Downs, Ann Gordon, Lynn Gordon, Rob Gordon, Rich Greenwald, Mike Hanagan, Chris Johnson, Sue Juster, Steve Leikin, Alf Luedtke, Genny McBride, Karen Mason, Melissa Meyer, Jane Pederson, Cathy Preston, Eve Rosenhaft, Tony Rosenthal, Ann Schofield, Ed Tebbenhoff, Mary Ellen Waller, Lynn Weiner, and Rob Weir were among those who contributed to my thinking. When I was in Vienna, Birgitta and her husband, Kamel Bader, were wonderful hosts as well, showing me their city's splendor and acting more like kin than friends.

At a crucial stage in my career, the Susan B. Anthony Center of the University of Rochester granted me a postdoctoral fellowship. The College of Liberal Arts; the College of Urban, Labor, and Metropolitan Affairs; and the Office for Research and Sponsored Programs of Wayne State University granted me research fellowships and sabbatical leave time. In 1995–96, the university awarded me a Career Development Chair, which gave me a year to work on the book. The Rutgers Center for Historical Analysis and the Institute for Research on Women at Rutgers University provided me with office space, computer support, access to photocopying, and intellectual community—a crucial ingredient in any scholarly endeavor.

Jackie Byars and her husband, Carl Michel, have been my family in Detroit/Ann Arbor, and it was Jackie who took me out for my first celebration on finishing the manuscript. My friend Jeanne Drewes talked about my sources as only a preservation librarian could and provided good company on many occasions. Her husband, Mike Moore, aided me in computer work, among other things. Gretchen Elsner-Sommer steered me through a summer of doldrums on long walks when we shared our writing and research; Ellie Feller encouraged me through the last summer of writing. Paula Nemes and her husband, Steve Rasmussen, are thanked for their hospitality; I will never forget the sweet dark bread, the pumpkin preserves, the goat burgers, or the mulberries. Natalie Reciputi rendered her support via letters but always managed to cook up humor, intellectual provocation, and stellar suppers during my visits.

My sister Annamarie gave me wonderful suggestions and concrete help at several crucial junctures but especially when she spent some time in the State Historical Society of Wisconsin. I still owe her a box of Christmas cigars; the trouble is that Frank Valesh's King of Trails hasn't been produced since 1920. Joe Turrini, Kimberly Welch, Patricia Singleton, Marion Romig, Emily Roche, and my niece Rebecca Jones traced down some research leads. My brother Jeffrey nagged me incessantly to write another book; finishing this one is no guarantee that he will stop. When I first moved to New Jersey, he and his wife, Alice, gave me a place to live and, during my two Rutgers years, provided mail service, rides to the airport, and home-cooked meals.

In closing, I want to acknowledge my family, including my other siblings (Deborah, Greg, and Charlotte) and the nieces and nephews who were born since the last dedication and who may not forgive me if I do not publish their names: Beatrice, Rory, Nora, Breanna, and Isaiah. I have personal thanks to give to those fictive kin who mentored me: Francine Moskowitz, Elisabeth Borders, and Doreen Savage.

This book is dedicated to my parents. The most important gifts they gave me and my siblings were love and the encouragement to labor honestly and to the best of one's abilities, to refuse the distractions of competition and peer pressure, and to know the difference between fantasy and reality—a knowledge even my flirtation with theory hasn't destroyed. Their lessons were not about theory but practice. This book is my thanks.

Writing the Wrongs

TRUTH-TELLING FICTIONS

Reconstructing a Life in Labor

In the summer of 1891, Eva McDonald Valesh was a popular lecturer on the Populist circuit and notable enough nationally to be asked to contribute a sketch of her life to *American Women*, a volume edited by Frances Willard and Mary Livermore, important social thinkers of the time. Valesh suggested that friend and fellow reporter Albert Dollenmayer be her "historian." After outlining the simple facts of her life, McDonald wrote to him that she had kept it short, "because you are well enough acquainted with my history to clothe the skeleton properly."[1] Every biographer is faced with the same problem of clothing the facts, according to the fashion of the time or in the current style. It is made more difficult when the subject of the biography was literate and provided her own literary interpretation. Eva Valesh was a professional writer who told conscious tales of how she, a working-class daughter, achieved success in the labor and newspaper worlds. As she proudly declared, she knew enough to give the press a good story. Like Valesh's writings, this book is a set of stories in which she figures as a major but not the sole character. I intend to tell both her story and the intertwined tale of class and gender politics that her story reveals.

I begin my stories of Valesh by noting three facts: She dyed her hair red into her eighties, smoked black twisted cigars, and wore green silk pajamas. In her attire and manner of living, she was an exceptional woman. An American-born daughter of a respectable Protestant Scots-Irish working-class family, she acquired an education and a profession—journalism—by accident and calculation. Under the penname Eva Gay, she set out to investigate the truth about working girls and their worlds. Responses to her first column ranged from appreciative editorials to charges that she was directly responsible for labor strife.

Speaking and writing for labor and Populist causes, McDonald soon became a nationally recognized figure. Soon after, she married Frank Valesh, a Czech immigrant trade unionist, who seemed bound for similar success.[2] For more than twenty years, in her role as journalist and organizer, Valesh illuminated the stage of labor and reform politics, where public debates and newspapers were forms of entertainment and persuasion was the key political skill. Her facility with language and her talent as an orator placed her in the ranks of middle-class professionals and gave her a career that was beyond the marriage, motherhood, and traditional women's work available at the time.

Filled with spectacular performances, provocative writing, and personal conflicts, Valesh's life captured the attention of many of her contemporaries. According to numerous admirers, she was "bright," "piquant," and even "comet-like." To her enemies, though, she was "a ravenous mouse," "a pest," and someone who "used her tongue in a lively way and taken all the benefit that her sex controls when in argument with a man."[3] In our time, she might be called a character. By 1952, when she was interviewed by the Columbia University Oral History Project, Valesh was a forgotten figure whose memories of the labor movement remained unmemorialized; but she is not so easily dismissed.

In this book I explore the career of Eva Valesh, one of labor's foremost publicists of the Progressive Era. In doing so, I incorporate two different genres of historical writing—the study of an individual life with an analysis of the changing character of American labor reform.[4] Reconstructing the life story of Valesh, who left behind few personal papers and a fragmentary public record, requires us to take this route. Given her broad range of political affiliation and achievement, however, we are able to see connections that often escape those who focus on only one institution or event. Seeing how Valesh was able to construct a public identity as the daughter of a workingman and as a workingwoman herself allows us to see how class as well as gender identities were reconstructed at the end of the nineteenth century. The expanding labor movement in the Gilded Age created a working-class public sphere and a broad-based effort to educate the public on the labor question. At the same time, labor reformers responded to shifts in work and political life. The massive influx of immigrants into the labor force and the struggle of women to break into male-dominated trades gave rise to a working-class politics of manhood that was anti-immigrant and pro–family wage, and the emergence of elite women as a political force recast the dynamics of difference among women to encourage cross-class alliances. All of these projects revealed the developing relationship between publicity—essentially, making the politics of class visible—and the political work of labor reform.

As a result, Valesh's career—from printer to trade unionist, Populist, labor reformer, and later club woman—depended on her ability and experience in mainstream and reform journalism. Our understanding of the past usually separates the history of journalism from that of labor and reform politics. And yet, as we shall see, Valesh's work as a newspaper reporter was crucial to her social mobility and political viability. Not only the careers of publicists like Valesh but also the evolution of political reporting and mainstream political culture hinged on investigative journalism and "truth-telling."[5] Oriented toward middle- and working-class audiences, Progressive Era newspapers came to feature prominently narratives of class, the impoverishment of the masses, the dangers of industry, the moral threat of working-class struggles, and the precarious perch of labor in a corporate political environment. As an authentic working-class voice, Eva Valesh had insights and political skills that were sought by newspapers and reformers alike.

At the same time, by virtue of her work, her social ascent, and her gender, Valesh's life exhibited the social tensions facing those who crossed the class divide and the contradictions of women who entered male-dominated trades and professions. In journalism, labor activism, and politics—even in her youth as an apprentice typesetter—Valesh made her living in the public world of men. She was trained as a skilled worker at a time when most workingwomen were domestic servants or semi-skilled factory laborers. She was politically active before women were much engaged in public life. She ran for political office even though women had only the right to vote in school elections. She was a prominent labor organizer at a time when labor unions routinely restricted women's access to unionized work. She took up journalism in the age of the reporter, a figure defined in the minds of the public and of editors as male. In her private life, Valesh was equally unconventional. At a time when women were supposed to be monogamous, married, and maternal, she bordered on the disreputable. She always knew, though, where the boundaries were and kept just within them. For all of her unconventionality, Valesh sought validation in the spheres in which she worked, proving to be a popular speaker and writer and leaving her own quiet mark on history.

Political Culture and Social Mobility

For individuals such as Eva McDonald Valesh, the age of labor and working-class publicity offered both new political identities as entrepreneurs and translators of class politics and new paths of social mobility. Reporting and public speaking became her means of social and political ascent. That social mobility also transformed her class identity. Like other working-class children of the time, Valesh found that her acquisition of and facility with language, public speaking and writing, and organizational skills were essential to her social and political success. Yet public speaking and writing are unstable venues for both social and individual mobility. Dependent on networks of patronage and communities of readers, cultural workers often assumed the role of chameleon, go-between, and mediator between the classes. For a woman of working-class origin, the role of public speaker and writer required mental and physical transformation. Education in political economy was only one aspect; being at home in politics, journalism, or the women's club movement meant taking on new dress, speech, and manners. Early on in her career, as she took up work defined as male, Valesh sought male mentors but often found masculine critics. Taking up cultural work meant abandoning, to some extent, working-class identity, in the service of a movement that was working class and masculine. Straddling class and gender identities, Valesh made her living at the interstices of political and cultural life.

The labor reform movement of the late nineteenth century provided an arena for both collective struggle and individual striving. Politics and reform were professions, just as they had been since the early days of the republic. Efforts to reshape industrializing America in ways that protected the weak, fostered and rewarded the productive, and ensured honest and equal government were also ways of consecrating one's life and making a living. For working-class men in particular, the call to organize workers, teach political economy, write or speak to the working-class public, or run for office on a workingmen's ticket provided social mobility.[6] What these men had in common was class identity and experience, which gave some the ability to mediate between the classes. Born into poor or working-class families, they apprenticed in a skilled trade such as printing, cigar-making, mining, or carpentry and worked their way into politics through their facility at translating the experience of workers into political and economic demands. Labor activism and class politics thus served as a means to individual mobility.

A classic example of these contradictions was Samuel Gompers, later president of the American Federation of Labor and Valesh's mentor and colleague. Born in mid-nineteenth-century London to Dutch-Jewish immigrants, Gompers migrated with his family at age fourteen to the United States. His early background shaped his career and outlook on class. As he was to recall, "Like all children of the poor, we early found our way to the city streets—the place where we began contacts and struggles with our fellows. It is the education of the street that produces that early shrewdness in the children of those who 'have not' that often leaves ineradicable differences between them and the children of those who have." Gompers learned the cigar-making trade early in his youth. As a young worker, he took up the study of political economy in the cigar shop. His trade had earned him "the mind freedom that accompanied skill as a craftsman." Married and a father before his eighteenth birthday, he quickly made his ascent in the trade. Like many of his peers in trade union-ism, his life story was marked by his origins in poverty and a dread fear of un-employment. By the end of his life, however, he politicked with wealthy cor-porate leaders in the National Civic Federation and even advised presidents on the conditions and needs of labor.[7] His dizzying social ascent from city streets to presidential advisor illustrates how labor activists could traverse the class spectrum in the course of their careers.

While many working-class advocates sacrificed money and time to the cause, so that the poor salary and deprived circumstances of some leaders be-came legendary, more often—having left the factory floor, the mine, or the craft shop—labor leaders were both of and outside their class. Upwardly mo-bile, the working-class children who became the leaders and cultural workers of the labor movement had trans-class identities. Crossing the boundaries of class, they could and did mediate and communicate working-class claims, ideals, and politics. Historian Mary Jo Maynes described European working-class autobiographers as "boundary crossers, highly self-conscious because of their experiences as organizers or movers up the social ladder. Their percep-tions and claims were marked by these positions." The working-class men and women who followed the path to labor reform in the United States felt sim-ilar tensions. Their life histories were set, as Carolyn Steedman noted of her own life and that of her mother, "on the borderlands" of working-class expe-rience. For working-class women, social mobility through activism was more rare, but the booming cultural industries of teaching, journalism, and even reform offered opportunities for them to achieve the same kind of social mo-bility as men of their class.[8]

All of her life, Eva McDonald Valesh wedded the heroic story of labor's struggle with her own narrative of upward mobility. Beginning with the strike that catapulted her into the public limelight and a career as a labor reformer, her life story was an allegory familiar to readers of dime novels and pulp fiction. Repeated years later in an oral history, Valesh's reminiscences telescoped the events of the heady spring of 1888, when she first gained public attention, with those of earlier and later developments. It was important, however, for Valesh that her career coincide with the "woman's strike" and that her discovery be fateful. As a narrative of social mobility, Valesh's life story emerged from the margins and moved toward the center. It was, in effect, the story of an out-sider's rise to visibility.

Scope of the Book

Recovering the life of a largely forgotten woman journalist has not been an easy task. Eva Valesh left no diaries and scant correspondence, and her newspaper writing and editing was often unsigned.[9] Reading through the surviving evidence, I came to understand that public and private had different meanings for the class of respectable tradespeople into which Valesh was born. Because she had little regard for her place in history, she left behind limited sources on her personal and professional life. From what survives, we know that Valesh was a prolific correspondent but had little regard for saving her letters. This owed less, I think, to her fear of gossip-mongers than to a view of her life that was very different from that of the middle class of her day. Despite her upward mobility, she shared working-class ideas about biography and individuality. Like the cheap novels of the nineteenth century, life stories for the working class—especially those of women—were not about the path of an individual. They were staged in the territory of allegory. Life stories were retold not for biographers or the purposes of history but for political reasons. Valesh told her story to interviewers with detachment—not so much describing her achievements and failures as providing a window on class and gender relations. The power of those stories—and of her story—drives the narrative of this book.

The text is organized chronologically to follow the story of Eva Valesh's life and the evolution of her world. Chapters 1 and 2 examine her early career in the context of an emerging working-class public sphere, the role of women within it, and the process of class fragmentation that pulled apart and reconfigured labor's political culture. Without a strong historical record of her early years, the story focuses on the pivotal events and formative experiences that transformed Eva McDonald, the daughter of a carpenter and labor activist, into a national political figure. Mentored by the local Knights of Labor leadership, she came to represent the growing presence of women in the labor force and labor reform.

Valesh's experiences as a speaker, organizer, and publicist in the Populist and labor movements follow. Examining the place of women in Gilded Age political culture through lecturing on the state Farmers' Alliance circuit and the public forums of labor reform, Chapters 3 and 4 raise important questions about women's political experience and their partisanship. As a trade unionist, Valesh had interesting insights on the relative strength of the Populist and labor movements and recruited from the podium as a woman from both worlds. From this arena, as I show in Chapters 5 and 6, she spent time as a labor editor and political reporter for commercial newspapers in the Twin Cities, and

I examine how she created and sustained a career against the backdrop of the new journalism.

Valesh's experience in the mass media put her in demand as a labor journalist, and it paid off when Samuel Gompers hired her as assistant editor of the *American Federationist*. At the same time, as I explain in Chapter 7, she found herself torn, as did many labor progressives, between the class language of conflict and new interest-group and coalitional politics. As Samuel Gompers's "right-hand man," Eva Valesh contributed to the development and translation of a labor ideology in which the appropriate subject and object of labor organization was constructed as the white, male, native-born (or naturalized) craft worker.

As a daughter, wife, and employee of craft unionists and a craft unionist herself, Valesh represented one path to women's integration into the labor movement: acceptance of an ideology that increasingly marginalized and subordinated women. Her identity as a worker caught her up in other contradictions. As a "Joan of Arc of the Women of the Laboring Classes," Valesh offered political skills, insights, and resources to a new cross-class coalition of women. They drew on her expertise to mobilize working-class women under their banner. By this time in her career, Valesh was herself removed from the shop floor; she was neither a member of the working-class community from which women factory operatives and clerical workers came nor a member of their ethnic community. In Chapter 8, I trace the origins of women's partisanship in the twentieth-century world, built as it was on a foundation of interclass cooperation in which corporate paternalism set the parameters. Her eventual withdrawal from the public realm into life as a private citizen sets up the Conclusion, wherein I analyze the intertwined strands of social mobility, class and gender identity, and working-class desire.

From the moment that Eva McDonald hit the public stage of the labor movement in the spring of 1888 to her final retreat from public life in 1920, she played the role of an icon in reform culture. She represented, legitimately or not, the cadre of working-class daughters who made their way in a workingman's world. She presumed to speak for the wider masses of workers who were faced with the social costs and individual risks of the industrial age. I trace her steps as an apprentice reporter, organizer, and performer on the local and national stages of reform politics. Class is a learned position in life as in politics, however; many of Valesh's gains and losses might be attributed to the shifting social climate of late-nineteenth-century America and the roles that a woman had to accept. At the threshold of her career, Eva McDonald thankfully saw no such limitations—only possibilities.

CHAPTER I

STEALING THE TRADE

The Making of a Labor Journalist

It was the *Globe* of St. Paul that published to the world that Minneapolis contained more poor working women employed at starving wages, who were compelled to work in mere hovels; and by these articles practically became the direct cause of the strike.[1]

—*Minneapolis Tribune*, 1888

Whenever she told her life story, Eva McDonald Valesh began with the event that turned her into a public figure, a now-obscure labor struggle, "the first women's strike in Minneapolis." Under the pen-name Eva Gay, she had been writing for the *St. Paul Globe* a series of articles on women workers. With an eye toward the melodramatic and comic stories of working-class life, McDonald led her readers on a journey that began with the "song of the shirt" in garment factories and explored laundries, printing houses, and government offices. Within a few weeks, however, the women at a firm she had been investigating walked out. When the strike dragged on for weeks, the *Minneapolis Tribune* claimed that Eva Gay had stirred the women to action. By exposing the conditions of factory life to the public, the *Globe* articles "practically became the direct cause of the strike."[2] The same articles convinced labor leaders that they had found a new champion for workingwomen.

As the daughter of a workingmen's advocate, Eva McDonald had grown up in labor circles in the Twin Cities, but it was the women's strike that catapulted her into the center of local labor politics. Invitations to speak and commissions for labor articles followed. Her sudden fame sparked her ambitions in both the newspaper world and the labor movement. As a reporter and publicist for the strike, McDonald learned the importance of good tales and the value and limitations of images. At the same time, she had prepared herself for these experiences. Her early life and apprenticeship as a printer were equally compelling sources for the ideas and stories she used in her life work. In this chapter I trace Eva McDonald's origins, education, and early work experiences. I explore her newspaper column and her participation in the strike that contributed to her popularity and provided her new career opportunities. By grounding the story of her success in the social world and labor culture into which she was born and matured, we can see how she gained her skills as writer and political organizer as women often did—learning the trade of labor advocate while pursuing another career.

The Daughter of a Workingman

Like many labor reformers of her day, Mary Eva McDonald Valesh had an uneven class background. She was born in Orono, Maine, a year after the Civil War ended, to John Louis McDonald, a Canadian immigrant of Scot and Irish descent, and Ellen J. Lane. "Practically an orphan," John was born in Nova Scotia and lived "in the family of a stingy old uncle who didn't treat him well."[3] Independent, John left home at age fifteen and learned the trade of carpentry and bridge-building. Nova Scotia had a growing economy, but the labor market in New England promised greater opportunity.[4] In 1862, at age twenty-six, John emigrated to Maine. The following year, he married Ellen Lane, an Irish-American woman five years his junior, in Bangor. Mary Eva was born on September 9, 1866.[5] Soon after, McDonald took a position as bridge-builder for the Boston, Bangor, and Aristook Railroad,[6] a job that lent stability to the household. Within the decade, the family had expanded to five children—Eva and her brothers Willis, Joseph, Ralph, and Charles.[7]

By the mid-1870s, the lumber industry in Maine was exhausted and its forests stripped of good timber. Eva's family, she told an interviewer, "had all been lumber people." When the industry moved west, so, too, did her mother's family, the Lanes. Lonely for her brother and sister, Ellen urged her husband to move the family as well. John McDonald "didn't object."[8] The wooden bridges on which he had worked were being replaced with ones of structural steel. Work became harder to find, and opportunity had shifted to the urban frontiers of the Midwest. The family of seven moved first to the boomtown of Stillwater, Minnesota. Two years later, they relocated to nearby Minneapolis.[9]

The city to which John and Ellen McDonald migrated in the late 1870s was a busy center of industry, marketing, and transportation. It had been settled by a New England elite before the Civil War, but in the decades that followed, Norwegians, Swedes, Germans, and Irish emigrated into the new metropolis.[10] The hub of a developing rural hinterland, Minneapolis had grown substantially. With a population of only 13,000 in 1870, it expanded to nearly 50,000 in 1880 and 130,000 by 1885.[11] In 1886, Albert Shaw noted that "urban development at once so rapid and on so liberal and metropolitan a scale, ha[d] scarcely been seen elsewhere in the country; and citizens who [were] witnessing the unfolding as if by magic of a ragged western village into a splendid and palatial city, [were] stirred to enthusiasm, however dull their native temperament."[12] Migrants to the city were attracted by the new industries of flour milling, lumbering, and railroads. Banking, wholesale jobbing, and light manufacturing made up an increasing share of the region's economy. Bookbinding, printing, and journalism contributed as well. The city's growth also sparked a building boom, in which carpenters were in particular demand.[13]

Like many craftsmen of his time, John McDonald moved back and forth between small business and contract employment. Having left bridge-building, he did a lucrative business in constructing working-class cottages and bungalows.[14] By the mid-1880s, McDonald owned a grocery but later returned to carpentry.[15] His real love seemed to be political economy. As his daughter remembered, he had "an innate love of books and learning, and he had some inventive faculty." "Quite a bookish man," McDonald's "formal education was somewhat limited, and as a youth he didn't get many opportunities. In later life, he was always writing to the newspapers concerning civic welfare."[16] Both education and trade spoke for John McDonald in the new environment, and he became active in the Knights of Labor and the Workingmen's Municipal Reform Association. He later served as president of the city Trades and Labor Assembly.[17]

Inasmuch as John McDonald looked toward organized labor, Eva's mother had different ideas. According to her daughter, Ellen McDonald was "quite aristocratic."[18] As Eva recalled, "My family objected decidedly to my speaking for the working people. My mother was especially full of disapproval." She added, "There was a legend that 'there had been money' on her [mother's] side of the family."[19] In contrast, Eva's friend Albert Dollenmayer wrote that she had inherited from her mother "whatever of poetry there [was] in her nature."[20] But, as Eva told her interviewer, she didn't have a happy childhood. Her mother was "the kind of woman who always adored her latest baby."[21] As the eldest child and only daughter for her first fourteen years, Eva was expected to take care of the younger children. In Minneapolis, two younger sisters were born, which probably added to her burden. But if Ellen McDonald depended on her daughter for childcare, she also had social ambitions for her. When the family bought a piano, Ellen insisted that Eva take music lessons, despite a distinct lack of musical talent. As Eva McDonald became increasingly involved in labor politics, her mother complained that "we've come to a fine pass when I've got to look at the morning paper to see where my daughter was yesterday."[22]

The daughter of a respectable working family, Eva grew up in an atmosphere best characterized as working-class domesticity.[23] She was herself probably cared for as an infant by a temporary nurse and as a child by maternal relatives. As an adolescent, she helped care for younger siblings, but the family had a maid and at times even a cook.[24] As an avid reader, Eva McDonald learned lessons about girlhood and womanhood from school readers, dime novels, classic literature, and newspapers. A newspaper editorial asked, "What constitutes a well-bred girl?" and answered predictably that "the perfection of her being" required gentle manners, proper modesty, and obedience to authority. She was to be above ostentation, not show "all her jewelry in the daytime," and not "wear boots without buttons or a frock that needs mending." A good girl did not "speak of her mother in a sarcastic way," but instead gave her mother "the loving deference that is her due." Above all, a well-bred girl did not "say she hates women" and didn't "want to be a man" or "imitate him by wearing stiff hats, smoking cigarettes, and using an occasional big, big D[amn]."[25] Like many working-class and middle-class daughters, Eva McDonald stayed with her parents into her adult years. By the end of the nineteenth century, this common pattern had lengthened the time both sons and daughters lived with their parents between puberty and marriage.[26] The expectation of marriage, and the limited horizons for working-class daughters in particular, must have felt confining to those who read of adventure in the serialized novels and daily newspapers.

Eva's first act of self-creation may have been the abandonment of the given name, Mary, for her middle name, Eva. By her own account, she was an outspoken child. As Dollenmayer wrote, she was "a bright child but full of mischief" and, Eva later recalled, "an awful tomboy."[27] She began school at four, had a bout with diphtheria, and remembered being carried "piggyback" through the snow to school by her Uncle Thomas.[28] As she grew older, Dollenmayer noted, Eva acquired "an annoying habit of saying unpleasant truths in a blunt fashion without respect to the feelings" of others.[29] Her family undoubtedly heard many unpleasant truths from her as she took on independent ideas about her future.

Eva had a good public school education and parental tutoring. She graduated from high school in Minneapolis just three months shy of her sixteenth birthday. Her parents did not consider giving her an education, but she pressed them to send her to teachers' training school, even though she "never wanted

Eva McDonald at about age twelve, ca. 1878. She admitted to being an "awful tomboy." Photo courtesy of Dolores Lautman.

to teach school." But, as she admitted, "I thought that it would get me away from the family."[30] While her mother was content with Eva helping at home, her daughter had different ideas. With her youthful looks, she was unable to get a job as a teacher. As a reporter later wrote, McDonald "was expected to assume the dignity of a school teacher at once. . . . [T]he Board of Trustees, after a glance at the boyish-looking young person in short skirts and pigtails, concluded she 'had not the necessary dignity.'" From her brief exposure, she concluded, "I didn't like school teaching anyway, and it has always remained in my mind as a type of the dreariest occupations by which a woman may earn her bread."[31]

At that point, her father took some of Eva's writing to a struggling weekly newspaper, the *Saturday Evening Spectator*.[32] A reform newspaper, the *Spectator* ran a nonunion printing shop. She took on the job of "collecting and writing society items."[33] Of greater interest to her was the opportunity to learn type-setting. In an era when printing apprenticeship took four or five years, getting experience, often with nonunion printers, was a first step toward the union card. Later she described her first day of work. On entering the *Spectator*'s office, she encountered an "oppressive odor of lead, printer's ink, and benzine." In the outer room, she saw two older men "smoking vile pipes in a very much crowded office." She went back to the office where Bill McCann, the foreman, was working. "A big red-headed girl perched on a high stool," McCann's sister, Mary, was "doing something with bits of metal from a tall case before her." Mary "obligingly taught me how to set type."[34] As a beginner, Eva could hardly have been expected to earn good money, and yet she received thirty cents per thousand and earned $6 to $7 a week. After paying her parents $2 for board, she spent the rest on new clothes.[35]

In the article "Girls Who Make Money," written a few years later, Eva described the process of learning, mocking her own supposed ineptness. Manual typesetting required memorizing the place of letters in large print boxes, the mastery of stick and rule in placing the letters right-side up, learning spacing and punctuation, and reading from often sloppy and even illegible copy. As Eva was later to write, "The gas light made my eyes ache, the sharp edges of the type took the skin off my fingers, my shoulders were as stiff as if I'd had the rheumatism for about ten years." Printing, a woman typesetter told her, was "very hard work. It require[d] quickness, and the lead type [was] apt to poison your blood," but the $12 to $18 a week that experienced women typesetters made was a strong incentive.[36]

The printing trade in the nineteenth century was a field in which women had gained only a foothold. While women had been printers since the eighteenth century, the growth of the penny press, story papers, and book publishing in the nineteenth century had not vastly expanded their numbers. In 1880, adult women constituted only about 12 percent of the book and job publishing labor force. Printers were, after all, one of the most highly skilled, best-paid, and powerful trades in the country. They successfully staved off the mechanization of typesetting until the late 1880s, and most newspapers continued to be typeset by hand. Hostility toward workingwomen and restrictive apprenticeship rules limited the number of women compositors. As economist Edith Abbott wrote, employer preference also kept women from apprenticing in the trade: "The girl, therefore, in the language of the union 'steals the trade'; that is, she learns it without undergoing the same course of instruction that is prescribed for those who enter the trade properly; and she is, in consequence, imperfectly equipped." Women compositors often were restricted in the kind

Publishing house employees, ca. 1880s. West Publishing, a large printing shop in St. Paul, exhibited a familiar sexual division of labor. The few women employees seated in the front two rows were probably engaged in sheet-feeding, folding, and book-binding, rather than typesetting. Photo by G. A. Ladd. Courtesy of the Minnesota Historical Society.

of work they did. Many knew only how to typeset "straight matter"—short, clean lines of type—and they were excluded from the better lines of work. The introduction of the linotype did not then or in subsequent years lead to a growth in their employment. Rather, women were assigned other jobs—press feeders and folders, the lowest-paid sectors of the trade.[37]

McDonald's apprenticeship as a compositor on a religious newspaper was typical for women who entered the trade. She learned her skills in a nonunion shop and only then joined the typographical union. Nonunion workers, however, contributed to a brewing labor dispute in Minneapolis. In early 1888, the four union printers in the *Spectator* shop walked out. They charged that the newspaper did not run "a strictly union office." Although C. H. Du Bois, the owner and editor, had experience among the cooperative coopers, he was not above employing nonunion labor, especially young women typesetters. Of twelve employees, only four belonged to unions. While Du Bois's editorials in the *Spectator* seemed "public-spirited and progressive," his shop-floor practices were different. Women in his office worked long hours for what one reporter called "starvation wages." While the paper provided supper on Friday evenings, it did not make up for the pay. The union printers ignored the women in their strike. Rather, they demanded a union shop and received strong support from the union's executive board. In defense, Du Bois responded that of the seventy-eight to eighty-three printing offices in the city, only eighteen were union shops. The boycott, he argued, was only a test case to put the city's printing offices on notice. Du Bois finally settled the dispute in arbitration in October 1888, on terms that allowed him to continue to employ nonunion women.[38]

For McDonald, learning a skilled trade opened doors and gave her security. As she later claimed, "In the more colorful chapters of my life, it was always good to feel that I had a real trade to fall back on."[39] Her *Spectator* essays opened other doors. In later years, a reporter wrote that McDonald "was obliged to leave off her work as a compositor" when "the lead type affected her health." Union activism and personal ambition, however, were probably more important. As "one of the army of factory girls in the Northwestern city," she looked for new opportunities. Time spent in factories and shops, however brief, exposed her to the conditions facing workingwomen. That experience McDonald later used as a crusading labor reporter. As both a laborer and journalist, she proved to be outspoken about inequities in the workplace. As she later recalled, "I was not exactly popular anywhere because I did not hesitate to tell the foreman what I thought of long hours and the unhygienic conditions of work. I also managed to get other girls dissatisfied. I was never discharged, for I was a quick worker, but I usually left soon to look for something better."[40] For McDonald, that "something better" was the world of labor journalism.

By the late nineteenth century, Minneapolis had a thriving labor movement.[41] Among the first organizations of workingmen was the printers' union, International Typographical Union Local 42, the local that Eva McDonald joined. Beginning in 1878, workingmen's organizations had begun to affiliate with the Knights of Labor in assemblies organized as trade union locals and mixed assemblies, or unions of workers from various occupations; trade unions also flourished. They supported, among other institutions, a local labor newspaper, *Northwestern Labor Union*, with more than 1,200 subscriptions, and they contributed as well to St. Paul's *Labor Echo*. Local newspapers carried labor columns as well. The building of a labor temple in 1886–87 signaled the local movement's growing national visibility. That year, more than seven thousand members in ninety-five assemblies provided support for the Knights' political affiliation with regional parties, such as the Union Labor party in 1888 and the Alliance Labor party in 1890.[42]

Throughout the 1880s, members of the Knights and the trade unions had self-consciously engaged in public education for political ends. As historian David Nord wrote of the abolitionists, the aim of labor radicals "was to keep their unpopular message constantly before the public until the consciences of the people were finally touched."[43] Truth-telling was equally important to labor's political culture. As one trade unionist later wrote, the labor movement "contributed considerably in educating that ephemeral quantity, public opinion, to the importance of the study of labor problems."[44] "In those early years," he recalled, "we recognized the advantage of publicity so far as the educational side of the work was concerned and notwithstanding that it was not very popular to be a labor leader in those days we worked the daily press to the limit for space."[45] Attentive to the growing number of workingwomen in the cities, the Knights founded two local women's assemblies. Exhibiting the "clear brains and honest heart" needed, the object of these associations was "to better every physical and moral condition of their sex." They regularly surveyed women's wages and working conditions seeking to expose the shameful story of workingwomen's exploitation.[46]

Newspapers became the forum for these concerns. Faced with stiff competition in St. Paul and Minneapolis, the *St. Paul Globe* was seeking to build its working-class readership with more extensive labor coverage and reap the political rewards. In 1888, responding to recent Knights of Labor reports on workingwomen, the *Globe*'s Minneapolis editor, John Swift, took up the challenge. The findings of the local committee on women's work never made it beyond the pages of the district assembly's proceedings or the occasional mention in the St. Paul *Labor Echo*. A larger sphere of publicity, calling attention to the low wages of women and their need for organization, was a prerequisite for engaging public opinion. Swift probably also thought it might serve to awaken workingwomen to their own plight.

In 1887, Eva McDonald was becoming involved in labor circles. Both she and her father had joined the Knights of Labor Building Association, and Eva served as one of the planners of the kirmess, a cultural event to celebrate the opening of the Knights' Labor Temple.[47] For these reasons and others, the Knights' Swift showed up at the McDonalds' house one evening. He announced that the *St. Paul Globe* "wants somebody to go and work in the factories, live in the homes, and give an all-round picture of how working people live."[48] Swift thought John McDonald's enterprising daughter could take on the assignment.

The work required many of the strengths Eva McDonald already possessed. Her acting ability, observations of work, and education made her an ideal choice. So, too, did the youthful looks that earlier had disqualified her as a teacher. She later recalled that "I had my hair cut short like a boy. Certainly I didn't look more than twelve or thirteen."[49] In one of her columns, she confessed that the direct method of approaching workingwomen to answer questions hadn't worked, so she resorted to disguise. "So next morning" McDonald continued, "I carefully fished out of the rag-bag a dilapidated dress, having borrowed a hat and jacket to match . . . and procured shoes and gloves with many holes in them. When my disguise was completed, I looked as if I hadn't eaten a square meal in a long time. Hoping that my wretched appearance would provoke pity, I presented myself at the office of the mill and asked for work."[50] She proudly asserted, "No employer ever discovered me—that was the odd thing—because they were looking for a tall, grimly efficient spinster."[51]

Among Girls Who Toil

"'Mong Girls Who Toil," the first article of the series published in March of 1888, gave McDonald the break for which she had been looking. As she later said, "This sort of newspaper article has become common enough but at that time it was a novelty and caused excitement, for I told unmincingly of conditions as they were."[52] Her eye for detail, the personal tone of the reports, and sense of humor all seemed to serve her in good stead. Written under the pen-name Eva Gay, her working-women series provoked a wide-ranging response from labor activists and newspaper editors alike.

The popularity of the Eva Gay series was due to its author's narrative flair, humorous bent, and dramatic tone. Each story began as McDonald described the factory or shop and led her readers up a back stair or through a locked door. After bringing the audience inside the working girls' world, she grimly rehearsed their low wages and poor working conditions. In badly lit, poorly ventilated factories, women earned their daily bread. The atmosphere smelled; women wore bandages around their aching heads and squinted in the dim light. As she wrote of one woolen mill, it was "the hardest looking work room in the city." The older part of the mill was "where the blankets and flannels [were] washed and dried." At first, McDonald could see no one in the dark, intensely heated room. Gradually, she spied women working by the windows. "I thought," she wrote, "if they could work in that place day after day, surely I could stand it for half an hour. The floor was dirty, and little streams of soap suds ran from the washing machines. Picking my way across the damp floor I found some girls working on heavy machines called 'gigs'; others were 'bushing,' or picking specks off the blankets when finished."[53]

In a commercial laundry, McDonald found similar conditions: The stone floor was "cold, wet and slippery. The steam filled the air and dripped from the ceiling and wall . . . . It looked more like a rat hole than a place where women were forced to work." Even in unionized cigar factories, the "strong smell of tobacco and the dust in the air" made her head ache. When she asked one of the women whether her health suffered, the woman replied, "Not if you're strong enough to stand it; some girls get sick and leave, but there are others who work for years at the trade. They get used to the work." Outraged, McDonald suggested to her readers, "This matter of 'getting used to the work' seems, in many trades, to take away all danger to their health—the girls often seeming to think when they are accustomed to any bad feature that of course it doesn't injure them."[54]

Exploring the lives of workingwomen introduced readers to garment workers, laundresses, cigar-makers, seamstresses, domestics, operatives in woolen and knitting mills and boot and shoe factories, telephone and telegraph operators, bookbinders, stenographers, and shop women. McDonald also showed readers the social distinctions among factory girls, domestics, and the "girls who wear gold-rimmed glasses and quote legal technicalities." One clerk, "a young lady of culchah" who had "read all the latest novels, or at least the titles of them, couldn't bear to associate with the common rabble." Telephone operators presented a similar "haughty and aristocratic mien" as they had a "perfect horror" of being classified among working girls. "Among themselves," McDonald observed, "they always seemed quite capable of having a jolly time, but let a stranger approach, especially one of the feminine persuasion, and they instantly assume an icy calmness of demeanor calculated to make a person of any age and experience flee in fear and trembling from their presence." Labor aristocracy existed even among women workers whose labor collectively was devalued and underpaid.[55]

At the same time, McDonald plotted the pleasures and dangers of women's lives. She found that novels, shared stories, and mutual aid partially compensated for isolation. Covering a wide range of women's occupations, she both provoked and amused her readers with tales from the working girl's life. If there was danger that women might stray from virtue, they also shared the innocent joys of Sunday promenade in the city parks. Women made work light by conversing over their machines, and they deeply resented when the privilege was taken away from them. Across worktables, they swapped novels, from Emile Zola's *L'Assommoir* to the thrilling tones of a Bertha M. Clay dime novel and James Fenimore Cooper's *The Spy.* Their sense of community was revealed in their sharing of not only books but also food and clothing. When one woman had no lunch at work, the others shared theirs, even when the meal was as meager as bacon on coarse rye. McDonald's ability to enter workplaces, accept positions, and interview women workers depended on their willingness to confide in her and to keep her identity secret. She frequently substituted for friends at work, which required both trust and cooperation.[56]

In all of her articles, McDonald stressed that the appalling conditions under which most women worked were amenable to change. Women in the boot and shoe industry and the printing trade and women who worked as government clerks earned living wages and lived independently. For the most part, she asserted, better conditions and earnings were a result of women's union membership. In a real sense, it was the same-sex solidarity of trade unions, the sense of individual independence supported through collective effort, that McDonald recommended for workingwomen. While she abhorred some of the divisions among women, it was their common plight and collective sensibility that suggested them as an apt target for organization.[57]

A Beehive of Industry

In "'Mong Girls Who Toil," Eva Gay wrote on the conditions in a garment factory, Shotwell, Clerihew and Lothmann. The firm was a difficult place to work, and this owed more to the owners' ambitions than to the nature of the work. Inspired, perhaps, by literature promoting investment in the city, the owners moved the business from Cincinnati to Minneapolis in 1884.[58] They soon added a manufacturing section specializing in workingmen's clothing—overalls, jumpers, shirts, and mackinaws—for the western market.[59] By 1888, the firm moved to a new building on the corner of First Avenue South and Second Street. Described as "a perfect beehive of industry," it was the workplace of nearly three hundred women by 1888. More than one hundred sewing machines were used in the making of shirts and overalls; others were dedicated to blankets and buttons. The factory was noisy and dusty and smelled of new cloth and sewer gas.[60]

As McDonald revealed, the workingwomen of Shotwell were among the worst-paid female operatives in the city. Paid on the piece-rate system, they received only three-and-a-half cents for every shirt, seven cents on overalls, eight to ten cents per pair of jeans, and thirty-three cents on mackinaws. Rates like these meant women carried home only three or four dollars per week on average. During the coat season, operatives could see ten or twelve dollars a week for a three-week stint making coats.[61] Such wages amounted to a standard of living at the poverty level. In the spring of 1888, the slim wage packets got thinner. The new manager, Eugene Woodward, introduced wage cuts that reduced piece rates from 20 percent to 33 percent.[62] Furthermore, he set new rules that prohibited singing and talking on the shop floor, and he refused the women breaks during working hours. One of the women declared she'd rather find another job than go back to the firm: "We will hunt work elsewhere. We have nothing to lose. A girl gets more wages at housework and work of that character than we did at Shotwell's. . . . Ever since Mr. Woodward has been manager he has been grinding our wages down and has been [as] disagreeable as a slave master."[63]

Woodward's defense against such charges was simple. He offered his women employees a better chance to earn good money by his innovations. As he told one reporter, "Our wages are as high as any other factory. If the girls don't draw enough to live on, it is their fault. I put the girls on the kind of work that makes them proficient in their work and enables them to draw more wages. Now other factories compel their workers to do several kinds of work, and no one can work as fast on several kinds of classes as they can on one. This benefit to the girls was some of my brainwork."[64] But while some employers would have made changes more slowly, the speed, rigor, and enthusiasm with which Woodward established his "foreman's empire" suggests that he was motivated both by the pressures of a failing firm and by dislike of his employees. Other supervisors seemed to have shared Woodward's prejudices. As one worker complained, "Mrs. Dexter, our forelady, says we are a lot of foolish, ignorant girls."[65]

When Woodward assigned the women a lower grade of work in April and further reduced their pay packets, they took their cause to the Knights of Labor women's assembly.[66] Although its numbers were small, the assembly was credited with having "done more for the workingwomen of the two cities than the combined influence of press, pulpit, and public institutions." On the eve of the strike, membership soared to 300.[67] The Knights' District Master Workman, Timothy Brosnan, stepped in to head off any labor conflict. Like many Knights, he considered strikes "costly luxuries" that led to the impoverishment of workers and the collapse of labor organizations. In exchange for the women's patience, he offered to intervene with the firm, but he was rebuffed.[68]

The next day, Alice Rooney led the grievance committee of fifteen to the Shotwell office. In a dismissive mood, Woodward refused to listen to the workers' complaints. If the women desired higher wages, he suggested, they could quit and find work elsewhere. In a city filled with unemployed women, Woodward added, the firm would have no trouble replacing those who left. Indeed, he later reported he would have "no trouble in hiring help," even if "the girls [would] probably make a strong effort through labor organizations and other influences to prevent others from filling their places."[69] Woodward closed the meeting with a parting shot. Did the committee represent the "art gallery" upstairs?

The act of wearing clothing too fine for women of the working classes was, from Woodward's point of view, a transgression of the class lines in factory and city. As one operative reported to McDonald, Woodward said "we girls wear too many feathers and fine clothes and threatens to cut our wages so we'll be glad to wear plain clothes by spring. He [said] we act as if we thought ourselves ladies."[70] His choice of "art gallery" to identify them was a subtle reference to city art expositions, in which well-dressed women appeared to make commercial use of public space. While pretending to be ladies, they acted instead as public women or prostitutes.[71] Hearing his rough language riddled with misogyny and disregard for their complaints, the women believed that Woodward sought to force them down the road of poverty, ill health, and prostitution.

Angered over Woodward's remarks, the women sought satisfaction from their employer almost immediately. The manager had insulted them, judging their manners too fine for their coarse circumstances and their work too lax for decent wages. The phrase "art gallery specimens" reverberated as they retold the confrontation with the foreman to McDonald. An operative added, "Woodward never imagined that the ornaments of his 'art gallery' would strike; for even though they dress like the daughters of millionaires, he didn't suppose for a moment that they could afford to take such a step."[72] The next day, the women stopped the machinery, took up their cloaks, and almost emptied the workplace. Idling not only the machines but the men who worked in the factory, they headed to the Knights of Labor hall, only a block away.[73] Once there, the strikers drew up a list of demands that included a restoration of wage cuts, a small raise, and an end to harassment by male employees. Woodward's condemnation of the women resonated with the behavior of other men in the factory; they, too, spoke with contempt of the women. As McDonald reported, the women declared, "If we go back, it will be with the understanding that the dude clerks shall stop ogling us and trying to mash us when we go to and from work."[74]

Dude Clerks and Working Girls

The "dude clerks" who erupted into the story of the Shotwell strikers suggest a side of the shop floor not even hinted at in complaints about wages and fear of poverty. The dudes of Shotwell's were bookkeepers, accountants, and salesmen who stood in similar relation to the sewing women as did Woodward. They, like he, were not from the class of operatives nor were they skilled tradesmen and laborers. Some, perhaps most, of the clerks hoped to make a career in a business with a better future, if not greater respect, than their fathers.[75] Yet in the rapidly expanding cities of the late nineteenth century, the clerks were "giddy mashers" and "Ah, There's." These dudes—and their female counterparts, dudesses—"lash[ed] vulgar ostentation" and displayed "airs and gewgaws."[76]

The clerks often walked the streets in search of female companionship, some too shy or broke to make the acquaintance of shop girls. One reporter described the typical clerk: He "spends about all he earns in purchasing loud and costly clothes, and then 'stands off' his landlady, or eats at a '15-cent joint' in order to make both ends meet. He is not particularly dangerous but is very tiresome. He is generally just the sort who will have just animation enough to smile in a sickly way and remark 'Ah, there' as the object of his adoration passes him on the street."[77] These "milk-shake mashers" stood in contrast to wealthier young men, who, as the writer claimed, "delight in being called 'rounders' and being considered 'deucedly sly,' don'tcher know" and "made a business of mashing" with "enough money to do about as they please." Money made success, according to this formula, as "old mashers" had better success seducing women with food, drink, and dress.[78]

At the very least, the growing number of women working increased the opportunity for male clerks and managers to "ogle" and "mash" women as well as to upbraid them for being in the public realm of work. Many men believed that women preferred companions with large salaries and more money. There were, the writer confessed, "but few girls who care to go anywhere with him [the clerk], as by experience they know that $6 or $7 per week will not go a long way in buying theater tickets and dainty little suppers." As clerks with only a weekly salary to distinguish them from piece-rate workers, the men of Shotwell carried their habits of staring into the factory. They eyed the young women who worked in the factory, "ever on the alert for a pretty face."[79]

The tensions between men and women in the Gilded Age workplace often set the context for other confrontations and grievances. If the dude clerks tried to prey upon working girls, inadequate wages were another potential source of sexual danger for women as the objects of sexual harassment and as the targets of seduction. McDonald's reports caught these tensions. Embattled by the supervisor, ogled by male co-workers, and threatened by a wage cut, one striker in despair told the reporter, "How can [a woman] live on such wages and live and dress respectively? She can't do it. It is impossible. She must either go without clothing or board or get money in a way I would blush to mention. Those who board along with friends for nothing can get along but girls earning three and four dollars a week cannot pay board and room rent and clothe themselves." Another striker asked, "Does Mr. Shotwell or anyone else think girls can live on such wages and remain pure? They can, of course, but it is sickness and death for people to do hard work without proper food and nourishment and life is so much more pleasant than a home in the ground."[80]

Workingwomen, labor advocates, and middle-class supporters used similar political language in their claims about the protection of the community. With the familiar metaphors of slavery and prostitution, they characterized wage labor as the selling of the body to an impersonal and immoral market. Dependency, and the resulting moral peril, was the consequence of women's unequal position in the marketplace. The ideology of the Knights of Labor complicated this representation, precisely because it allowed for an alternative vision of womanhood in the workplace and labor movement. "Labor's True Woman" could be a woman wage-earner as well as a wife, a printer or seamstress as well as a daughter. Yet as historian Susan Levine has argued, this ideal was contradictory and ambiguous. The Knights of Labor viewed women as only temporary wageworkers and unionists. Furthermore, labor drew on an older system of metaphors—prostitution, wage slavery, the public market—that made women the central symbol of the evil of competition. The language reinforced the image of female moral peril in public wage labor. To many reformers, domestic and family labor was a better choice for women, who could be insulated from the public exposure and individual peril of wage work in private homes and businesses. Within the family shop and farm household, women could be protected from the contamination of public money, public space, and public intercourse.

In the essay "The Factory's White Slave," written in response to working-women's plight, McDonald expressed the underlying fears of workingwomen. The essay follows the conversation of two men girl-watching on a busy city street. One woman catches a gentleman's eye. Although she was "neatly and plainly dressed, deported herself modestly and didn't carry a lunch basket," he can tell she's a working girl. His friend badgers him to reveal how he knows. The discerning gentleman returns that "anybody who is familiar with the types of humanity seen on our city streets can easily pick the working girls from the throng." As the six-o'clock whistle blows, the young men begin to name women by their occupations. A young clerk with "her dress neatly arranged, eyes bright, complexion clear" unconsciously "walks with that dragging step peculiar to clerks who have stood behind a counter all day." "[U]ntidy dress, tawdry hat and frayed jacket" betray a laundress suffering from consumption. "A bevy of girls . . . chattering like magpies and laughing heartily" were poor factory drudges forbidden to talk and laugh at work, so their "merriment bursts forth as soon as they get free." The "pitiful droop of the mouth and reddened eyelids" signal a girl looking for work, and another woman had a "hesitating, cringing manner," which revealed she routinely bore "petty exactions" from "tyrannical foremen." Only one woman with "bright glittering eyes" and immaculate dress stood out from the crowd of working girls, but she was marked with the "coldly cruel expression and defiant air" of a woman of casual virtue. Through their choice of dress, women sought insurance against those who would insult them as working girls. Unlike the city dudes who ogled them, women believed their work should be a object of respect, not derision.[81]

As McDonald found, workingwomen themselves made distinctions between the Victorian middle-class ideology of respectability (which made work dangerous and fancy dress temptation to a life of sin) and the working-class belief that work and clothes made one respectable. The practice of dressing for church, changing into one's street clothes for the walk home, or donning a servant's uniform that separated employer from employee signaled the connection between clothing and social status. Because they understood that insult and disdain were linked to clothing that was plain, worn, or old, women tried to avoid wearing work costumes on the street for fear of being pointed out. Furthermore, not having the money to "clothe oneself" made one undressed, ragged, naked, and thus vulnerable. It contrasted with the state of being dressed respectably and thus able to interact and partake. Honor, for the middle class, was the reward of the workingwoman in rags; dishonor and shame, for workingwomen, were the result of not having money to clothe oneself. Being dressed respectably was a matter of both pride in and protection of the self.[82]

Apart from the wage cuts and dude clerks, the workers' most serious grievance was Woodward's abusive behavior toward them. The "sewing girls" held him responsible for wages set at "New York standards." The fear of poverty resounded in voices that said Woodward hoped "to reduce them all to the miserable condition of those women for whom the song of the shirt was written."[83] Furthermore, Woodward had insulted them. He made them stand in the street, a sign of disrespect. He denied them passes to leave the shop even when they were sick, and he threatened them with physical violence. His hostility escalated the conflict. As one striker reported, "When one section of lights went out by accident last fall and the girls made for the elevator, Mr. Woodward drove them back like a lot of cattle. He took hold of one girl and shook her roughly and swore at her." Another added, "Mr. Woodward told one girl that if she did not go back to her seat, he would kick her down stairs."[84]

These heroic tales of workingwomen confronting an immoral boss and his unbridled dude clerks carried with them the anxieties and pleasures of the age: glimpsing, staring at, ogling the opposite sex in the new spaces of the modern city; finding discomfort and excitement in men and women mixing in public, not only in churches or families but in factories, streets, and theaters; getting tangled in the class mixing as well. Clerks, factory operatives, and shop girls were roughly on the same footing. They worried about the boss, unemployment, and the simple lack of spending money. The city had become a vast marketplace; department stores, streetcars, theaters and restaurants pulled working people inexorably into a city life organized around consumption and service. The garment strikers, like McDonald herself, signaled changes in the new urban world.

To Get Justice

During the course of the strike, the submerged organization of the working-women surfaced in the newspaper reporting of Eva McDonald and others. As one journalist wrote, "The small army of striking shop girls still stand in solid phalanx determined to secure better wages or declare eternal war on their irate employers. . . . The young women regard these days of their first experience in striking as holidays, and all of them donned their holiday toilets"[85] in celebration of their unity. The factory's very closeness—the machines packed tightly together on tables, the lack of time to go out for breaks, the pass system that kept women inside the building—had contributed to the growing labor solidarity among the women. During the long protest, their retelling bound the strikers together in a single purpose. As one told McDonald, "It's only at meetings like this where we talk, then we try to arrange plans to get justice."[86]

The strike committee developed into an efficient operation. Headed by Alice Rooney and Jessie England, it started to negotiate with the firm and begin the major task of raising funds. Having no strike fund initially, they needed to find sources to support the many self-supporting women among them. The Trades and Labor Assemblies of Minneapolis and St. Paul and other unions generously gave of their treasuries.[87] Within days, the strike committee also collected union dues from the wages they received after the walkout began. They further organized one committee to handle publicity and another to study the women's wages and the effects of wage cuts. And they published a newspaper asking sewing girls to stay away from the firm.[88]

The support of trade unions proved crucial to the women's strike. Early on, they passed resolutions that condemned the firm's actions. The Knights of Labor and trade unions were behind the call for a boycott. Labor leaders spoke out against the industrial system's abuse of women workers. They demanded newspapers cover the strike fairly, a demand that led to some of McDonald's investigations. If workingmen did not entirely believe in women's right to work and expressed ambivalence about strikes, they "express[ed] loathing and contempt for the man who would build up a fortune on the ruins of female happiness and virtue." Labor advocates used every avenue they had toward ending the strike, including donations of time and money, publicity, guidance, and political pressure. As they asserted, "The girls have acted in perfect accord since the strike began, and it proves that they have it within their power to better their conditions through organization. Society has made it necessary at last for working women finally to resort to methods so long employed by working men."[89]

Workers in the North Star Woolen Mills, ca. 1905. This was one of the factories investigated by Eva Gay in the late 1880s. The photograph shows the working conditions she exposed. Photo courtesy of the Minnesota Historical Society.

Newspapers were essential in building public support for the strike, and here McDonald was crucial. The *Globe* claimed responsibility for raising the issue of workingwomen's wages to the public. While the *Minneapolis Tribune* condemned the *Globe* for its sensationalist articles, the *Globe* responded that it would not falsify reports simply to sustain the firm: "If the sustaining process means the wreck and pauperization of women, then we say, in God's name, let Eastern firms do our manufacturing, rather than have Minneapolis blighted by a large class of women whose lives must be cursed by penury or blasted by prostitution."[90] The *Irish Standard* commended the *Globe* for "its enterprise in exposing the hardship, poor pay, and bad treatment of the operatives in some of the factories. The daily press of the city should co-operate with the *Globe* in its humanitarian work and rid itself of professional jealousy in this work of crying injustice."[91] The *Standard* called on clergy to support the effort.

The most enthusiastic displays of public support were two meetings at Harmonia Hall. Arranged by clergy and concerned women in the cities in alliance with the strikers, the first meeting on May 10 was designed to pressure the firm into arbitration with the striking workers. The audience that night was faced with a drop curtain onto which were pinned various pieces of workingmen's clothing. The strikers had attached labels to them with prices paid for their making: a blouse marked Shotwell—6 cents, St. Paul—9 cents; overhauls—12 cents; St. Paul—14–1/2 cents.[92] The Reverend William Wilkinson spoke on a religion of common sense. He confessed that he did not believe entirely "in preaching about the hereafter or reading articles about how to reach the laboring classes. The way to reach them was to help them." "Monssini Baker" (printer Thomas Clark) sang "The Workingmen's Marseillaise," and Clara Holbrook and Mrs. E. M. S. Marble, president of the Minneapolis Women's Christian Temperance Union, gave short addresses.[93]

The main speaker that night was Charlotte Van Cleve, a member of one of Minneapolis's oldest families and founder of the Bethany Home, a rescue mission for reformed prostitutes. Van Cleve had been interested in the strike from its beginning. She was part of the "crusade for working girls" that raised funds for new boarding homes; during this crusade she wrote a report on domestic service for the state Bureau of Labor Statistics. In her early statements about the strike, Van Cleve argued that women's low wages were "temptation to theft" and cited cases of women "driven to lives of crime to obtain the necessaries of life."[94] Her public address, "Inadequate Wages for Women," declared "that woman is underpaid is patent, and God never meant that man should prosper and woman should starve." Van Cleve concluded with a call for action: "Friends, mothers, fathers, brothers, I call upon you to take an interest in this matter of women's wages; I call upon you to feel your responsibility in this matter. Girls, I advise you to be careful." The meeting supported the strikers' efforts to attain better wages and improved workplace conditions, but above all it reinforced the sense of moral danger faced by women at work.[95]

Responding to the newspaper reports and public forums, the public pressured the firm to negotiate. Its owners proved both unresponsive and resistant to the strikers' demands. At first, the manager tried to wait out the strike, expecting the women to return to their jobs when they needed wages.[96] When the partners tried to hire new help within a week of the walkout, they could find only twelve substitutes. At the same time, the firm made overtures to the committee, promising that the wage cuts would be restored. Rumors that not all of the strikers would be rehired led to a vote to refuse the firm's offer. Two weeks after the strike began, the women issued a manifesto stating their wages. When the committee proposed arbitration, the firm withdrew its offer, and the labor unions called for a citywide boycott of its goods. More than seventy-five establishments had joined the boycott when the firm declared bankruptcy in June 1888.[97]

The Power of the Story

For more than a year after the Shotwell strike, Eva Gay's "travels" through the world of women workers continued to stir readers' imaginations. Every story raised a new and controversial issue as she took her readers on a tour of women's workplaces—from the steamy atmosphere of commercial laundries to the high-brow world of government clerks and private homes where women served as maids and cooks. Sometimes McDonald recited statistics on the appalling wages for which women worked. Other times she told of the workers' "Sundays out," the times of laughter and gaiety that surfaced during the mostly grim workdays, and the women's experience of harassment and fear of losing their livelihood. Her newspaper tales thus opened a window onto the lives of women workers and helped to spark the interests of both labor advocates and middle-class reformers in helping the working girl.[98]

McDonald thus joined a new corps of women writers and labor investigators who reported on working conditions for the metropolitan press.[99] As historians John Andrews and William Bliss wrote, "The field of investigation but recently entered by many government labor bureaus and state factory inspectors was . . . occupied by several sympathetic writers like Nell Nelson, Ethel Allen, and Eva Gay, who were unconsciously following in the footsteps of 'Shirley Dare' and Virginia Penny, of the previous generation of writer reformers."[100] Unlike these pioneer women journalists, McDonald found herself not only recording history but also making it. The strike at Shotwell was only the first of many labor conflicts in which she would play the role of instigator as well as witness, organizer as well as reporter.

As for McDonald's first story, the women's strike at Shotwell, Clerihew, and Lothmann had several unintended consequences. The firm's management simply wanted to cut costs in a highly competitive industry. It was surprised by the opposition from its women employees and from the community. It was not only the boycott but also the tightening of credit that had led to bankruptcy. The example would hardly have gone unnoticed by local merchants and small manufacturing firms. Businessmen—once supporters and even members of the Knights of Labor—now viewed with alarm the increasing power of organized labor in the city. They were more wary of the power of banks in shaping the market and curbing the expansion of upstart businesses. These perceptions, combined with the increasing gap between rich and poor, heightened class conflict and contributed to the realignment of local class politics.

For the reformers of the Knights of Labor, the strike had held both danger and promise. Committed to the path of arbitration, convinced that women in the workplace were permanently hobbled by their sex, and timid in the face of declining numbers, Knights of Labor leaders sought to end the strike before it began. And yet once the women left the workplace, the Knights fully supported the women's decision. While the strike continued, local assemblies committed resources to strike pay and publicity and declared a boycott. They helped organize a short-lived cooperative garment factory and sought to use what little political muscle they had to support the workers. Although "the Shotwell strike gave a brief impetus to organization among women," membership in the Knights of Labor began a slow decline.[101] For the women of Shotwell, the strike's impact was the loss of jobs, which for many meant a curtailing of personal autonomy. Some workers returned to the round of jobseeking that was a prelude to marriage, while others returned home to live with their families.

The most visible and best-known fate was not that of any of the striking workers but of the woman reporter who "discovered" their plight and reported labor conflicts in great detail. Having spent her apprenticeship in the printing offices and factories of Minneapolis, Eva McDonald had found the path to a career, and it would not be associated with teaching or marriage, as her mother desired. Taking up the cause of workingwomen, the woman whose "spicy observations on labor matters . . . made her one of the most popular lecturers"[102] had a career in front of her as a teller of tales, a speaker of truths, and a writer of fictions for a public hungry for stories of urban life and a labor movement seeking a new voice. Eva McDonald eagerly sought to be that writer and to provide that new voice.

CHAPTER 2

"An Object of Solicitude at Election Time"

The Knights, Partisanship, and Working-Class Politics Revisited

I know that much relief can be gained through politics, but politics
will never solve the problem and only opens up avenues for design-
ing men, who enter the order for selfish ends, to create dissension
and finally disrupt us.

—John F. Cronin, secretary,
District Assembly 79, Knights of Labor, 1887

Following the garment workers' strike, Eva McDonald, the rising star of labor reform journalism, stepped into the spotlight again. That fall, she became the first woman candidate to run for school board office in Minneapolis since school suffrage had been granted to Minnesota women a decade before. At twenty-two, McDonald was the candidate not of the Prohibition party that launched women school superintendents in a handful of counties across Minnesota or of the emergent woman suffrage movement.[1] Instead, she ran on the Democratic workingmen's ticket. Her rise first to labor orator and then to political candidate demonstrated the strength and vitality of working-class culture at the time.

In this chapter I explain the political culture that supported Eva McDonald's career. Workingmen's political associations raised the most difficult problem of the day—the labor question—in the context of a democracy founded on private property, circumscribed by the demands of the market, and legitimized by cultural authority. As economic uncertainty undermined the political clout of the producing classes, power was increasingly concentrated in the hands of the wealthy. Local Knights of Labor addressed the changing environment with plans for cooperative industry and land reform, and they engaged in political alliances with both municipal reformers and farmers. After the collapse of several cooperatives in the mid-1880s, however, labor advocates began to ask themselves how they could base their political citizenship not in cooperative production but in wage work. The answer was to enlarge political capacity through electoral reform and the eight-hour day. The Eight-Hour League they formed was the first step in transforming labor's political culture, but they ultimately contributed to the demise of the local power of the Knights of Labor. With "Eight Hours for What We Will" as its creed, trade unionism became the banner under which the local labor movement sought legitimacy.

Eva McDonald was both an actor in labor's political culture and a symbol of its goal of attaining equal rights in civil society. Given labor's commitment to a politics of manhood in which class demands and political rights were seen in male terms, the choice of McDonald as working-class champion took imagination and faith that the "crusade for working women" was intimately connected to labor's future. Like the labor radicals who mentored her, she represented the capacity of the working classes to make their voice heard in the growing cacophony of the public sphere. The popular press, moral and urban reformers, conservative employers, and the middle classes already could be heard loud and clear in the public arena. Could labor make working-class demands heard among the contending voices of late-nineteenth-century politics? Adapting to changing circumstances, working-class advocates and their new disciple, Eva McDonald, agitated to retain labor's access to the political world.

The Girl Orator

After the 1888 strike, McDonald turned her time as an investigative reporter to good use. She had gained notoriety for calling attention to the plight of women workers. More important for McDonald, writing the Eva Gay columns gave her the equivalent of a "tramping year" in her trade as a journalist, an apprenticeship designed for a woman making her career in the competitive worlds of journalism, labor organizing, and politics. Reporting on the labor question exposed McDonald to social problems at an experiential level. It lent a tone of authenticity and realism to her writing that was hard to obtain from formal study of political economy. It also provided an opportunity to learn to listen to others and gave her words a common touch that many more seasoned reformers did not have. Drawing on these experiences, she spoke with great facility on the questions of political economy and education facing workers. Because she had spent time talking to working people where they lived and worked, she could speak to them in their own language.

The transformation of a young woman in her twenties into an accomplished speaker was not, however, effected through her exposure to "authentic experience" alone. While the gritty realism of newspaper detective work gave authority to McDonald's articles and speeches, other skills—self-presentation, persuasion, and political analysis—had to be learned. Unaccustomed to publicity and often untutored in public speaking and politics, most women of McDonald's time had little knowledge of what it was to speak to mixed audiences with a range of backgrounds, interests, and expectations. What she needed, and received, was tutelage from speakers and writers who had spent a lifetime in reform. In her political campaigns, labor organizing, and eight-hour agitation, McDonald had excellent teachers. The first such group, known as the Athenaeum of Crude Philosophers, was responsible for the girl reporter becoming a girl orator.

McDonald's first tutor was John P. "Jack" McGaughey, a man with a long history in the labor movement and political circles. Born in Mount Vernon, Ohio, McGaughey first became active in the labor movement in an 1873 strike of locomotive engineers. A yardmaster in Memphis, Tennessee, he migrated to Minnesota in the 1870s. As a brakeman on the Chicago, Milwaukee, and St. Paul Railway, McGaughey lost an arm in 1879.[2] Hired as a car accountant for Omaha Freight, McGaughey joined in 1882 a Knights of Labor assembly that was later known as the North Star Labor Club. Within a year, he was elected master workman of the Knights of Labor District Assembly and remained in the office until he resigned during the 1886 election. Popular with fellow workers, McGaughey was later reelected master workman in 1889.[3]

As a public figure, McGaughey had a reputation for honesty, plain speaking, and mastery of political economy. "In the circles of organized labor in Minneapolis and the state of Minnesota," one reporter claimed, Jack McGaughey was recognized as "a conservative thinker but fearless when his mind [was] once made up, and possessing a tireless energy and quick perception, he [was] apt to see a point or grasp an idea with more than ordinary rapidity." John Lamb, the state labor commissioner and a Knight himself, wrote a letter in support of McGaughey for deputy labor commissioner. Lamb asserted that McGaughey was "prominently identified with the cause of labor in this state, and possess[ed] . . . the necessary qualifications."[4] Above all, McGaughey was familiar with political economy and the condition of workers.

An accomplished public speaker, capable of moving audiences with his logic and wit, McGaughey, the "one-armed ex-soldier, scholar and poet," appeared before audiences as a local labor giant. At a Knights of Labor gathering in Hastings, Minnesota, he spoke for two hours on the history, object, and aims of the order. "Oft interrupted by applause," his address "electrified the audience" and provided "a grand intellectual treat." In appearance, McGaughey had "a light form, medium height, and carrie[d] on his shoulders a well-balanced head; blue eyes, light hair, a pleasant face. In manners, gentlemanly, courteous, and easy. . . . His voice [was] clear, musical, and full-toned. . . . His eloquence [was] of the impassioned, impressive character, lofty and sublime, always argumentative, clear and distinct."[5]

Some sixty years later, McDonald recalled that she met McGaughey in the vestibule of a union hall during a strike meeting: "I had heard of him vaguely as a fine speaker and a man active in helping to get better conditions for workers. Someone introduced us. He said, 'I heard your talk to the girls. Now look here, I think you'd make a good speaker. Would you like to try it? I might help you.'"[6] As he further explained, "I learned a great many things by experience, and I am willing to pass them on to you as far as you will accept them."[7] Already active in local labor circles by that time, McDonald probably knew his reputation as an orator. She consented to study with him.

What McGaughey taught McDonald was his own style of oratory, which relied on clear presentation, conversational style, and what he called "a basis of facts."[8] He was a harsh teacher. As McDonald later remembered, McGaughey believed she had talent but also thought her "glib of tongue." She recalled him saying that "you've got much to learn about how to present your matter seriously to your audience."[9] Much of his advice was basically to enrich her store of knowledge by learning political economy and mastering social statistics. McGaughey taught her basic elements of verbal persuasion and prose style—balancing the story and using plain cases and vivid examples. He advised, "When you talk about abuses that exist in factories, never fail to point out that there are some employers who are absolutely good, honest and fair to their employees." He added, "Be as earnest as you like, and always speak the truth."[10] She also was to speak without any notes. As she recalled, McGaughey "said if I didn't know a thing well enough to speak extempore and make my points clear to the audience—Well, I didn't know it. I have since proved the value of that test."[11] Over the year that they jointly spoke at public engagements, McDonald learned her craft by constant practice. "You speak first," McGaughey said. "No matter how much you stumble, you must learn to speak without notes. If you can't do it, you don't know your subject. Then I will come along and pick up the loose thread and make your effort seem a pleasant talk."[12]

In June 1888, Eva McDonald made her "maiden speech" in front of an audience of Duluth trade unionists. As a way of setting the stage, she introduced herself not as an expert or an orator, but as "one of the people." She had "worked for [her] living so long, and . . . seen so many abuses" that she felt it necessary to "raise a voice in protest against the conditions under which women now work and endeavor to make them a better condition of affairs." Her talk that night was passionate, if a little incoherent. Because she was inexperienced and not well-schooled in political economy, McDonald presented stories of the moral dangers to which workingwomen were exposed rather than propose remedies for their situation. Playing to the crowd, she spoke of women who could not "get respect in the workplace" and foremen who gave them every "open and covert insult." Often faced with the choice of tolerating abuse or quitting work, women lacked the means to demystify their wages or educate themselves into better work. Far from being "noble and holy" (in the language of the Knights), women's labor was often used to "degrade" and "lower" them in "the eyes of the people." Much of McDonald's speech reflected the complaints of the women strikers that spring. With a flourish, she concluded with a call for action: "Let the girls band together, so that no girl need be insulted when she works; let her be paid what her services are worth; let them go out evenings and get a practical education. Let the men and women band together and give working girls their share of this world's good, so that life, instead of being drudgery, may be one of peace and happiness."[13]

McDonald's sense of herself as a speaker emerged in constant practice. A few months later her second speech met with approval. The *Mankato Review* deemed it "a true exposition of the wrongs under which only too many of our working girls labor." That evening, McDonald "displayed an earnestness which carried conviction to the hearts of her audience." McGaughey followed with his own speech on "the wrongs of working men."[14] McDonald told a reporter years later that, "though my apprenticeship as a public speaker was very trying to me—and, I doubt not, to my audiences—I yet acquired a knack of speaking at any time and in any surroundings and also learned to speak to working people in a simple and direct manner that they readily understood." Bristling at McGaughey's not infrequent criticism, McDonald often wanted to quit. Still, she returned to his tutelage time and again, becoming "as much at ease while speaking from a dry-goods box as a town hall platform or from the stage of an opera house."[15] One evening, her familiarity with McGaughey's topics gave her the ability to give his speech rather than her own. Afterward, he announced that she had "graduated." It was the end of her lessons.[16]

The Athenaeum of Crude Philosophers

McGaughey was only one of a circle of local labor intellectuals to whom McDonald referred as "the Athenaeum of Crude Philosophers." In an 1895 newspaper story, she recalled the times "when Brosnan, McGaughey, Clark, Lamb, Doc Finnegan and myself used to hold a little session every day in a dingy little office. 'The Athenaeum of Crude Philosophers' someone sarcastically styled our group. We were crude enough, but we were terribly in earnest. We studied and discussed the labor question as if the fate of the universe hung upon our decisions."[17] The group's public persona was as local assembly 805, also known as the North Star Labor Club. It was a circle of printers, reformers, and labor intellectuals who, as McDonald recalled, "shaped Knights of Labor policy locally."[18] Its members included McGaughey; Timothy Brosnan, the Knights master workman; John Lamb, labor commissioner; Michael Finnegan, a doctor and political activist; George William Morey, a radical printer; and Thomas Clark, a printer and songwriter.[19] Over their careers, they—like McDonald's father—shifted in and out of craft work, sometimes running small businesses and sometimes working for local governments.

By 1888, the Athenaeum adopted McDonald as their latest protégé. They took care to engage her in public debates, even though she "was the youngest both in point of age and knowledge." Three of its members figured prominently in McDonald's education: Lamb, Clark, and Brosnan. Their life stories provide the backdrop for the Knights' political developments. Born in Peru, Illinois, in 1853, Lamb moved with his family first to St. Peter, Minnesota, and then to the Twin Cities. As a young man, he worked his way through the state university and took a job as a surveyor. Eventually, he returned to Minneapolis, where he became a draftsman. Later elected statistician for the local Knights,[20] Lamb contributed editorials to the mainstream and labor press and militantly advocated a labor party. His editorials appeared in local newspapers as well as in *John Swinton's Paper* and the *Journal of United Labor.* His ideas were framed, much as those of the other labor radicals, by a mélange of labor republican, producerist, and nativist thought. An "earnest advocate" of organization for women,[21] Lamb commissioned the first report on workingwomen when he became head of the state Bureau of Labor Statistics.[22]

If Lamb's forte was intellectual engagement and statistical prowess, Clark, one of the many printers in the Athenaeum, was known for other talents. In labor circles, Clark was known as "Monssini Baker," a singer and songwriter who was a welcome presence at local labor gatherings. On holidays and political gatherings, he led the Knights in "The Workingmen's Marseillaise" or "When Knights of Labor Men Shall Rule." Inspirational hymns to labor were not Clark's only talent. When the decision was made to build a labor temple, Clark founded the Knights of Labor Building Association. Over the years, he served as official printer for government agencies and published pamphlets, flyers, and campaign materials for the Democratic party, the Knights of Labor, and the state Farmers' Alliance. He also published, along with his songbook, two labor novels, Eva McDonald's *A Tale of the Twin Cities* and Henry Gantt's *Breaking the Chains.*[23]

By contrast, Brosnan invested in practical experience as a labor organizer and political activist. Born in Athens, Ohio, in 1854, he "attained manhood in its different stages in Tennessee, Massachusetts, and southern and eastern states" before settling in Minneapolis in 1885. There he found work as a clerk and later joined the Knights.[24] Known for "his sterling honesty" and "the gift of dispassionate judgment," Brosnan "saved the more impetuous ones from many a blunder." Furthermore, as Eva Valesh recalled, it was Brosnan who was the main impetus of the Athenaeum's efforts at public education: "Somehow our philosophers' circle was broken when Brosnan moved away and one by one we drifted into more active lines of work."[25]

Like the utopian proletarians of Jacques Rancière's *Nights of Labor,* the labor radicals of the Athenaeum were simultaneously working class and bourgeois. Joining the Knights of Labor for explicitly political reasons, they engaged in working-class culture with far greater enthusiasm than they had for the market economy. While their life histories were riddled with contradictions, the men of the North Star Labor Club were able to find a path toward labor modernism from the utopian and popular republican designs of the Gilded Age.[26] Yet in creating a working-class political culture committed to utopian ideals, they also acted as hardheaded and practical politicians. Their politics was rooted in an understanding of manhood and citizenship in which anyone dependent on wages could not be a whole man. To them, such dependents lacked the autonomy and civic virtue required of citizens in a republic. It was those sentiments that they sought to pass on in their adoption of McDonald as protégé.

Among the Crude Philosophers, the central tenets of labor republicanism still held sway as late as the 1890s. Their growing fear of the wealth and power increasingly concentrated in the hands of corporations was framed in traditional republican language that condemned political corruption and vested interests. Seeking the means to economic autonomy from dependence on wage work and the market, they opted for cooperative means where possible. Their own version of republican virtue was rooted in "producerism," a popular version of the labor theory of value that saw all worth stemming from the labor of a broadly defined group of producers. Only those dependent on the largesse of state and private charity, those underage, and those living off the work of others (bankers, liquor salesmen, and sometimes lawyers) were excluded.[27] For the Athenaeum radicals, independence was the defining mark of a citizen. They were prepared, in adopting McDonald, to see women take up the role of citizen as well.

The Political Functions of Citizens

Both locally and nationally, the Knights of Labor exhibited ambivalence about what constituted viable political strategies for the producing classes. How, in an era of concentrated wealth, could workers hope to use the state to ameliorate their problems, or must they rely on economic solutions alone? While many, including third-party advocate John Lamb, were dubious about the efficacy of politics, the Knights of Labor became invested in a wide range of efforts to achieve working-class political ends. Locally, the use of police in strikes, the eight-hour movement, and free textbooks caught the attention of workingmen, who came out to support a range of parties and candidates. It was the high tide of such political activism for labor. As historian Leon Fink has shown, the Knights launched nearly two hundred labor tickets between 1886 and 1888, in addition to supporting workingmen who ran for office as Democrats or Republicans. Labor politics came to mean endorsing the political capacity of ordinary workingmen who ran for office themselves.[28] At the same time, politicians thrived on the reputation of being "the friend of the workingman." As one newspaper wrote, "The workingman [would] always be an object of solicitude at election time, and the average municipal candidate is lavish in his promises to be watchful of labor interests should he be elected."[29]

Despite labor leaders' reservations about party politics, the workingmen's cause in Minneapolis was linked to both national political ferment and local conflict. In 1888, the year of McDonald's first public successes, the sound and fury of political parties was devoted to booming speeches about the tariff and torchlight parades as "the dinner pail brigade" (the Democrats) and the Grand Old Party (the Republicans) once more charged the political arena in mock combat. Carrying banners aloft, the electoral warriors fought it out on the local scene in "bloody shirt campaigns" that called on Civil War loyalties and "dinner pail" skirmishes in which class conflict played a major role. Pursued through parades, rallies, and picnics, elections resembled street fights more than debating societies. If the social violence that disrupted antebellum politics had diminished in intensity, party races still used the language of military virtue as candidates contested issues, arrayed forces, and won campaigns. Manhood was tested on the field of electoral battle, where men ganged together in partisan armies.[30]

Labor's political strength was characterized by the continuing vitality of the working-class public sphere and lingering adherence to republican beliefs among the skilled workers, labor intellectuals, and small businessmen who formed the core of Knights leadership. At the same time, their educational efforts did not supersede other aspects of Gilded Age politics. Even a relatively new urban area like Minneapolis had a political machine that fostered and rewarded loyalty among workingmen. The head of the local machine was Albert Alonzo "Doc" Ames, city mayor for four nonconsecutive terms. Like many of the workingmen's advocates who followed him, he pursued his political career through the most convenient channels. First an alderman and then city health officer, he was elected mayor in 1876, 1882, 1886, and 1900. Described as "one of the most handsome men that ever lived in the city" and "a commanding, soldierly figure, erect, with an eye that drew people," Ames was genial, loyal, and generous. He thought of himself as a "man of the people" and "friend and champion of the laboring people."[31] Later profiled as one of the bosses in Lincoln Steffens's *The Shame of the Cities*, Ames became known for political corruption, bribery, and graft. In the 1880s, however, he drew the loyal support of workingmen in the Democratic party, and many of the Knights owed political allegiance to him.

Workingmen's advocates benefited from the patronage of the machine and the Democratic party more generally. Richard Shadrick, the first Knights organizer in Minnesota, edited Ames's party paper. John Swift—McDonald's benefactor and a construction worker, officer in the Knights of Labor, and political boss—became a county commissioner. Michael Mogan, another active Knight and a machinist, became city jailer. In 1889, McGaughey was accused of seeking a place on the police commission and later became assistant labor commissioner; McDonald herself sought and received a clerkship in the State House.[32] In a political system where elections were decided by thin margins, the voting power of urban workingmen guaranteed that some of their leaders would be granted spoils.

Workingmen's politics were thus sustained by realistic assessments of the resources the political system both granted and rescinded. The power of workers' votes at the local level made possible individual careers in politics and expanded the potential uses of the state. If patronage was one aspect, so, too, was enlarging the functions of government to bolster education, regulate employment, find facts and promote legislation, and provide city jobs for the unemployed. Labor ideologues did not understand such efforts to entangle them in what they viewed as a corrupt political system but rather as the first step in reforming that system. When, for example, the state legislature established a bureau of labor, the candidate to fill the job of labor commissioner was John

Lamb, the statistician of the local Knights, a match of skill to position but also a political gift to "workingmen."[33]

Lamb's appointment created within the realm of the state a source—sometimes the only source—of information about women and child wage-earners, the prevalence of strikes, industrial accidents, and labor union membership—information vital to the creation of public policy and the regulation of employment. It also served to educate the public to labor's needs. The Democratic party, third-party advocates, and labor's political pressure supported the creation of the Bureau of Labor Statistics and benefited from it in ways unrelated to reform. In essence, this model of politics, what one might rightly see as the predecessor of interest-group politics, was created and practiced at the heart of the Workingmen's Democracy of the Knights of Labor. While Lamb argued that in patronage politics "the proper object and function of the state is perverted and abused, and the state loses its utility as an agent of defense, and becomes an engine of oppression to the common people,"[34] he and other workingmen's advocates were deeply invested in using the government's largesse for the good of workingmen.

The Unnatural Discontent of the Wearers of Dirty Shirts

The presence of workingmen in politics gave rise to heightened class hostility and ridicule in the public sphere. The cartoons of Thomas Nast portrayed the working class as animals and their political leaders as thieves and monsters. The stories of Mr. Dooley, which regularly lampooned the laziness and intelligence of Irish immigrants, equated poverty and foreign birth with cruelty, dirt, disease, and moral turpitude. In these and other ways, Gilded Age culture sanctioned the economic depredations of the age. Resurgent biological racism damned the immigrant masses to generations of poverty and blamed their plight on inherited traits, while conservative religious ideologies gave their blessings to indifference and rationalized wealth. Knights leader Terence Powderly himself argued that workers should strive for respectability. Only a "professional agitator . . . denounces a clean boot and a white shirt as badges of the oppressor and rails at all neatness and cleanness in personal appearance." For Powderly, it was a "contemptible notion that the workingmen should wear overalls and a grimy face at all times and that the labor advocate appear on the platform in rags."[35] Despite labor's claim of legitimacy, many upper- and middle-class citizens saw working-class political activism—even when dressed in white shirts and clean boots—as threatening not only to the social order but also to the human race.[36]

In the 1888 campaign, Republicans displayed contempt and hostility toward workers as a whole. In the *Tribune*, a local Republican newspaper, Democratic picnics and parades were characterized as the gatherings of barbarians and boys. A barbecue was attended, so the reporter offered, by "a few leading Democrats, a number of respectable, ordinary everyday voters, and the rest of the rabble of the town." The rabble "smashed every plug hat" in sight, "threw chunks of brown bread" at the wearers, and raised false alarms in the crowd. Entertained by bands and speakers, they wandered from stand to stand and "many carried huge ox ribs, from which they gnawed the raw flesh."[37] In a similar fashion, the *Tribune* portrayed the Democratic parade a month later as "an awkward, straggling, and unpicturesque mass" compared to the orderly, powerful, and well-dressed assembly of Republicans. Those attending the rally were represented as "a number of the unwashed Democracy who might well be called 'back numbers.'"[38] By the campaign of 1888, whatever class truce might have existed in local politics obviously began to break down. On the excuse that the Democratic campaign for Ames in 1884 had been marred by "thugs" throwing rotten eggs at Republican opponents, the political exchange in 1888 had escalated to new heights of party and class hostility.

Eva McDonald undertook her first political campaign in the wake of her newfound celebrity. Her candidacy for school board had as its backdrop the nasty class politics, prejudices, and policies of the period. As a working-class woman, she was praised for bringing labor's views to the school board election and reviled for daring to enter the political fray. For the first but not the last time, both reformers and politicians criticized her association with labor politicians and the press. More than that, the candidacy of a young working-class woman raised opposition among newly mobilized women voters in a local race.

More than just social class factored in the local elections of 1888. In the school board election, charges of religious prejudice and political corruption and the first attempt at mobilizing women voters steered campaign rhetoric away from American manhood toward women in politics. Early estimates showed a vigorous registration effort in the wards, including the registration of women voters seeking to exercise their school suffrage rights. A week before the election, more than 35,000 voters were registered. While the figures were exaggerated, press coverage sparked additional interest among women.[39] It was not just the novelty of women voters that called forth predictions that local voting might reach 50,000. Rather, the school board election campaign brought up charges and countercharges of political corruption and ethnic conflict.

The school board campaign offered urban reformers one of their best opportunities to affect the political process, and the reform slate was particularly strong. In coalition with the local Women's Christian Temperance Union (WCTU), the Prohibition party actively campaigned for local candidates, especially in the school board races. That year, the Prohibition party's city convention drew strong response from women who had the right to vote in school board elections.[40] Suggestions that the school superintendent or the board candidates were engaged in self-aggrandizement, religious interference, or simple inequity seeped between the lines of political debate. A fomenting, if vague, anti-Catholicism surfaced on the local scene in the discussion of school board policy and the election.[41]

Years later, Eva Valesh remembered her campaign for the school board as inconsequential. She had been nominated in a burst of enthusiasm at the local Democratic party meetings even though, as she claimed, "I was a woman; I wasn't yet twenty-one years old; I lacked the judgment to deal with educational matters."[42] In an interview, Valesh asserted that "the nomination was a matter of some surprise to me, as I had no knowledge of any such action. . . . I intended to resign at first, but after carefully considering the situation have concluded to allow my name to remain on the ticket."[43] Her modesty in the press was not matched by reluctance to speak on educational issues. She appeared several times that fall to lecture on "the school question."[44] On the platform, McDonald was not as naive in educational matters as she pretended. In a later letter to Blue Earth County School Superintendent Sarah Christie Stevens, McDonald wrote that she could "talk theoretically about school teaching by the yard" and considered herself fully qualified to promote educational reform. During the election, she wisely praised the professionalism of women teachers while criticizing the parochial character of the school board, its corruption, and its ethnic and religious prejudice.[45]

Popular response in the newspapers tended to favor reform-minded middle-class candidates. Editorial writers cited McDonald's youth and inexperience and her connections to labor circles as reasons to vote against her. They also attacked her for willfully distorting facts, airing personal grievances, and practicing partisanship. Her defenders emphasized her record and integrity and condemned her opponents' prejudices.[46] Her candidacy and that of other working-class activists provoked a strong opposition from the local WCTU. Followers accused McDonald's fellow labor advocate, the Reverend Falk Gjertsen, of a "brutal assault" on WCTU President Frances Willard. Although a "broad-gauged, liberal-minded, and thoroughly Americanized gentleman," Gjertsen had disgraced himself when he "referred to this noble and best of women [Willard] as 'a platform harlot,' who stalks around the country giving speeches [and] has done irreparable injury to the temperance cause, assuming man's position." Such accusations did not endear the workingmen's ticket to the reform community.[47]

Early signs of a Republican victory prepared local Democrats to lose city and county offices. They looked wherever they could for small victories on the local front. No doubt McDonald's reputation in labor circles and the opportunity presented to capture some part of the women's vote sparked her nomination to the school board slate. At the same time, as she remembered years later, party regulars discouraged her from campaigning. McDonald's only speech was at the Democratic gathering the night before the election. As she recalled, "The meeting was held in a large theater. It was packed. For the first and only time in my life, I felt stage-fright. Dr. Ames, the genial candidate for mayor [actually he was the outgoing mayor], introduced me as the 'pride of Minneapolis and the job of the Democratic party.' My speech was brief and well-received. Of course, I wasn't elected."[48]

The mass meeting that night represented the hope that the Democratic party would be able to stave off disaster. Publicity in Minneapolis's streets and the newspapers called for a lively meeting with attendance sure to exceed 5,000. Later reports were that 10,000 men marched through the streets shouting for the democracy. The *Globe's* editorial claimed that the gathering was "never equaled in either numbers or enthusiasm" and anticipated the Republicans "retir[ing] in dismay" at the large turnout. Transparencies carried aloft declared that "We Are All Registered, You Bet," "The Democratic Party is the Workingman's Party," and "The Dinner Pail Brigade Is in Line." Under the light of colored fires and fireworks, Democratic ward and ethnic clubs from across the city marched in line behind the party regulars, as Danes, Norwegians, Poles, and Bohemians were "out in full force."[49]

The People's Theater, where the party faithful—including many new women voters—gathered, was filled to the rafters. Mayor Ames called the audience to its feet with his stirring declaration that the Democratic party was the people's party. As he confessed, "Some people forget that they came from the people, but I do not, and I thank the old 'dinner pail' brigade for my elevation. When I saw the demonstration of tonight I leaned back and waved my bandanna in admiration." His references to the old soldiers' vote, to the reunion of blue and gray and the rights of workingmen, and the redemption of the people through politics were familiar themes to his audience. In the midst of wild cheering, Ames then introduced McDonald, "the product of Democracy." McDonald's reported speech was quite brief. She admitted that her candidacy was historic, for "never before in the history of this city has a woman been permitted to take the stand in a political meeting." She spoke of the condition of the public schools, but her words were fairly measured and uncontroversial. The rest of the evening speeches were intermingled with attacks on the Republican party and its tax policies.[50]

The coverage of the presidential race and even the attention devoted to McDonald obscured the fact that local issues dominated the election. Charges of corruption endangered the mayor's reelection campaign, and ethnic conflict, hidden in the reform rhetoric of the school board race, surfaced in the political realm. The party machinery and the threat to or promise of patronage brought supporters out to vote in great numbers. As one reporter declared, "There was one fact that stood out in bold relief, and that was the city election dwarfed and overshadowed everything. The hacks were all for the city candidates, and most of the work at the polls was to the same end, much to the disgust of many candidates on either side." The hacks' presence was evident in the high level of split-ticket voting, as local party men encouraged the use of pasters, or stickers with the names of alternate candidates, and scratched candidates in an effort to ensure some division of offices.[51]

The Republican candidate won the mayoral election by 3,000 votes. Scandal had undermined but not defeated his campaign. In most other races, voters divided their votes among multiple parties, because of the presence of local Prohibition and Alliance-Labor candidates. Alliance-Labor candidates showed surprising strength, and many previously Democratic wards went Republican. Most of the races were taken by small margins.[52] While McDonald and her Democratic running mate lost by more than 8,000 votes, more than 12,000 voters cast their ballot for her as the first woman candidate for school board.[53]

In such an election, the novelty of a woman candidate might have swung the school board vote in the Democrats' favor, but no one had counted on the opposition to McDonald from women voters. Their opposition provides some insight into women's involvement in Minneapolis's political parties. Out in numbers for the first time since granted school suffrage, woman voters caught the attention of the press. One reporter wrote, "The ladies were out in full force, and walked up to the polls and dropped in their ballots 'like little men.'" Another pundit declared, "The woman in politics has become an amazingly prominent figure within the past few weeks, and the lords of creation are beginning to be sorry they allowed her even a shadow of a vote." In the "final act of the comedy," the woman who "dare[d] to own her true age" "dare[d] to stand in line and wait her turn to cast a vote."[54]

In the new world of women voters, McDonald's partisan allegiances to labor did little to help and much to hinder her candidacy. Even in Democratic wards, women mobilized to vote against her. According to the local press, women voters publicly and demonstrably opposed McDonald. The *Globe*, McDonald's own newspaper, reported, "When Eva McDonald tickets were tendered them one of them seized the ballot, tore it in two and stamped the bits of paper into the mud, while her eyes flashed with the anger she seemed to be anxious to display rather than to conceal."[55] In the school board race, McDonald had earned the opposition of urban women reformers simply by her association with labor's cause. Being a workingman's candidate did little good for a woman interested in one of the few public offices available to her.

Eight Hours of Work in a City of Idle Men

Defeat in the 1888 election did not discourage the forces of urban reform or workingmen's advocates. The labor and Populist campaigns that followed drew much of their energy and resources from the coalition between such groups and the Farmers' Alliance. Politics in the local community, however, was not strictly confined to workingmen's campaigns in local or national elections. As members of the Knights of Labor knew, it was important to keep the working-man's plight in front of the public. In the years between elections, major educational and lobbying campaigns were launched to support the principal concerns of workingmen's advocates: the eight-hour day, abolition of convict labor, and public work for the unemployed. In these campaigns, McDonald was a central figure. At the same time, the question of political capacity—access to the political realm and unfettered ability to participate in public debate—was at the heart of labor concerns.

Eight-hour campaigns held a place of honor in the constellation of working-class politics. Conducted in the 1880s by a Knights of Labor/trade unionists coalition, the eight-hour workday campaign sought voluntary compliance from private and state employers—that is, labor advocates pressed these employers to reduce the number of hours that they required their employees to work. Joining the national movement striking for an eight-hour day, Minneapolis local assemblies pushed the issue in public forums and private negotiations. Publicity was seen as vital to the effort. As a labor writer declared, "The leading difficulty in the way of shortening the working day is that of not being able to get a hearing. Facts by the thousands can be furnished to prove the benefits and the necessity of devoting less time to bodily toil and more to education, recreation and improvement in health, morals and manners."[56]

Shortening working hours was vital, and not simply because leisure was workingmen's chief aim. Rather, it was a matter of self-determination. As Jack McGaughey declared, "The working people have a perfect right to say just how many hours they will work. The establishment of the eight-hour day is a step toward solving the labor problem. I believe that the two hours would be spent in study, not in the saloon." Moreover, he added, "a shortening of hours has always caused an awakening of intelligence in any craft where applied."[57]

The health of the nation—both mental and physical—was at stake. As one labor advocate wrote, both insanity and suicide were the result of the laboring and business classes working long hours without leisure: "Facts prove that a very large proportion of the deplorable intemperance of the time is caused by the mental and physical exhaustion of the overworked classes, and the right way to fight intemperance in the use of liquor is to give up, first, the more baleful intemperance of excessive, slavish toil."[58] Athenaeum member Michael Finnegan, a physician, argued that the eight-hour system was necessary for "physiological reasons." There would be, he claimed, "fewer paupers, fewer drunkards, and fewer broken-down men and women if that should become the rule of life."[59]

The declining electoral fortunes of labor led to the formation of the Eight-Hour League in 1889. Organized by representatives of both the Knights of Labor and trade unions, the "purely educational" campaign "to create a sympathetic public sentiment in behalf of the eight hour day" engaged the local labor movement for the next four years. Shortening the workday became the working class's central issue and absorbed the energies of many of its most experienced members as well as the up-and-coming generation of labor unionists.[60] In the Twin Cities, the Eight-Hour League recruited both McDonald and Frank Valesh, a young cigar-maker and union leader. In frequent public meetings in union halls, picnic grounds, public squares, and street corners, the league sought to educate the public for a shorter workday and organized ward clubs in support of their demands.

The Eight-Hour League undertook nonstop agitation to educate the public about this issue. Throughout 1889, it held numerous meetings in front of ready-made audiences of local Knights of Labor assemblies and trade unions. As McDonald later recounted, the campaign had a romantic cast. Representing herself as a "'a committee of one' to educate public opinion on the subject of the eight-hour day," she cited her pioneering efforts in the campaign, which included "wheedl[ing]" her father into letting her use "his horse-drawn light delivery wagon as a platform."[61] John McDonald "sat on the tail board of wagon to see 'that no one annoyed me.'" Her younger brothers, by now adolescents, made signs with ink made from lamp soot, and she bribed them with "cakes from the pantry . . . to distribute the bills." Neighborhood boys were paid in small change "to carry the transparencies" down Washington Avenue.[62] "Somehow," she remembered, "the newspapers got hold of the meetings and regarded them as news, and so my friends the reporters came. They gave me 'good press' partly because the campaign was a bit of a novelty and partly because I was one of them and always tried to give them a good story."[63] More

Eva McDonald as Populist orator, ca. 1891. Appearing in an *Arena* article on women Populists, this is the most familiar photograph of Eva Valesh. Photo by Rugg. Courtesy of the Minnesota Historical Society.

realistically, her stump speeches for the shorter workday were part of a wider campaign. Alongside eight-hour stalwarts such as T. H. Lucas, McGaughey, and H. B. Martin, McDonald delivered speeches almost nightly. At one meeting, she spoke "with characteristic eagerness and eloquence" and "pleaded for unity and organization of effort to shorten the hours of labor." Given her strenuous efforts, in 1889 McDonald was appointed an organizer for the local Knights of Labor.[64] From this point forward, her career was carried by popular appeal, a knack for publicity, and the goodwill of political friends.

Utopians and Pragmatists

Reading about the political campaigns of 1888–89 renews questions about the politics and practicality of the Knights of Labor that have been the source of much debate in labor history. From the view of labor historian John Commons that the Knights of Labor were mere utopians and dreamers, the group's reputation recovered in the new labor history as local studies of it found a richer, more engaged, and infinitely more practical circle of workingmen's advocates than older studies suggested. In particular, this revival benefited from the work of historian Leon Fink in reinterpreting the group's political activism. He argued that the Gilded Age labor movement used politics in four ways: to express class conflict; to serve as a hedge against police intervention in labor struggles; to create class legislation, especially in public works, and to transform class politics into social movements.[65] Fink's formulation described the wide range and uneven success of working-class politics in the era.

Eva McDonald's rise to labor advocate and political candidate suggests interpretations different from Fink's. Even a cursory glance at Gilded Age working-class politics reveals its use as ritual, as an instrument of individual and collective social mobility, and as constitutive of working-class manhood. The Athenaeum of Crude Philosophers provides a good example of these complementary functions. Its members debated, often and vociferously, on the legitimacy of political action, but they remained convinced that politics was important in and of itself, whether in republican duty (citizenship as political activism) or as an arena to achieve honor and value apart from the employment nexus. The question of what the functions of government ought to be were ever present in their labor newspapers, columns, and forums.

It was not, however, a high-minded debate about the uses of the state that absorbed these men but a conflict over pragmatic and material ends. Although the Knights of Labor did not presume that the government should own property, they used their political clout to fight for public jobs and insulation from the vagaries of the private economy. They did so using a language of manhood that they shared with their opponents from across the political spectrum. In the 1880s, the demand for eight hours of labor and a day system in public work represented labor's attempt to regulate working conditions. Workingmen's advocates also sought to elect public officials who condemned the use of police in strikes. They wanted to stem the class hostility of local courts and improve the public school system with better facilities and free textbooks.[66] Given this history, we might modify Fink's conclusions to expand the uses of labor politics to include its instrumental aspects in patronage and individual mobility and its cultural and symbolic power.

The quest for political power by both workingmen and businessmen had a masculine cast.

The eight-hour movement provided another vehicle from which to view the state's powers. Labor history has usually understood the movement as solely directed toward workplace issues and reflective of the shift toward labor modernism in its focus on wage work. The reinvigorated eight-hour movement suggests two other possibilities. First, while the campaign to limit workday hours sought to address the imbalance between workers' and employers' power in the workplace, the movement was most effective in setting the conditions for public employment and government work. Frustrated with court and police hostility and private employer resistance, working-class political activists turned to the state. Their attitudes toward state intervention, while deeply ambivalent, demonstrated investment in and belief in working-class ownership of the public realm.

Furthermore, a long-neglected dimension of the eight-hour movement was its power to directly address one of the most charged class issues of the time—the declining ability of "the people," whether the producing classes or simply workers, to engage in a meaningful politics. In contrast to the growing and visible power of moneyed interests in public life, workingmen's political leverage seemed to disintegrate with each turn of the wheel. By restricting labor to eight hours a day, labor advocates hoped to increase working-class political capacity—by encouraging workers to use their increased leisure time for education, political debate, and civic involvement. Symbolically, controlling the hours of labor meant that a man could limit his own obligation—and perhaps dependency—on waged employment. Devoting the best of his energies to the political realm, a workingman could restore his manhood in political striving.

From this perspective, the interesting twist in late-nineteenth-century political culture was that the new visibility of workingwomen, woman suffrage, and temperance agitation raised questions about how women would fit into workingmen's politics. Working-class women had no manhood to gain or lose through wage dependency. Although only in the early stages of her career, Eva McDonald became a symbol of the Knights of Labor's efforts to integrate education, workingwomen, and women's issues into the traditional agenda of class politics. Extending patronage to women, as they had to McDonald, was one way in which workingmen's advocates signaled their desire to incorporate women into the polity. Yet several obstacles stood in the way. Women did not have full suffrage and would not for another thirty years. Workingmen's attitudes exhibited genuine ambivalence toward women's claims for equality, especially with regard to wage labor. Women's advocates themselves, bound in a very different kind of class politics, viewed with suspicion the emergence of a "working girl" as spokesperson not only for workingmen but also for women as a whole. The conflict between the politics of class and of gender would continue to trouble the labor movement, as did the shifting ground of class-based political action and the fragile alliance of producers. As a workingwoman in a social movement of workingmen, McDonald had struggled for and gained political and personal success. Her showing in the school board election and her work in the eight-hour movement rapidly moved her to the center of local labor politics. The question was whether it was possible for a woman, even as the clever daughter and student of workingmen, to sustain her place among them.

CHAPTER 3

TELLING *TALES*

Labor Conflict, Class Politics, and Lawlessness in the Great Streetcar Strike of 1889

> The men are getting tired of having just and reasonable requests
> treated with contempt. When the limit of their patience is reached,
> a strike is likely to follow.
>
> —St. Paul *Globe*, April 7, 1889

In 1889, Eva McDonald's alter ego, Eva Gay, made her last appearance when *A Tale of the Twin Cities: Lights and Shadows of the Street Car Strike in Minneapolis and St. Paul* was published. A recounting of the cities' recent and explosive labor conflict, the book purported to be neither "an artistic literary production" nor "a sworn statement of facts occurring during the strike" but "a souvenir of the incidents which made this strike one of the most remarkable events in the history of the North Star state." McDonald asked that any "lack of continuity," "absence of polished phrases," and "dearth of imaginative power" be attributed to her "belong[ing] to the sex whose members are popularly supposed not to have any abilities outside of that involved in managing a kitchen or choosing a spring costume."[1] Despite the disclaimer, McDonald used Eva Gay as an effective narrative voice to overcome public hostility toward the strikers and their sympathizers.

A Tale of the Twin Cities was published by Thomas Clark in a first print run of 12,000 copies. It was advertised in local and national labor newspapers. The success or failure of a publication, however, cannot convey either its meaning to the audience or its purpose, which might give us insight into the ways in which the labor movement sought to express, transmit, and spread its ideas. *A Tale of the Twin Cities* was primarily designed to invest the newspaper-reading public in working-class political struggles. Its author invited citizens—strikers, signers of the mass petition, and boycotters—to take *A Tale* home as a "souvenir" and thus remember that the labor question was not simply about labor but about the common welfare. Interpretations of the strike, even so soon after its end, were subject to the precarious memories and shifting alliances of a distrustful and politically divided reading public that was fragmented along class lines. Labor's side of the conflict thus competed with other stories from the press and politicians. But if *A Tale of the Twin Cities* represented the possibilities and limitations of cultural production in solving the labor question, it also revealed how McDonald had learned to use both literary and political means to advance labor's cause.

No Wheels Turn

In the spring of 1889, still heady from her rapid ascent as star in the labor community, McDonald abandoned her Eva Gay series to become labor editor and general reporter for the *Globe*. A popular speaker, she spent an increasing amount of time working on the eight-hour campaign and educating the public on labor's political agenda. Her speaking schedule brought her to social science forums and evening lectures on public education, ballot reform, and workingwomen. The Knights of Labor district assembly appointed her organizer, and her association with the labor intelligentsia brought her numerous opportunities to speak in front of audiences on the questions of the day. As her career escalated, though, she was increasingly drawn into the local conflict between streetcar workers and their employer.

In the spring of 1889, the longstanding tensions between Thomas Lowry, president of the Minneapolis and St. Paul Street Railway Company, and the Street Railway Employees Protective Association came to a head.[2] The introduction of coal-driven motor lines and the switch to an electric cable system to reduce costs set the stage for renewed labor conflict. Lowry sought to cut the labor force and resented that the union had forced him to hire more conductors.[3] Deciding to seize the opportunity to move against the union, Lowry discharged the older men and posted a wage reduction of 15 percent. Only three years before, the union settled a strike against the Minneapolis company with an agreement that guaranteed wages, working conditions, and job security.[4] The wage cuts effectively revoked that contract, which was not due to expire until mid-May; in St. Paul, such actions preempted any negotiation. Explicit in his desire to break the associations, Lowry presented his new employees with an ironclad agreement, which required them to pledge not to join a labor union.[5]

What was less well known at the time was that Lowry had already sold a controlling share of the streetcar company to eastern bondholders. He continued to run the company as his own, but he needed to meet the demands of his investors and the bond interest payments. Elsewhere in the country, companies worked to consolidate streetcar franchises and tighten expenses to increase profitability.[6] Throughout the strike, labor leaders argued that Lowry orchestrated his actions with these national efforts. The introduction of split-shifts and the push to eliminate conductors were central to the campaign.[7] Supported by an investigator's report, local labor leaders publicly denounced this "war against labor." Lowry's actions, they argued, signaled that "an aristocracy of gentlemen, a plutocracy of grasping parvenus, ha[d] arisen" and purposefully sought to widen the chasm between the classes.[8]

Whatever the cause of Lowry's cuts, the motormen in Minneapolis walked out on the morning of April 11, when the bill outlining the new wage cuts was posted in the streetcar barns. The news passed down each streetcar line. As members of the union boarded cars and conferred with drivers and conductors, the men abandoned their cars or returned to the barns. By three o'clock, the last car had returned; and the car starter reported the news to the company.[9] The next morning, St. Paul streetcar men joined their brethren in a joint city strike that closed down the streetcar lines. More than 300 St. Paul and 600 Minneapolis streetcar drivers went out on strike.[10]

The strikers' chief grievances focused on the wage reductions and the firm's anti-union activities. The strikers argued that Lowry "had been discharging good men and cutting wages since last November, without any apparent reason except that it seem[ed] easier to take new men and make them submit to arbitrary conditions than those who are more experienced in their work." Furthermore, "the men [were] getting tired of having just and reasonable requests treated with contempt." The company attempted to justify wage cuts on the basis of declining revenues and the need to raise money for new cable lines—an argument that outraged the union. One member declared that Lowry could not be losing money; "there [was] not a driver or a conductor in his employ who believe[d] it." The claim that there was no money to expand fell short of convincing an unwilling public. Pleas of poverty, many thought, merely served to cover Lowry's desire to expand his holdings, for they knew "if any one is to pinch or go hungry it must be the men."[11]

Newspaper and labor supporters responded with a new satirical view of "King Lowry," a drop box with a penny slot for "Poor Tom" to pay for his streetcar lines, and references to "the lordly tyrant Lowry."[12] Suffragist Marietta Bones referred to him, the company president, somewhat incongruously, as a "sycophant and lickspittle" of eastern capital. Striking workers wrote a burlesque on the ironclad contract that the company sought to enforce. At strike headquarters, they posted "Lord Lowry's Contract," which stipulated that workers belonged to "Lowry, body and soul, for all time to come." It was "signed with my heart's contempt" by "Sam Nobody, John Loafer, Peter Wontwork, and Jim Donothing, scabs."[13] In its public response, the local trades and labor assembly expressed skepticism. Lowry's history of watering company stock, they argued, represented "one of the most gigantic schemes of plunder that ever sacked a city under the forms of law."[14] Pleas for public support sounded hollow in the face of his actions. Similar tones of suspicion and ridicule later surfaced in McDonald's *Tale of the Twin Cities.*

More to the point, the working-class public—the streetcar drivers, their union supporters, and public sympathizers—had serious grievances against Lowry. He had a history of breaking union contracts and political maneuvering; the strike further put him in violation of his agreement to provide public transit. Ten thousand people gathered in Bridge Square on the night of April 11 to protest Lowry's actions. Drawing on labor's most charismatic speakers, the program included McDonald, labor advocate Thomas Lucas, and local firebrand J. W. Arctander. Ridiculing Lowry's public rationale for his drastic wage cuts, Arctander said that he had "read in the papers the other day that my friend Tom Lowry is going to the poorhouse, and [he] came down to console with him." Although, as one reporter noted, his rhetoric was charged, "it remained for Miss Eva McDonald to stir up the assembly. . . . She was quite plain in her advice. In fact, her language was of a very strong character and would have done credit to a Chicago anarchist."[15] While McDonald's comments were measured, they supported the general call for a petition campaign to urge the city to revoke Lowry's franchise for the streetcar lines. In petitioning government officials, citizens raised the stakes of the strike from contract arbitration to renegotiating public transportation. With a strong bid for city ownership of the streetcar line, labor leaders and reformers had merged community and workplace, public and private welfare, into a single fight.[16]

Public Sphere and Publicity

Not surprisingly, leaders of the Knights of Labor, the Eight-Hour League, and the federated trade unions became involved in the strike's publicity and political organization. Having spent the spring lecturing on the eight-hour day, McDonald now served as acting secretary for the streetcar employees' executive board. Reminiscing some sixty years later, she modestly described her role: "I was invited to attend the private meetings of their executive board and to act as general advisor in the conduct of the strike."[17] Yet it was her closeness to the strike's leadership that made possible the insider narrative of *A Tale of the Twin Cities,* her unsigned *Globe* reports, and her coverage of board meetings. As "the most popular newspaper slave present" at meetings, she did more than record the minutes. She spoke at several public meetings. Her denunciations of Lowry and the evils of the competitive system and her "pretty and graceful address" created a great demand for her on public platforms.[18]

Like the Eight-Hour League agitation, labor's publicity in the streetcar strike relied heavily on a voluntarist—and discursive—model of politics. Labor leaders chose a public forum to air their grievances and sought private arbitration between the company and its workers. They hoped that the public petition to end the use of special police, condemn strikebreakers, and revoke the Street Railway Company's franchise would pressure Lowry to negotiate. Speaking to mixed-class audiences, sympathizers sought to persuade their listeners of the rightness of the streetcar men's cause. During the strike, such speakers as Arctander, whom one reporter called "the Sancho Panza of the fair field of chivalric debate," invoked comic and corrupt images of authority in criticizing the competitive system.[19] Referred to as a "fiery Norse orator" and complimented for "his delightful Parisian accent" [*sic*], Arctander was a local favorite. McDonald, William Morey, and Jack McGaughey were described with similar enthusiasm for—or depreciation of—their appeal to the masses. In many ways, the meetings served as "veritable labor symposiums" to educate the public. They were pageants as well, as leaders appeared with "gorgeous badges, to distinguish themselves from the rank and file."[20] Throughout, labor reformers sought to stress the link between the fate of the working class and that of the citizenry in general.

Newspaper publicity was vital to the strikers' petition drive to revoke Lowry's street railway franchise. Published in the *Northwestern Labor Union,* the "monster" petition circulated throughout the cities, carrying about 20,000 signatures of citizens or "registered voters." Presented to the city councils in the second week of the strike, the petition demanded that officials ask the state legislature to allow them to purchase the street railway franchise. The Minneapolis council split its vote on the measure, while the St. Paul city council voted in favor of the petition. The House passed a version of the law, but the Senate voted overwhelmingly against it. After the vote, the Street Railway Company made a concerted effort to start the streetcars running again with replacement workers. On that day, sporadic street protests turned to riot.[21]

Civic Order and Urban Disorder

Most protests against the Street Railway Company took place on the street-cars, in the streets, and in neighborhoods far removed from both the streetcar barns and city hall. Striking drivers and conductors took part in the action, but the community was substantially involved, as newspapers were quick to report. Apart from withholding labor, striking drivers and their allies managed to keep replacement workers, nonstriking drivers, and special police from running the cars. In effect, the collective and cumulative actions of individuals talking to drivers, small groups throwing stones or unhitching horses, and large crowds obstructing streets and car lines publicly enforced the strike.

Using ridicule and physical intimidation, crowds during the first week de-railed cars, forced drivers and conductors off them, and kept the streetcar company from its regular service. "Mobs," "crowds," and "riots" occurred on a daily basis. Only the rain seemed to act as a deterrent. There were direct attacks on strikebreakers, from assault with a wrench, roughhousing, and "guying," or ridiculing, to community refusals to serve the "cowboy" strikebreakers food or allow them to eat unharassed at a local restaurant. By the end of the strike, not even labor meetings were safe from escalating public disorder, as "young hoodlums" interrupted speakers at a labor gathering in support of striking workers.[22]

In these public protests, women played a central role as the moral voice of community standards. They served notice, in public statement and crowd action, that they did not approve of the company's actions. From the very beginning, local women's leaders took part in public debate. Journalism school head Maria Sanford and the Dakota suffragist Marietta Bones joined in to urge Lowry to agree to arbitration with the union.[23] There were more widespread protests as well. On April 19, women in North Minneapolis, "indignant at the action of the police who were charged with clubbing an old lady," charged them with being drunk on the job. Gathering in a neighborhood hall a few days later, the women declared a public boycott of the streetcar lines.[24] Throughout the strike reporters noted that the crowds included not just "citizens" but "a great army of hoodlums and roughs, some women, and a good many children." The protesters not only shouted "scab" and "bread stealer" at the cars but threw stones, eggs, and bricks; placed paper caps and torpedoes on the rails; piled timbers on them; and unhitched horses. Other women tried to keep men from the cars by bribing them with money and food.[25]

The breadth of community responses suggest that the streetcar conflict was not only a struggle between capital and labor. General class resentment against Lowry played a role, and the strike operated as collective repayment for

Looking down Hennepin Avenue from Fourth Street, Minneapolis, ca. 1888. The open vistas here suggest a frontier feel, but the streetcars and commercial buildings show the city's rapid expansion. Streetcars such as these were involved in the transportation strike the following year. Photo courtesy of the Minnesota Historical Society.

Lowry's real estate dealings and his unseemly wealth. The streetcars reminded the working class of growing class privilege and division, as not many of those who stood at the bottom of the social scale could afford to ride them. And yet, in controlling urban transportation and public space, the street railway had become a presence in everyone's life—from pedestrians who choked on the fumes of its coal-burning cars to those whose lives were disturbed by the noise, the snorting of horses, and the shouting of passengers. Because streetcar lines tended to run through working-class immigrant neighborhoods, these areas particularly suffered from the noise, inconvenience, and danger of the new monstrosities. Furthermore, streetcar and rail lines—along with lumberyards and riverbanks—were just about the only places that working-class children could find to play. Children's deaths from these new machines—like that of Mr. Anderson's five-year-old son in the fall of 1888—incensed the community. If the daily newspaper censured Lowry's street railway company for "killing little children," it was not legally held responsible for such deaths. The lack of access to decent housing and the premature death of children raised issues about the ownership of public space, intensified class hostilities, and, as in the streetcar strike, sparked open conflict.[26]

Cowboys Who Never Saw a Cow

The urban disorder caused by the strike evoked images of the Wild West, a memory and an experience not far from the urban threshold of the Twin Cities in the 1880s. Indeed, McDonald's newspaper, the *St. Paul Globe*, kept a vigilant eye on developments in the Dakota territories and especially on the "Red Men" who appeared in its columns as signers of treaties, entertainers in Wild West shows, and stereotypes of violent, childish, and duplicitous behavior. At the same time that the streetcar conflict occupied the front pages, so, too, did the Oklahoma land rush, women politicians in Kansas, and sightseeing Dakota on their way to a tomahawk-throwing exhibition.[27] It is little wonder, then, that the disappearance of public conveyance evoked a "return to the days of stage coach service," whose driver was "a six-footer wearing a regular wild-west, broad-brimmed white hat." A *Globe* reporter who was undoubtedly McDonald wrote, "The whole get-up was 'Western' in nearly all the details, and the only thing lacking was the absence of a big gun slung in a holster to the side of the driver."[28]

In less than a week, the friendly cowboy driver was replaced by another image of the Wild West. As the streetcar company cast about for workers to replace its striking drivers, it recruited some men from Chicago and some local workers, most of whom promptly left the company's employ. The majority of new men came from Kansas City, first as thirty or forty individuals, then as the more numerous "gang of cowboy drivers."[29] It was the latter group, "an armed mob at the beck and call of a corporation," that provoked some of the most severe Lowry criticism and crowd violence during the strike. Twin Cities newspapers decried the use of outsiders in a local conflict, but at issue was more than the simple introduction of imported strikebreakers. Ethnic prejudices were also at play, as the cowboys, many of whom might well have been native-born southerners, clashed with immigrant and northern counterparts. Dressing to intimidate, the cowboys also "carried their big revolvers with them." Wearing "their hair long and drink[ing] poor whisky," they embodied outlaws of dime novels and western myths.[30] In *A Tale of the Twin Cities*, McDonald wrote, "They certainly looked vicious, and irate citizens promised them plenty of opportunity to display their boasted determination." Other writers were taken with the "dusky, sun-burned men wearing large-rimmed sombreros and chewing about four pounds of tobacco per minute." At the same time, "the Knights of the Lasso" were ridiculed "something scandalous" as working-class "idlers" were not intimidated by mean looks. The only real cowboy "stood on the platform with the reins in his hand and a devil-may-care air about him that protected him from insult or jeer. He knew how to drive and could give some of the old drivers pointers."[31]

The strikers and their sympathizers believed that Lowry hired "cowboys and toughs" explicitly to "frighten the men into an acceptance of the company's conditions." Some of these "cowboy desperadoes" were professional strike-breakers. In a *Journal* interview, Matt Ford, an engineer hired to work on the motor line during the strike, "boasted he had been a non-union man for 15 years." Another scab, a veteran of the cattle range wars, declared, "We didn't come here for fun. We have a reputation and we will keep it. This is the crowd that took the books from Cimarron to Engles in the Gray county seat war. There were a number of men killed at that time; so you can see we mean busi-ness." Only a few months before, the *Globe* had covered the raid of "notorious roughs and cowboys" in Gray County.[32]

The image of lawlessness that pervaded newspaper columns was clearly ex-aggerated. The cowboys were merely strikebreakers dressed in the guise of he-roes. As such, they became the subject of satire. Accompanying the article on desperado strikebreakers was a caricature of "Skinny Brown," his revolver en-larged and tucked into the back of his pants. *Journal* articles on sabotaged at-tempts to run the streetcars had cartoons of "cowboy conductors" who bel-lowed and shot off their revolvers in warning, of Lowry as a mother hen giving birth to an egg from which a cowboy emerges, and even racist stereotypes of "savage Indians" come to drive streetcars. The "big, bad men from Bitter Creek" might, as the *Journal* suggested, not be "cowboys" or Pinkertons but "a delegation from the great families of Oklahoma come north to spend the summer at the Lake."[33]

Distinguished from manly streetcar conductors, who stood apart from the swirling social violence, the strikebreakers were perceived to be, as one labor speaker declared, "scabs, bums, loafers, criminals, and jailbirds." Moreover, such cowboys "never saw a cow except when they looked in the looking glass." In their violence and meanness, they embodied "depravity and degradation" and thus were not really cowboys but "rustlers, hoss thieves, cheap gamblers, tramps, and close herders who have been digging post holes all winter for their board." As Broncho John Sullivan declared, "there wasn't a genuine cowboy in the crowd." Cowboys, he asserted, "don't go around taking another man's job from him. Cowboys are honest, hard working men, and they wouldn't do what this crowd have done for all the money in town." Nor did they "come into civilization carrying their guns and looking for a fight." Rather, like Bron-cho John, cowboys "want justice done to the boys."[34]

As a symbol of lawlessness and reckless disregard for community morals, the Kansas City men served as provocation to men whose jobs were on the line. The *Globe* reported that their presence stirred crowd action. They seemed less cowboys than thugs. As the article noted, "The revolvers taken from them are of the latest make, and, in the hands of desperate men, would do terrible execution. The feeling that the men are not cowboys at all, but simply toughs and men who have been picked up in different places is gaining ground all the time. The police declare such is the fact."[35] In the urban disturbances to follow, wherever the cowboys appeared—at a restaurant in a working-class neighborhood, on a streetcar, or on the street—they brought personal or collective violence with them. Even honest cowboys were not safe from being hooted and insulted on the street.[36]

Woven into the narrative of the strike, the images of masculinity and militancy were complex and often contradictory. Popular culture drew images of cowboys and coppers, strikers and strikebreakers, soldiers and citizens, which were then deployed to explain and illuminate labor struggle and political conflict within the evolving city. The contest, at times, seemed to be over which men best embodied manhood. Certainly, the strike echoed the political contests of the day in raising the banner of manhood on the field of conflict. In the streetcar strike, this orderly array of representations turned to riot. There were Kansas City cowboys (or traitors); laboring men, idle or unemployed, presenting the image of either class solidarity or dissolute carnival; skilled, respectable workingmen manfully refusing the wage cuts of Lowry, the hard-driving parvenu, who was either hardworking and deserving or mean, greedy, and corrupt. Respectable manly citizens came to the aid of respectable workingmen with the petition drive and the forceful demand for justice, which was, in the end, turned down by the mayor, who was either a crook or a gallant defender of the free-market economy.

It was the cowboys who brought on the worst incidents of violence and destruction of property during the strike—the Easter riot. Early on Easter morning, April 21, a small group of unemployed men in the Riverside district began tearing up streetcar rails. Soon they were joined by a crowd of laborers from the neighborhood—men idled by the holiday who had gathered along the streetcar lines. Amid the church bells of Easter Sunday, the Minneapolis Street Railway Company began to run cars to take parishioners to services. The cars that ran north along the contested lines were staffed by returning workers and policemen. In what was probably a calculated move by the company, the Kansas City cowboys were assigned to run the cars through the immigrant Riverside neighborhood. Some of the drivers wore their revolvers in full public view. It was on this line that crowds stopped cars and overturned those delayed at sabotaged signals. They also hurled stones, cast timbers on the rails, and tore up the track. By the end of the morning, police arrested more than twenty men from Riverside alone, picking up even longtime residents in a sweep of the area.[37]

The conflict between the company and the workers had spread to encompass a struggle between outsider outlaw-cowboys and idled immigrant workingmen, women, and children. The police sought to reestablish formal order by enforcing long-abandoned ordinances prohibiting the destruction of railroad property and the gathering of more than three individuals on public streets.[38] They came down particularly hard on the Riverside crowds, in part because the violence was more severe and the crowd more disorderly than elsewhere in the city, but also, one suspects, because, to the courts, immigrant laborers represented public disorder. Lacking any direct connection to the strike, they, too, were outsiders in the contestation over public space and public privilege. The Riverside rioters undoubtedly bore the mark of difference both from the cowboys and from the police, who probably had more in common with the native-born tradesmen and skilled workers protesting in other areas.[39]

They All Walk: Public Conveyance and Public Order

The strike had consequences beyond the immediate community of streetcar workers, their unions, and the crowds of laborers who participated in the strike. In the first place, in the years prior to the strike, real estate developers expanded into new neighborhoods. The streetcar lines had become vital arteries between these additions and commercial and industrial areas.[40] Lowry was the chief beneficiary of such development, as he both built the streetcar lines and sold real estate. Caught up in this trajectory of city-building, he made his fortune in selling real estate parcels and orchestrating the addition of land to the city as both investor and lawyer.[41] His dealings made him a powerful voice in city politics and a symbol of an emergent urban elite. It was Lowry, moreover, who had plotted to revoke an earlier eight-hour ordinance on city work.

During the strike, both business and casual riders had to find alternative sources of transportation or walk, which most could not do from more distant neighborhoods. Camden, a mixed-class neighborhood, was eight miles from the city center; so, too, was the "gold coast" area around the city lakes, where middle-class families bought homes. Because shoppers could not easily get transportation in and out of the city, business also experienced a downturn during the strike. The slack taken up by wagoners, horse-drawn bus drivers, and freelancers could not cover the thousands of daily trips into, out of, and around the city. More than 25,000 passengers a day had been served by the streetcars. The sense of disorder—of idle men, of potential violence, and of massed people—served as deterrent against casual visitors, shoppers, and sightseers, even as other spectators came into the city to see the massive crowds. Yet despite the fear and inconvenience, both men and women regularly attended mass gatherings in support of the strike and petitioned in significant numbers for the repeal of Lowry's franchise.[42] The signatures of one-third of the city's adult citizens was strong and fairly persuasive evidence of community support and of the suspicion with which residents viewed the company and its owner.

By 1889, the monopoly franchise granted to Lowry for use of the streets had become a boon for him and his partners and a means for them to dominate city politics. While the aldermen were dependent on ward support and thus showed support for the strikers, the city mayors had undue power to veto city council resolutions on any measure concerning the streetcar lines. The citizen petitions were not heard. In *A Tale of the Twin Cities*, McDonald wrote of their destruction in the basement of City Hall. The state legislature's failure to act on the will on its citizens gave rise to additional skepticism about the uses of politics. The role of politicians was captured in one of the better passages of McDonald's *Tale*, where she paints a picture of the state legislature. Her protagonist, Mary Burr, comments that the legislature was "much like an elaborately furnished school room and the Senate like a badly disciplined lot of students." From this august body, no good could be expected. Like the petition campaign, the decision to work through the state legislature was "misdirected energy."[43]

By the end of the strike, political fights over the franchise were put aside. Control of police and courts supplanted them.[44] During the streetcar conflict, harsh treatment of strikers and sympathizers was sanctioned by state ordinances prohibiting citizens from congregating around rail and streetcar facilities, interfering with public transit, and destroying railroad property. Collectively, these ordinances amounted to the use of police as strikebreakers. Policemen rode the cars sent out from the car barns, sometimes served as drivers if cars were stalled or derailed, and intervened in crowd actions. Furthermore, the mayor's decision to invoke sections of the state penal code on railroad and street railway operation gave license to the police to arrest not only those destroying property but also anyone interfering with streetcar workers, including those who yelled "scab" or refused an order to "move on" from streetcar lines. The police's wide-ranging authority was particularly evident on the days leading up to and encompassing the riot. Of more than 120 arrests reported in the daily newspapers, the vast majority were of persons refusing to cooperate with the police. Although some offenses were of a more serious nature (throwing stones, bricks, tearing up rails or derailing cars, unhitching horses, pulling the linchpin on a cart to obstruct traffic), most agitators were charged with disorderly conduct for shouting "scab" or resisting the order to clear the streets.[45]

The spectacles of the Easter riot and its attendant arrests were enough to cause doubts about the effectiveness and prospects of success among the strikers. Intimidation by the police caused a noticeable drop in the number of people willing to engage in crowd actions, to interfere with streetcars, or even to quietly persuade working drivers to leave their duties. Like many labor conflicts of the day, the Twin Cities streetcar strike did not fail catastrophically. Rather, the motormen who began the strike voted to return. They were followed by individual drivers who could not afford to lose their jobs. Other drivers and conductors were hired, and the executive committee of the strike abandoned headquarters. Some labor radicals created a cooperative line of "People's Herdics," or horse-drawn busses, that could substitute for Lowry's monopoly; but they had neither credit nor sufficient service to best the competition. The company took most of the workers back with reduced wages, but they did not sign Lowry's ironclad contract. A hard core of strikers continued to meet throughout the summer of 1889. "The Men Weaken," the *Journal* proclaimed; the *Globe* answered back, "Strike Stricken Out."[46]

Why Quiet Reigned

Many attempts were made to discern what had gone wrong with the Easter protests. Some argued that the riot turned public opinion against the strikers, but the "riot" was not the first collective action against the company's property. Indeed, the first few days of the strike witnessed several incidents of streetcars and motor trolleys being overturned, men unhitching horses and leading them back to the barn, and agitators talking conductors and drivers off cars. The petition drive continued successfully through a weeklong series of confrontations.

Despite pressures on newspapers, the press coverage of the strike was even-handed, as even labor advocates like McDonald believed that their reporting had to be balanced. While the Minneapolis Board of Trade suggested that the papers should suppress any and all pro-labor sentiment and limit their coverage of crowd actions, there was very little muckraking or exposés—or even radical critique—of Lowry's methods, motivations, or private resources. No investigator even revealed that he was no longer the owner of the streetcar line, and the cursory mention of his large house did not come close to drawing attention to Lowry's salary as president, the numerous real estate deals that evolved from his streetcar ventures, or his stock holdings.

At the same time, both Lowry and the streetcar drivers sought to shape press coverage of the strike. The battle between business and labor over journalism in the Twin Cities—as elsewhere—had gone on for a long time. Trade unionists boycotted nonunion newspapers,[47] and labor reformers used the promise and threat of working-class subscribers to elicit greater and more favorable coverage of trade union and reform activities. The classic critique of "the hireling press" surfaced in labor and Populist papers alike. As early as 1880, labor speakers argued that "without distinction, the press was the mouthpiece of the moneyed interests of the land" and condemned it for "subserviency."[48] Labor turned to its own devices to force the press to give adequate—and occasionally favorable—coverage.[49]

Still, by simply covering the strike a newspaper could bring on itself accusations of hostility toward Lowry and antipathy toward the streetcar drivers' peaceful return to work. The Minneapolis Board of Trade condemned equally strike coverage by the Republican *Tribune* and Democratic *Journal* as "imbecile and criminal" even though—as the rival *Globe* pointed out—they were "diametrically opposed in their treatment of the strike." While C. J. Buell, a labor editor, "scored the police for acting as streetcar drivers," the board passed resolutions condemning the strike before the end of the first week. Board members later claimed that the trades assembly had passed resolutions "of an incendiary character" and "encouraged a spirit of lawlessness." While debate ensued over trade unionism, the board was almost unanimous in blaming the newspapers for the riot, for they had not adopted "an attitude in favor of law and order and in condemnation of lawlessness." Not knowing "what devil controls them, the typographical union or what," a board member labeled all papers "contemptible, treacherous, outrageous—damnable." Following this, J. M. Bartlett declared that "the reporters that go out to get news are members of labor organizations and give us no truthful reports of what happens." Furthermore, "whatever blood is shed and trouble made the papers and especially *The Journal* are responsible. The great trouble in all such affairs here in Minneapolis is the presence of these miserable papers. They are guilty of all the bloodshed. They do not take the honorable and upright course on public questions."[50]

To this "board of trade riot," labor leaders replied by asking "to what assembly the reporters of this city belong." If Eva Gay's reporting had somehow served to balance coverage of workers and the labor movement, the press nevertheless hardly "belong[ed] to labor organization[s]" or "distort[ed] facts to suit the views of organized labor." Such accusations were "a total surprise in labor circles, where the impression has always prevailed that reporters were quite impartial toward both sides of all questions where capital and labor are concerned." Newspaper editors agreed. If some might label their prose and cartoons "imbecile and criminal," it was simply one more "illustration," one editor sardonically wrote, "of the general proposition that the people who know best how to run the newspapers are those not engaged in the business."[51]

Public opinion, whether shaped by a negative or neutral press, was not the chief cause of either strike failure or company victory. While the magnitude of the Easter "riot" may have convinced the public that the union men had gone wrong, a better explanation might be found in the exhaustion of means to force Lowry to a settlement. Once the bid to strip him of his franchise failed, the state legislature barred the door to further action, and the police continued to support the company in the face of public criticism. It is unclear what more might have been done to push Lowry to arbitrate or begin a new system of public transportation. The People's Herdic Company failed in November, less than six months after it started,[52] and electoral revenge against the mayor and the courts was a good year off.

The key to strike failure was precisely in the growing class division, conflict, and fragmentation of the Gilded Age.[53] Local businessmen, who might well have forced Lowry to the bargaining table, refused to intervene. Only a few years before, in 1886, they cooperated with the streetcar union in providing community support for their strike. The intervening years, however, saw the decline of the Knights of Labor, an uncertain federation of craft unions, and the political agitation of the Eight-Hour League. The Shotwell, Clerihew, and Lothmann strike demonstrated working-class power through the boycott and forced a well-known firm into bankruptcy. All this probably suggested to local businesses—and their national backers—that it was time to stop bargaining with labor. Competition from local and national firms, pressure from financiers and creditors, and the troublesome vision of an empowered laboring class presented an ultimatum to local capital—either team together or be driven apart by the demands of finance on the one hand and labor on the other.

Questions of legitimacy also played a role. In the context of a liberal state, which privileges property rights and leaves no certain role for labor organization, the actions of the streetcar drivers clearly infringed on the contract and property rights and violated laws to which the workingmen implicitly consented. Gilded Age businessmen increasingly participated in an emergent middle-class culture strongly influenced by social Darwinism and the competitive work ethic and imbued with a formal legalism. To them, the rhetoric of the workingman's republic must have sounded demonic: The idea that labor could intervene in the private economy—in a contract between the respectable Thomas Lowry and two city governments—amounted to breaking the laws of nature and society.[54]

The strike narrated in *A Tale of the Twin Cities* was one of the final stages in the disintegration of the class coalition among small businessmen, labor reformers, and skilled workers represented by the Knights of Labor. It came at a time of increasing fragmentation within both the working class, with its growing contingent of immigrants of various ethnicity, and the middle class, which was seeing industrial and finance capital become increasingly at odds with small retail and manufacturing firms. By the end of the nineteenth century, such fragmentation was the basis of a new political configuration in which skilled workers, organized labor, and finance capital joined together in such associations as the National Civic Federation. The transformation of class politics required that capital become more concentrated and the working class become splintered.[55]

Ultimately, for the new class of businessmen engaged in commerce and manufacturing on a small scale, the political route to resolve the streetcar strike—pressuring aldermen, petitioning local and state government, and passing laws revoking streetcar monopoly franchises—had the ring of illegitimacy. Streetcar strikers and their supporters sought to intervene in a private contract by extraneous—in this case, political—means, just as they had intervened in the garment industry with their communitywide boycott. By the turn of the century, the boycott, along with sympathy strikes and community support, was widely viewed as an illegal means of coercing business and illegitimately entering into the employment contract. Trying to pry the franchise from Lowry's hands was no less illegitimate an act in the eyes of his colleagues, his business partners, and his friends.

Within the local government arena, there was not much labor could do either. In the words of H. B. Martin, editor of *Northwestern Labor Union*, "Many things have occurred during the past few months to cause the honest citizens of Minneapolis to feel that their proud city was being most shamefully disgraced and damaged by the gang of boodle politicians that have managed to seize control of the city government." The city officials, he continued, were of "such a character as to arouse the disgust and fear of every citizen who has the honor and welfare of the city at heart."[56] Still, it was a legitimate and elected government. The mayor's control over the police meant he had the right—and, some would argue, the duty—to protect Lowry's property, help run streetcars to provide transportation during the strike, and come down hard on the strikers. While the labor press parodied judges as "mortals who have donned the ermine, unraveled knotty points, and laid bare the fact that legislation protecting labor—and that only—is class legislation" and targeted them for refusing to place "privileges enjoyed by rich individuals and wealthy corporations"[57] under the same scrutiny, labor was subject to this same system of justice. During the strike, local judges demonstrated their commitment to property rights and ruled against community participation in the strike, passing down stiff fines and sentences during crowd actions. Passage—or invoca-tion—of ordinances prohibiting citizens from interfering with the operation of streetcars, destroying any property, and conspiring with others in those acts strengthened police power.

The police and court crackdown during the strike was unmediated by workingmen's political protests or public opinion that the arrests and sentences were unfair. Indeed, the adoption of a new patrol and signal system in the city in 1886 indicated that the city government had prepared for such contingen-cies as mass strikes and crowd control three years before the crisis.[58] Protect-ing property—and the lives of citizens, once the Easter riot had occurred—was sufficient sanction for police action. Because the city had a powerful mayor, labor's political options were few. After the strike was defeated and the union broken, workingmen could only organize for municipal reform and hope to be able to change the rules for the next confrontation.

Class and the Urban Public Sphere

The saga of the streetcar strike brings us back to the prose experiment of Eva McDonald, her *Tale of the Twin Cities*. In her story, the Burrs, a migrant fam-ily from rural Maine, arrive in the Twin Cities on the first day of the strike. They are respectable "country folk" who trace their lineage to the Mayflower and their politics to the New England town meeting. Their son, Mark, has never read a dime novel, and their daughter, Mary, pines for marriage with her now absent love. Father Hezekiah is philosophical and foolish, not radical; "Mother" is the salt of the earth, all-knowing if not all-disclosing. Their stum-bling into the great strike provides both a comic opening and an opportunity to gain the insights necessary to combat the growing anti-union feeling in the Twin Cities.

Within the "lights and shadows of the streetcar strike" that Eva Gay/ McDonald constructed there was considerable concern not merely for the out-come of the strike but for the shape of a future society and the role of citizens within it. The Burr family—Hezekiah, Mother, Mary, and Mark—served as precursors and archetypes of this world, as did the streetcar men, cowboys, Lowry, the mayor, and Mary's beau, John Dean. Each had a role to play in rep-resenting either the old order of monopoly, privilege, and corruption or the new order of cooperation, voluntarist politics, and the workingmen's republic. Only the collapse of monopoly power could make such a new world possible—hence the importance of John Dean as the agent of the People's Herdic Com-pany, the last cooperative venture of the utopian Knights of Labor in the Twin

Cities. In the battle against government corruption (Mayor Babb and crooked aldermen and senators) and industrial tyranny (Tom Lowry), only collective efforts could succeed and bring about collective security and personal happiness.

So it was that the hapless "country boy" Mark ("who never was allowed to read thrilling detective stories from dime libraries, and consequently hadn't that ardent taste for city life which usually characterizes a country boy")[59] found his manhood and independence on the route from accidental strikebreaker to petition-gatherer, from jailed rioter to respectable subscription salesman for the People's Herdic Company. Mary, his sister, underwent a similar transformation. Having been abandoned by her "accepted lover," she found her "womanhood" in working as a secretary for the executive committee of the strike, a position in which McDonald also served. In contrast to her mother, Mary was both publicly active and economically independent, a situation not unlike McDonald's own. In the pursuit of this goal, Mary stumbled on to feminist thought and rediscovered her lover, whose disappearance was due to a cousin's trickery. Their marriage brings artificial closure to the *Tale*, as Mary and John settle on a farm in Michigan and Mary's parents return to Maine. Incongruously, the urban tale ends with the return to rural life and republican virtue.

These representations were the medium of a political message—about the necessity for class solidarity and the increasingly vicious conflict between the classes. They were truth-telling fiction, a political fable dressed as a novel, through which both novelists and reporters, political thinkers and social reformers were creating and re-creating American politics. As such, they were not in the end without material meaning and political consequence. The mayor and the Board of Trade were in a sense right when they condemned the newspapers for their irresponsible presentation of the "facts" of the strike. Newspaper strike coverage had helped to mobilize not only workingmen but dependent women and children. The authorities would have equally disdained McDonald's strike fiction. They believed that the playful nature of the reporters' prose was an invitation to the carnival of the streets.

Neither book nor carnival could forestall Thomas Lowry's streetcars, stop the use of the police, or even revoke Lowry's streetcar franchise to defend the rights of the people and fulfill their desires for fair treatment of the strikers and resumption of service. In a real sense, the legal system that underwrote property rights, granted privilege and monopoly in state charters and franchises, employed police to defend such laws, and provided courts to persecute their violation was the villain of the strike. No caricature of cowboys, coppers, or judges resolved political and economic inequalities, even as they might undermine the adherence to certain forms of traditional authority. Because the political culture of working-class people did not directly challenge the legal structure upholding property rights or directly assault the hegemony of law and order and the demonization of "lawlessness," it could not begin to address what would, in the next half-century, undermine every serious effort to organize the working class into unions and engage them in political struggles. The strike also had its lessons, not just for the local labor movement, which turned increasingly to trade unionism, but for Eva McDonald, whose own politics moved, over the course of the next decade, to the conservative edge of labor. In labor conflicts, she had the memory of the streetcar strike and its failure on which to base her own remedies for and reactions to the labor protests to come.

CHAPTER 4

"They Walk on My Collar in Their Party Organs"

Women, Partisan Speaking, and Third-Party Politics in the Late Nineteenth Century

> She is a *reporter*—a Printer—& the greatest little "Labor Agitator" in the West, & a nice good, sensible little girl—She is now also State Lecturer for the Alliance & speaks on all the "Economic Problems." Makes the best speeches I have heard.[1]
>
> —Sarah Christie Stevens, 1891

Kansas Populist Annie Diggs described Eva McDonald Valesh at the beginning of her career as a political reformer. In addressing the question of women's right to be at the rostrum, Diggs reported that Valesh "hoped to be able to speak for women's cause as long as there were homeless, voiceless women, helpless to cope with the hard conditions of life," despite those who wanted her to be silent. A woman in the audience shouted, "You are at home now; you are in the sphere for which God intended you."[2]

Debates over women's proper place in public life were nothing new in the history of women in the United States. The question of whether women had the right to free speech was first triggered by the transgression of custom that separated the sexes in public—first by the radical politics of Fanny Wright and later in the abolitionist address of Sarah and Angelina Grimké. Present at forums and organizations for public education, informal lobbying and petition, and critical-rational debate, women acquired a veneer of legitimacy. While not unknown among women, partisanship in the late nineteenth century, however, still carried with it masculine connotations of rough-and-tumble conflict and political corruption. During the 1850s, women speakers had become something of a reform signature, their presence in—and labor for—voluntary associations and informal politics a given. When the agenda was moral reform, temperance, abolition, or women's rights, women speakers were likely on the program.[3] In time, the debate over whether women had the right to the public rostrum moved to a different venue—partisan politics. It was in these places, where press and politician meet, that Eva McDonald established her career while still in her mid-twenties. In doing so, she confronted political opposition based not only on an ideology, program, or personality but also on her gender. Hostility toward her activism as a woman in the partisan realm was expressed in the same trope of separate spheres that originally defined all public life as masculine and now claimed party politics as male domain. There was not so much an elemental divide between the ways in which men and women conducted political business as there were two distinct political cultures in American history: one centered in partisan politics, the other in reform.[4]

As a consequence, by the late nineteenth century, political practices were no longer determined solely by gender; instead they were defined by one's relationship to and attitudes about the party system. Even as voter participation soared and party participation was at an all-time high, men increasingly turned toward nonpartisanship, seeking the paths of independent and split-ticket voting; by the twentieth century, many would choose not to vote at all.[5] Women could be found not only in nonpartisan efforts of the woman suffrage movement, temperance, and moral reform but also testing the waters of party politics. They made use of electoral as well as educational means to ends and paraded, campaigned, and lobbied as partisans, albeit primarily in third parties.

Eva McDonald was a partisan. Raised in a trade union family, solidly Democratic for most of her political life, she ran on a party ticket for the Minneapolis school board, as we have seen, and experimented with Alliance-Labor and People's party politics. Just as the Knights of Labor's Jack McGaughey had introduced her to labor reform circles, prominent Populists played crucial roles in mentoring McDonald as an Alliance speaker. Women Populists such as Annie Diggs promoted McDonald as an orator and writer. Moreover, Populist politicians Ignatius Donnelly, Jerry Simpson, and William Peffer saw in McDonald a solution to the division between the rurally based People's party and the urban masses. She had her own ideas, however, about the role she would play. She sought and received patronage and continued to build her journalism career on political ties. Contradicting the expectations for women in reform, McDonald's partisan ways cost her the support of Donnelly and other important allies. In the end, her personal life, more than political defeat, brought her to choose labor over populism as a vehicle for her career.

A Pupil of Considerable Promise

The loss of the streetcar strike did little to weaken McDonald's ambitions or her career in labor reform circles. In the ensuing political turmoil, the Twin Cities labor movement renewed its efforts in both the political and economic arenas. In May of 1889, the Eight-Hour League reported that "the recent strike in the Twin Cities had seriously interfered with the eight hour agitation," but the group sought to find new ways to "carry on the educational work."[6] As labor advocates debated the future directions of their work, they reexamined earlier failures in campaigns under the Union Labor party. The growth of the Farmers' Alliance in Minnesota promised better fortunes for joint farmer-labor politics.

Looking toward the formation of a state federation of labor as the first step, labor leaders called a meeting in January 1890. Among the attendees were McDonald and Frank Valesh. Another prominent figure at the meeting was Ignatius Donnelly, the sometime Alliance member and perennial politician. In 1888, the Union Labor party had nominated him as their gubernatorial candidate, with Jack McGaughey as his running mate. When Donnelly withdrew from the ticket to accept another nomination for state legislature, he alienated many of his labor supporters. Stumping for Republican gubernatorial candidate William Merriam in 1888 cost Donnelly the labor vote and encouraged the development of a pro-labor, anti-Donnelly faction in the Farmers' Alliance under R. K. Hall. By 1890, Donnelly needed allies to help him unite the Alliance and labor under his leadership.[7]

In this context, Donnelly "discovered" McDonald at the labor meetings. Both Donnelly and his editor-ally, Everett Fish of the *Great West*, sought to sponsor her as a means to resolve difficulties within the Alliance. Like her earlier tutelage under McGaughey, McDonald's relationship with Donnelly, in a political retelling of Pygmalion, was another form of apprenticeship. Both Fish and Donnelly claimed they had transformed Eva McDonald, the working girl, into a girl Populist. In describing his recruitment of McDonald, Fish recalled that he envisioned a great future for her in the women's movement, but her vehicle was not to be suffrage agitation. Instead, she would become a leader in the Populist cause. While Fish saw trouble in McDonald's anticlerical views, opposition to prohibition, and skepticism toward greenback politics, he also appreciated her talents. Through Donnelly's—and Fish's—support, McDonald could help to organize the state and gain access to a national audience.[8]

As we saw earlier, political mentoring had an essential role in making women's public activism possible. Despite the presence of an earlier generation of women reformers, young women had few role models. Discontinuity and isolation were endemic to women in the public sphere. Women reformers with experience were confined for the most part to the stage of the women's rights movement. As Mari Jo Buhle has argued, women's political activism of the time—indeed, their fight for political and economic rights—was carried on in social movements whose primary mission was not suffrage. The Women's Christian Temperance Union (WCTU), to cite the best example, was the largest women's organization in the late nineteenth century, and women in social reform, farm, and labor organizations outnumbered those in suffrage organizations. No one of these causes, however, stood alone; rather, they comprised what historian Michael Goldberg refers to as "the reform matrix," often combining labor and farm protest with militant suffragism and a radical critique of women's condition. It was as if Frances Willard's call to "Do Everything!" was the slogan not merely of the WCTU but of all Gilded Age reform.[9]

In such an atmosphere, mentors in the life ways of reform were invaluable in helping such working-class talents as McDonald make it to the state and even national stage. Jack McGaughey and his cronies in the Athenaeum of Crude Philosophers had educated McDonald in contemporary political economy. By McDonald's own proud admission, McGaughey trained her as a platform speaker, and her apprenticeship in urban investigative journalism lent strength to her prose and poignancy to her political fables. Her education was now completed during speaking tours with Donnelly, arguably one of the best-known speakers of his time, and working alongside Populist stalwarts William Peffer, senator from Kansas, and Congressman Sockless Jerry Simpson. Simpson himself called McDonald "a pupil of considerable promise." On their tour of New York, he showed her "a few things about managing the dear public." McDonald was not loath to accept such tutelage, as she knew Simpson could "do a good deal toward putting me a few rounds higher on the ladder if he [chose]."[10] At least in the beginning, the same latitude was extended to Fish and Donnelly. McDonald willingly became their working girl–turned–Populist protégé.

At her first Farmers' Alliance meeting, McDonald gave her maiden speech as a Populist orator. The room was "jammed to the ceiling" with those eager to hear the labor reformer. In Fish's words, "Miss McDonald came to them as the daughter of a working man and as a working girl herself in the cities. And her later work in places where toil is ill-paid and ill-fed and where her pen has thrown light upon the cruelties of our commercial system has prepared her to talk with feeling upon these subjects. Her first sentences warmed every heart to her—especially the mothers present, whose daughters make up the great working girl population of these cities."[11]

Her speech that night focused on the central themes of her Populist career. She regularly targeted the industrial system, seeing its origins in serfdom and slavery. She castigated bankers, lawyers, and economic parasites and offered political organization as the remedy for such evils. Her critique of capitalism contrasted with political economists who sought to obscure the source of inequality and poverty. One newspaper reported, "Miss McDonald in a very unassuming and lady-like manner took up the speeches of the previous evening and logically proved the fallacy of their conclusions. She spoke nearly two hours. No offense was given to anyone, yet all were charmed by her eloquence, convinced by her logic, and melted to tears by her description of the poor in the great cities."[12] Annie Diggs later wrote that McDonald was "quite as much at home on an improvised store-box platform on the street corner, speaking earnestly to her toil-hardened brother Knights of Labor, as in the drawing room, radiating sparkling wit and repartee. All places and all experiences fall naturally within Mrs. Valesh's versatile sphere." Her charisma, ease on the podium, ring of authenticity, and wit were enough to persuade the New Auburn Alliance to make her a member.[13]

Public rallies and campaign speeches were one facet of McDonald's work for the Farmers' Alliance. As in labor reform circles, she became known for her ability to communicate complex ideas to a reading as well as a listening audience. In her column in the *Great West*, McDonald wrote, "We have so few publications which tell us just how wretched we are, and actually to what extent we depend upon capitalists for permission to exist, that the cry is constantly for more light, more knowledge, more education." Taking as her subject the "new political economy" of the Populist movement, she sought to demystify the workings of the capitalists system for her readers. As she wrote, "Political economists of the past century have been so busy justifying existing conditions and making them seem right that they obscure teachings in a mist of inexplicable terms and arguments, so that the average mortal gave up the study in despair." She stressed that there were reasons why farmers were impoverished and "railroad corporations, real estate speculators, stock gamblers, and professional politicians" became wealthy off the labor of others. "There was a reason," she continued, that farm children abandoned their fathers' occupation and chose instead to "go to the city in order to get their living in some more 'respectable' way."[14]

In her columns, speeches, and articles in the reform press, McDonald strongly emphasized the value of education and the importance of debate. Focusing on Populist issues such as greenbacks, the cooperative commonwealth, and the condition of labor, she was able to make connections between the farmers and workers who constituted "the great industrial army." Consigned "to a more or less deplorable condition of industrial slavery," those who worked on farms, in households, and in workshops had a common plight; they must now make common cause. As she observed, "Little by little a sentiment has been growing on both sides, in favor of some plan by which the farm laborer and factory operative could combine so as to protect all common interests and yet not interfere with each other's local affairs." As an organization of both producers and consumers, the Alliance opposed the privileges of "the class of nonproducers" who profited off the labor and misery of the laboring classes. "The unity of industrial interests" would ensure that farmers and workers were represented in the "national halls of legislation" and their demands fairly met.[15]

McDonald's public lectures and writings attracted both men and women to the Populist cause. An organizer for the Knights of Labor and a member of the new State Federation of Labor, McDonald spoke to farmers as a specialist on the industrial question, education, political economy, and women's labor. In his role as state lecturer and as president, Donnelly saw the potential for McDonald to bring together urban labor interests with those of farmers. He rooted this potential in the knowledge McDonald gained through her experience as a workingwoman. As Donnelly wrote in his diary, "Miss McDonald is a very bright girl—quick and apt, not poetical; her mind bearing the traces of the hard battle by which she has raised herself from the living grave of the factory room."[16] It was the "authentic" self-presentation of McDonald as working girl–turned–reformer that enabled her to engage, excite, and inspire both rural and urban populations.

In Ignatius's Wake

In the spring and summer of 1890, Donnelly and McDonald took their place as stump speakers in the election campaign. Races for local offices that year held out the promise of an increasingly influential Populist voice in state politics. The state Farmers' Alliance backed the efforts of Donnelly to revitalize the organization through this political campaigning; McDonald and other assistant lecturers offered up the chance that rural constituencies could join urban forces for reform. They organized a thousand suballiances that season.[17] In Donnelly's diary, he carefully noted the conditions, costs, and benefits of as well as the response to the lecture tour that month. He paid careful attention to McDonald's presence and showed interest both in how she performed and how the audiences responded to the Populist call. Their mission was to get as many Alliancemen elected to the state legislature as possible, but it went beyond that: They sought to connect in the public mind the inequities of the economic system and political corruption and to bring about reform through a people's mobilization. As advocates of radically different forms of political and economic organization, Donnelly, McDonald, and other Populist speakers had to break through cultural deference and indifference of voters and nonvoters alike, to persuade them of the possibility of change, and to make concrete to the public the means of achieving such change. This was not an easy task.[18]

Educating the public in the political economy of populism entailed both mental and physical labor, conducted under difficult circumstances at best, financed out of daily collections and minuscule speakers' fees. It meant an unrelenting grind of public speaking. In the space of a month, Donnelly and his lecturers each had two or three speaking engagements daily. From June 13 to June 28, for example, Donnelly was present at more than twenty meetings throughout the southern and western tier of Minnesota. At most of these meetings, McDonald accompanied him. Fatigue and hunger often plagued them during the hours of travel. In one diary entry, Donnelly captured the hazards and disappointments of the reform life. When he and McDonald showed up at an Inver Grove Allianceman's house, they found "no provision made for our entertainment." The next town offered little better, as they had to drive out of town for their dinner: "We ate the raw ham with many misgivings, but the family we found lives on it constantly, & so being hungry we risked the *trichinae*."[19] Even then, when they drove to the meeting, only four people were in the audience. As historian Frank Heck wrote, "Campaigning in a newly settled corner of Minnesota, even in the 1880s . . . was no child's play, though the hardship experienced by candidates and speakers in reaching their public simply measured in a rough way the difficulties many of their constituents had to face in the necessary task of getting their grain to the nearest railroad point."[20] McDonald later remembered these days as a Populist lecturer as ones of plain food, plain clothing (like many farmers' daughters), and plain transport, often in freight train cabooses instead of passenger cars. She shared stories, coffee, and sandwiches with train crews as she rode from one engagement to another.[21]

The rigors—and sometimes scant rewards—of Populist speaking were ever-present that summer and fall. McDonald spoke in numerous courthouses, theaters, churches, and parks to ever-growing numbers of farm folk. Her "sharp hits and bright sayings" amused many audiences and newspaper reporters. As one wrote, McDonald "is one of the best posted persons in the state regarding labor statistics. Her fort [*sic*] is addressing laboring men, more than farmers, but she acquitted herself nobly, and made a fine speech. She was particularly severe on bankers and lawyers. We looked and trembled, thinking a roast might come on editors, but the fair Eva in mercy let us go. But to tell the truth, Miss McDonald is well-known to most every newspaper man in the state, and is a great favorite with them. They would have to do something awful wicked before she would hurt their feelings."[22] Humor aside, McDonald's presence on the lecture tour, as she bolstered the political chances of Alliancemen and sought to bring the Populist message to the rural public, brought her fame of a limited sort. It also was hard labor in the cause of reform. Mostly patient, she still complained to Sarah Christie Stevens, a woman compatriot, that "the farmers expect me to be in four different places at once as it is."[23]

In the course of the campaign that year, McDonald got to know Stevens, a prohibitionist and the Alliance candidate for school board in Blue Earth County. Although McDonald neither supported temperance nor practiced religion devoutly, she was comfortable sharing her political resources and public stage with Stevens. The wife of a hard-pressed farmer, Sarah Stevens was thoroughly versed in the Populist creed and tried to make the most of it in her run for office. A generation older than McDonald, Stevens was "one of those cultured women whose energy and executive ability equal[ed] her culture." "An ardent friend of cooperation and the federation of social reform forces," she had the support of women throughout the country. The popular "girl orator" Eva McDonald was her ace in the hole. In late October, McDonald and Stevens gave a series of talks throughout the county. Lecturing twice a day for a week, McDonald spoke on the industrial question, workingwomen in cities, and educational policy. Stevens directed her attention to women's school suffrage and the need for free textbooks, improved schools, and better teacher preparation. They drew appreciative crowds as Stevens took advantage of McDonald's reputation to bring new support to her cause. When the election returns came in for Blue Earth, Stevens won the office of school superintendent by a scant 301 votes from nearly 7,000 cast. Although many immigrants (primarily Germans and Scandinavians) voted against her on gender grounds and city women gave most of their vote to main-party candidates, Stevens outpolled her opponents in rural districts.[24]

The work brought results, as the 1890 election was the most successful in the Alliance-Labor party's history. It also built McDonald's reputation and standing in the state organization. She was, in effect, owed political favors—a rare occurrence for women partisans. Campaigning for Stevens made McDonald a new ally and friend. She was satisfied that she had helped elect the older woman and many other Alliance candidates. As she wrote Stevens, "I feel a little personal pride in having contributed to the result. I see my legislative candidates in every district I spoke have been elected." Similarly, Stevens shared her appreciation for McDonald, "the greatest little 'Labor Agitator' in the West," with friends and family.[25]

Farmer–Labor Alliance

Success in the 1890 election gave the state Farmers' Alliance the balance of power in the Minnesota legislature. Candidates running on Alliance-Labor party tickets outpolled Republicans and Democrats in 22 of 79 counties and ran second in 11 additional counties. They received 58,000 votes of the 240,000 cast and—in coalition with the Democrats—controlled both houses of the state legislature. The distribution of Alliance-Labor party voting mirrored the organizational strength of the alliances in the wheat-growing regions and the cities of Minneapolis and Duluth. Populist weakness in rural dairy regions reflected the very different needs of those regions.[26] Electoral success, however regionally skewed, promised a bright future for Populist politics. Still, the Populist showing in state elections was not to be repeated, despite the subsequent creation of the People's party and its slate of popular candidates in the 1892, 1894, and 1896 elections.[27]

The failure of Populist legislators to fulfill their election promises was one reason for the rather precipitous decline in voter support. This legislative failure was reinforced by the growing factionalism and divisiveness among Alliancemen. Just as McDonald had been a major contributor to 1890 electoral victories, so now she could be blamed for some of the divisions in the state. The 1891 Minnesota Alliance meetings began with the election of Ignatius Donnelly to the presidency and a conflict over the state lectureship between Donnelly partisan Everett Fish and another opponent. Fights between the factions threw the state lectureship to McDonald, whom Fish had already tagged as an enemy. By this time, Donnelly was also having his doubts. His wife, Kate, believed that it "lowered the office" to have the girl orator elected. Kate Donnelly wrote that McDonald would be "'tanky' & troublesome" and tip the balance of executive board votes in favor of the opposition. Subsequent conflicts with the Hall faction led Donnelly to oppose McDonald's participation in state and national meetings, as "that vicious little pest" sided with the opposition.[28]

Some historians argue that these divisions reflected the radical-conservative split within the state Farmers' Alliance. The conflict between such far-seeing (if impractical) thinkers as Donnelly and Fish, who proposed radical changes in political economy, and figures like Sidney Owen and the labor reformers of the Twin Cities (among them McDonald), who envisioned a different politics of redistribution, intensified in both organizational matters and in political work. Donnelly's support for both the People's party and the subtreasury plan are sometimes used as evidence of his radicalism in the face of such division. In contrast, the Hall faction was characterized by its support of nonpartisan strategies (the Alliance as public-interest reformers) and attention to urban labor. Still, the two factions were divided by important issues that cannot be simply characterized as radical or conservative. They hinged on the constituency, activism, and ideas of reformers such as McDonald as they came to represent women in the Alliance and labor in Populist reform generally.

To begin with, the union of labor and the Farmers' Alliance that brought McDonald into the movement proved fragile, just as it had nationally. Historians such as Lawrence Goodwyn have argued that labor in "the Populist moment" was incapable of organizing and sustaining a democratic political movement. It did not and could not accept the radical critique of Populist thinkers or follow them along the route of independent political thinking. Subsequent studies have shown state arenas in which the Populist-labor coalition was mutually sustaining. Moreover, as we saw earlier, the Knights of Labor demonstrated their capacity for independent political action.[29] The instability of the coalition between farmers and their labor allies had more to do with the often-contradictory needs and demands of their different constituencies. Core proposals of the radical Populist program were designed to bolster the farm economy through government-sponsored farm credit. Inflationary pressure in the form of increased food prices would have hit the urban working class first. The long-term benefits of such inflation was a hard sell to workers whose real incomes seemed to stagnate. Similarly, support for state-sponsored binding twine and jute bags made by prison laborers was not exactly a compelling reason for campaigns in working-class neighborhoods. Labor demands clashed with farm interests, too, as the eight-hour day was resisted by farmers. Farmers had little sympathy for impoverished urban masses (except, perhaps, in states with small differences in ethnic composition, as in Minnesota) to bolster support for labor laws and union protection.[30]

In "Strengths and Weaknesses of the People's Movement," McDonald (writing under her married name, Valesh) characterized these problems. If her original motive for joining the Farmers' Alliance was to help build "a political movement for real industrial progress," she viewed the coalition more skeptically from the vantage point of a movement worker. In particular, the Minnesota experience—in which Donnelly and his supporters were able to effectively exclude urban reformers from the Alliance—must have been foremost in her mind. At the great convention of the People's party in 1892, city workmen were, she argued, virtually unrepresented. That was the greatest weakness for any people's movement: "For if the People's Party, in its ultimate development, only represents one class, no matter how large that class, its work must necessarily partake of a sectional character and, from lack of breadth and depth, fail to accomplish those great reforms which mark epochs in civilization." Some Knights of Labor leaders did attend, but their presence signaled only "the personal endorsement of intelligent and far-seeing leaders rather than an assurance of the assent and cooperation of the masses of city workmen."[31]

The problem for any farmer-labor coalition was the difference between farmers and workers in their political attachments. Nascent trade unions, quickly coalescing into the American Federation of Labor, remained outside the Populist movement. Taking their cues from judicial resistance and the experience of the Knights of Labor in electoral politics, the AFL viewed all political work as potentially divisive and pragmatically ineffective.[32] For farmers, as Valesh noted, the "tendency [of labor] to depend on systematic agitation and organization, and even to wait patiently until public opinion concedes the justice and utility of their reforms, seem[ed] . . . unexplainable and a waste of energy." Only if trade unions overcame their reluctance and made common cause with the people's movement could both sides capitalize on their joint bond as consumers and producers of commodities—the future basis for joint political success.[33] What McDonald left unsaid was that these interests were not wholly compatible or common.

Differences over political strategies and goals such as labor's role in the Populist movement had sparked the initial conflict between Donnelly and McDonald. Organizational competition enhanced it. By mid-1890, because of their substantial disagreements over monetarism and the politics of distribution, Everett Fish had counseled Donnelly to distance himself from McDonald. When McDonald, popular throughout the state after her triumphal lecture tours, was elected to the Alliance state lectureship in 1891, Fish took it on himself to launch the crusade to disqualify her or hound her from the post.[34] He began at the Alliance meeting when McDonald was elected, pointing out that women were barred from membership and that she had no credentials. The Farmers' Alliance constitution in fact allowed women to belong to the Alliance as wives and daughters of farmers and also as Alliance employees.[35] Voted down at the 1891 convention, Fish followed his attack with a barrage of articles categorically denying that McDonald even held the post, caricaturing her political efforts, and associating her with patronage politics (over a printing contract that Fish lost)[36] and journalistic corruption. In his words, McDonald was "a salaried reporter for one of the most contemptible plutocratic sheets in the world—the St. Paul *Globe*—and is not, and cannot be, a member of a local alliance."[37]

In his attacks on McDonald, Fish insisted that the issue was not women's participation in the movement. McDonald was simply "too acquainted with the state house, political atmosphere of the daily press and is a partisan of the Hall faction"—that is, she did not support Donnelly.[38] As Fish proclaimed, "It will not do for the Alliance to be carried away by the novelty of having a lady as state lecturer. There may possibly arise a time when a modern 'Joan of Arc' is needed in this cause, but it is not now and if that time does come, the 'Joan' will be a farmers' daughter whose life will bring her fully in sympathy with the lives of the farmer."[39]

And Not a Woman among Them

McDonald's strident advocacy of labor and women's causes in the Populist movement distinguished her from most organizers and writers in Minnesota and nationally. While she was neither the only nor the most prominent woman speaker in the Populist cause, McDonald symbolized the promise of coalition with urban labor reform and the advantages and drawbacks of women's new partisanship. Her way had been paved by women in reform movements and by the specific roles of such figures as Annie Diggs and Mary Elizabeth Lease. Their visibility as speakers, journalists, and organizers was made more evident by the relative absence of women in the political arena generally. At the same time, the unevenness of women's participation in the Farmers' Alliance was a product of state differences in membership eligibility and constituency. Given the period's prevailing conditions of economic hardship, southern and western agricultural regions would seem to be a poor setting for mobilizing women. Yet because women's labor was central to the farm economy, they played a major role in the work of the Alliance.[40]

McDonald's stance on women and populism, like her defense of labor's demands in the political economy, proved to be a contentious issue within the Alliance. At the Minnesota Alliance convention in 1890, McDonald expressed her views on farm women. Up to that point, she had focused on "the cruelties of the industrial system" for both farmer and urban workingman. Her experience in the almost entirely male world of the Farmers' Alliance led her to analyze the conditions of farm women and to suggest their organization. McDonald noted the absence of women from the gathering. As she wrote, "I felt rather subdued on seeing over five hundred delegates assembled to represent the farmers' interests and not a woman among them." She continued, "Is it because Minnesota farmers' wives don't have to work and consequently know nothing of the evils to be remedied? Or are they convinced that a woman's place is in the home?" Was only "the superior male intellect" capable of grasping "the political situation, the twine trust, the railway transactions, and the spoils of the wheat ring"?[41]

Nationally, the Farmers' Alliance in Kansas, Texas, North Carolina, and the Dakotas accepted women members, and women visibly contributed to Alliance political education, social solidarity, and economic goals. Leaders such as Leonidas

Polk and others worked to increase women's participation. In Minnesota, women's position was more ambiguous. McDonald argued, "If I were convinced that the women of this state were carefully educated, well clothed, well fed and not over-worked, I wouldn't say a word about their absence from the convention." As it was, women's burden was double. At times, "the wife and daughter go out into the fields and do the work of men" in addition to taking on domestic labor. As farm wives, their position, "from personal observation and remarks dropped by delegates," as McDonald wrote, was determined by their husbands and was "always a little worse of the two."[42]

Concretely, there were ways to ameliorate women's condition and give them greater political voice—support for woman suffrage, temperance legislation, admission to membership in the Alliance, and even women's auxiliaries, for "in industrial organizations women have proven themselves the equal of men in every respect." Furthermore, McDonald suggested the development of educational and social programs and temperance legislation—issues certain to mobilize women into the Alliance. As she claimed, "The uncertainty and poverty so prevalent among farmers and wageworkers of the cities is the direct cause of a large proportion of intemperance and every kindred vice."[43] Her speeches repeatedly called attention to the unequal place of women in the Alliance and urged their participation—a judgment she delivered on evenings devoted to women's work and at the 1891 Farmers' Alliance convention in Omaha.[44] McDonald's reception indicated that there was a female constituency for populism. As Donnelly himself noted, "It was interesting to observe how the women gathered around her at the closing of the meeting—a curious exhibition of feminine sympathy." He depended on McDonald's appeal to a rural women's audience to aid in his own efforts to lead the Alliance into the future of the People's party. The question was whether Donnelly and others within the Alliance could continue to allow McDonald political latitude and space on the podium, not to mention political patronage.[45]

Ironically, it was McDonald's appeal to general rural audiences that led to both new responsibilities and the growing factional division within the Alliance. In a short time, McDonald had become a nationally recognized leader of Minnesota populism. That recognition led to difficulties with both Fish, who had wanted the state lectureship for himself, and Donnelly, who aspired to state and national office. Within six months of their lecture tour together, McDonald and Donnelly were at odds in a conflict born of ambition and popular support in different segments of the Farmers' Alliance. Their short-lived collaboration had given rise to the most successful electoral effort of the Farmers' Alliance in Minnesota, but it was not a collaboration that led to legislative success for Populist reform, repeated electoral triumphs, or long-lived political partnership.

A Mouse to Stand between Him and His Ambition and Happiness

McDonald's election to the state lectureship of the Minnesota Alliance happened at the exact moment when Donnelly was having doubts about whether she was a help or a hindrance to his political ambitions. On the lecture circuit in the summer of 1890, Donnelly originally imagined that he would provide the fireworks for the Alliance revival, laying the groundwork for his own ascension to the U.S. Senate or even the presidency. If McDonald could pull in the audience, ease tensions with the urban and labor faction, and serve as a willing pupil, then she was well worth the sacrifice of an assistant lectureship and the daily expenses. But as they traveled through the rural alliance circuit, Donnelly found press coverage and audience appreciation somewhat lacking. He was ridiculed and criticized for his pompousness and the staleness of his delivery. At the same time, McDonald was a drawing card among the same farm population that found Donnelly's lectures overly familiar and tiresome. While McDonald received raves, Donnelly's notices—and he had been performing on the rostrum for more years than McDonald had lived—were terse, sarcastic, or simply dull.

In one article, a reporter caricatured "a typical Donnelly speech." Donnelly "abused Senator [William] Washburn, denounced the railroad companies, roasted the last legislature, anathematized the supreme court, attacked the character of Gen. [James] Garfield, abused the business men, lawyers, doctors, and editors, and in fact almost everybody in general who is not a member of the alliance . . . and besides a good many very extravagant and reckless statements, gave the farmers some good advice intermixed with much that was not good." Another Donnelly address was characterized as riddled with "back history" and "gray-bearded anecdotes," many of which were familiar to his audience. The reporter summarized the reaction of his listeners: "While they thought much of what Mr. Donnelly said was true, they had heard and read the same speech fifteen years ago and in the same dress."[46] In light of his own deteriorating popularity, Donnelly must have found his protégé's favor with rural audiences alarming.

The clamor for McDonald's stories of the great poor in the cities and for her assurances that the farm laborer and the factory slave could find unity of purpose marked a sea change in the tastes and interests of the rural population. No longer satisfied with Donnelly's "elocution," they preferred McDonald's "conversational" style and the newness of her thoughts and experiences.[47] If politics in the nineteenth century was a form of entertainment, the audience was demanding a change in the program. Rather than listen to "chronic wailers" (as the *New York Tribune* labeled William Peffer and Jerry Simpson), they wanted something different. In the case of McDonald, her popularity was rooted in that difference—conversation versus elocution; workingwoman, not genteel reformer; city stories versus country fables. McDonald's accessibility, her humor, and even her public modernity as a reformer who did not repudiate change or insist on looking backward attracted audiences.

Even if egotism and ambition for the plaudits of press and listeners alike had not interfered in the relationship between Ignatius Donnelly and his proclaimed protégé, the fractious politics of the Farmers' Alliance certainly would have. McDonald belonged to the labor circles that Donnelly had offended in 1888. Worse yet, they identified with the cities, where urban interests and political preferences stood in opposition to the Republican-leaning Donnelly and his third-party experiments. Donnelly, "the white-handed idol of the horny-fisted tillers of the soil," might have been "the king of utopia," but he came up short as the representative of workingmen. In Shakespearean tones, the *Pioneer Press* described his "predicament." With the presidency of the state Farmers' Alliance now in Donnelly's possession, he could aspire to be senator or even president. The farmers' movement might carry him from local fame to a national one; his speeches at the National Farmers' Alliance meetings only confirmed his place at the table of reform. Still, there was "an overdose of gall and wormwood in the cup, and even now he has found out that the fruit of ambition, fair and tempting without, is but ashes within. His crown of glory is but a crown of thorns, and withal he must perforce sit 'like patience on a monument, smiling at grief.'"[48]

The cause of Donnelly's troubles, according to the *Pioneer Press*, was Eva McDonald, "a mouse of ceaseless energy and a bitter, persistent, aggravating, and totally irreconcilable spirit." She thwarted Donnelly's ambitions, if only through her determination. McDonald, the reporter explained, was "a bright, intelligent, young lady, possessed of an all-absorbing desire to emancipate the sons of toil from their thralldom." She exhibited "a fierce dislike to be patronized or domineered over" and "possess[ed] that species of irreverence which mocks at those outward attributes to awe and majesty wherein to the major portion of mankind 'doth lie the dread and fear of kings.'"[49] The press's rhetoric captured the essential conflict within the Farmers' Alliance political effort. Claims to legitimate leadership were anchored in moral superiority, experience, commitment, and rhetorical skill, but also in the legitimacy of self-presentation. The authentic self that McDonald presented on the platform—daughter of the workingman, crusader for the causes of farmer and laborer alike, witness to the common suffering and disparate reward of productive labor—was sanctioned by the connection between that experience and its political voice. It was a legitimacy that Donnelly could not hope for, nor hope to attack, lest he be perceived as a brute, an opportunist, or simply not a man.

It was less an issue of chivalry than simple decency, as Reverend Gjertsen found out when he attacked Frances Willard as "a platform harlot." Clearly, if Donnelly were to emerge the winner and take his rightful place as leader of both the Farmers' Alliance and its national political efforts, he would have to find another way to diminish—or tarnish—the glint of McDonald's authentic political voice.

A New and Terrible Force

Behind many of the criticisms of McDonald among Donnelly's circle and in later trade-union disputes was the recognition that she began her career as "a paid agent" of the capitalist press. The connection between money and corruption, newspapers and political chicanery played undoubtedly on republican themes familiar to most nineteenth-century voters; but the negative associations that linked the press, once considered free, and capital was of newer vintage. In political battles over both ideas and reputations, newspapers took on ever more power—far more perhaps than they had when the newspapers were only patronage sheets.[50] Also, the number of subscribers and voters was growing ever faster. The character of journalism, in the era immediately preceding the yellow journalism of Joseph Pulitzer and William Randolph Hearst, was already bending in that direction, with a profusion of sensationalist headlines intermingled with political debate and business reports. The final factor was, however, that big-city newspapers—the mainstream press—had some reform interests but little sympathy and rather more ridicule for reformers themselves. Whether it was "the Reform Chorus," a harpooning of the moral reformers of the day, or a caricature of Donnelly, "the Sage of Nininger," the slings and arrows of the newspaper corps were directly aimed at what journalists increasingly regarded as the self-righteous opportunism of reform. Reporters knew how to play off the suspicions—if not outright cynicism—about politicians that even reform supporters harbored toward the ambitious. As J. L. of Sparta, Wisconsin, wrote in *Farm, Stock, and Home*, "In politics especially have I seen the crafty and selfish gather about [reform] movements, and under the most glowing asseverations for the public good direct them to their own unhallowed purposes."[51]

When social reformers condemned the press as corrupt and dangerous, however, they ran the risk of undermining their own means of livelihood and communication. In a politics of truth-telling,[52] the credibility of the messenger and the message meant everything. Political movements from the Greenback party and the Grange to the Farmers' Alliance, the Knights of Labor, and the Women's Christian Temperance Union were all heavily dependent on both reform and commercial newspapers to relay information and debate the issues. Many reformers made their careers—and their livings—patching together speaking tours, book deals, newspaper editing and reporting, and occasional political appointments. As a career, it was filled with risk. Limited positions and chancy rewards heightened the stakes in factional fighting within the reform movements. The loss of an ally often meant that fewer rewards would come one's way; gaining an ally could mean having to share the small rewards with yet another person.

Reform did not, in effect, pay well, except for the very few. When some reform solution did begin to accrue monetary value as well as political significance—as in the selling of hail and fire insurance by the Northwest Alliance in the Dakotas and Minnesota—everyone wanted in, including party politicians who invested in the companies.[53] The five-dollar-a-day position of state lecturer, the much more lucrative enterprise of campaigning for a mainstream party at $100 an engagement, the return one could get from being an editor of a newspaper with a regular dues-paying membership, or patronage gained by being hired to print ballots, flyers, pamphlets, constitutions, and other literature made the difference in sustaining a life of reform.[54] To criticize or verbally assault the means by which one earned a living was to somehow both reveal and diminish one's means of getting a living.

Donnelly's 1892 lawsuit against the *Pioneer Press* for publishing an embarrassing letter was another case in point. As McDonald wrote to her friend Albert Dollenmayer, "the $1.00 verdict in the *Pioneer* suit has completely queered Donnelly's chances for the presidential nomination"[55] of the newly formed People's party. Donnelly's Omaha convention speech, which made him a major figure in national Populist politics, had virtually guaranteed him the nomination. Now, he believed, the combination of the "hireling press" and the "ermine of the bench" denied him his prize. After the suit, as the reelected president of the state Farmers' Alliance, Donnelly devoted a portion of his address to "the lying capacity of the newspapers of America." In an amazing speech, he attributed the difficulties encountered by the People's party movement to the press's being used as the tool of capital. Because moneyed interests could not control the people's votes, they sought to control people through the commercial press. Echoing other reform press critiques, Donnelly explained that capital's "only resource [was] to deceive . . . through the agency of newspapers, which enter every house and penetrate into every mind."[56]

Donnelly compared the press evil to Lucifer. The only defense against the deceits of the press was to stop buying newspapers, for "the citizen who takes a plutocratic newspaper into his house commits an unpardonable sin against himself, his family, the republic and posterity. He might just as well call up a red-hot fiend from hell, and set him on his shoulder, to talk into his ear . . . an endless string of lies and slanders."[57] Press mendacity was, as Donnelly proclaimed, "stupendous . . . illimitable—it takes away the breath of simple virtue and bewilders honest truth into a paralysis. It threatens all our conceptions of primal right and forebodes the destruction of civilization. It is a new and terrible force of which antiquity knew nothing."[58]

That Eva McDonald, the darling of labor circles and favorite of the press, was a newspaper reporter did not enhance her reputation among Farmers' Alliance leaders. As Everett Fish, himself a reform journalist, pounded away at her appointment as state lecturer, he reminded supporters that "the astounding grief of the state and city press over the fact that Miss Eva McDonald is not the State Lecturer of the Minnesota Alliance, is assuring. . . . It demonstrates that today there is but one party in Minnesota, but one cause, one platform, that of the Alliance, and *The Globe* is its name." These challenges were answered by a press that found as much amusement in Populist wrangling and the humiliation of Ignatius Donnelly as it felt outrage at McDonald's treatment. In articles like "Donnelly as a Dictator" and "Only a Woman, but She May Have Stood between a Sage and His Ambition," the press punctured the balloon of serious reform.[59] At the same time, McDonald's investigative reports were the very tools with which she could elicit the support of thousands, bring Populist ideas to the public marketplace, and persuade the opposition. It was the single most important vehicle for her long career in reform.

Growing Ambitions

Despite growing opposition from Donnelly's supporters in Minnesota, McDonald (now Valesh) became an assistant lecturer for the Farmers' Alliance. This appointment, which came to her at the national meeting of the Alliance in Omaha in January of 1891, brought with it the opportunity to lecture with some of the leaders of the movement, to travel across the Midwest and into rural New York, and to publicize her own considerable writing and speaking talents. Scattered reports do scant justice to what must have been a lengthy speaking tour, which was interrupted only by McDonald's marriage in June to Frank Valesh.

Only a year or two before, McDonald met Valesh during the Eight-Hour League campaigns. The same age, they had approached the same stage in their careers. Eva was an organizer for the Knights of Labor, and Frank was an officer in the St. Paul local of the Cigar Makers' Union. As she recalled, "We found ourselves congenial."[60] Emigrating from what had been Bohemia in

Frank Valesh, ca. 1900. This is the only extant photograph of Frank Valesh as an adult, taken during the years of his separation from Eva Valesh. Photo courtesy of Dolores Lautman.

1874, Frank came to the United States on the steamship *Pomerania* with his mother and brother.[61] As a member of the Cigar Makers' Union, Valesh had inherited the traditions of that trade in its respect for book-learning. He wrote articles for labor newspapers, but—as Eva noted—"he hadn't any gift as a speaker, much to his sorrow."[62] Their off-setting skills and "hearty sympathy" made the two a strong match as a political couple. They married in June of 1891 in a ceremony witnessed by family members.[63]

Soon thereafter, Frank took up his duties of inspection as deputy commissioner of the state Bureau of Labor Statistics, and Eva left for the Populist summer tour of industrial expositions and farmers' encampments. She spoke across upstate New York, primarily in Allegany County, the only county with a substantial Alliance membership. She also lectured in Ohio, Indiana, Illinois, and Nebraska, giving speeches that were often only documented with a brief reference or reminiscence years later.[64] In Indianapolis that November, she spoke on the same platform with Annie Diggs and Mary E. Lease on the evening devoted to women's work.[65] The publicity that Diggs's essay on women in the movement generated for McDonald, her tour through the states in the summer, and her frequent appearances in Alliance–Knights of Labor meetings promised a bright future. As Valesh wrote her friend Albert Dollenmayer, "I become more eager, that now I have met the best of them, I think without egotism that I could stand side by side with them and hold my own."[66]

Valesh's performance that summer as a lecturer seemed to bring recognition. As she wrote Dollenmayer, opponents (Republicans in this case) "walk on my collar in their party organs in a manner that is perfectly delightful. They evidently don't know the value of the advertising they are giving me."[67] National Alliance leaders also "strayed into the country occasionally," and her speeches called her to their attention. Invitations to attend their inner circle followed, especially as Valesh had to raise her own expenses for these tours by taking up collections at meetings and occasionally accepting freelance assignments from the *Tribune*. Writing Dollenmayer about the possibilities of writing more sketches for his newspaper, she reported, "Simpson, Peffer, Mrs. Diggs, Mrs. Lease, Weaver, McCune, Ayers, and 'a few of the best of us' are going down to Old Colonial Beach at the mouth of Chesapeake Bay Sept. 1 to hold a council of peace on the industrial problem and incidentally to catch crabs and go surf bathing. I am not sure that I can afford to spend my time and shekels in their aristocratic inner circle, but I would like to and if I do may have some good stuff for you."[68]

Traveling as part of the Populist entourage in the non-election year of 1891 offered both possibilities and limits. While Valesh was never less than ambitious, her marriage that year brought new demands on her time and made her somewhat less open to the constant vagabonding of a career in social reform. In letters to Dollenmayer, she complained about the rigors of campaigning and the physical separation from Frank. Reflecting on the distance between them, she concluded that "to find your other self, 'the partner of your soul' as some writer puts it, means utter wretchedness when you are separated from that person. No amount of philosophy avails to reconcile me to the situation and I think I must have had an attack of temporary insanity when I arranged for this trip." Frank's own frequent absence from home was the only consolation. Yet, as Eva wrote, she was doing good work, and the time away enabled her to focus. To Dollenmayer she wrote, "I hardly think marriage makes the difference to a man that it does to a woman. Marriage opened so new and full a life to me that I felt bewildered and unbalanced and this time of solitude, while not at all pleasant, is giving me time to regain that mental balance that is so essential to the philosophic temperament."[69]

In subsequent letters, Valesh paid lavish attention to her colleagues, showing the social and personal side to a movement culture mostly seen from a distance. Absence from her husband was barely mentioned among the attractions of upstate New York and the attentions of movement leaders like Peffer, Lease, and Simpson. By the end of the tour, Valesh was writing Dollenmayer about the conflict she felt between her private life and public ambitions. Of Frank, she wrote, "It is a hard struggle. I hate to leave him and I'm unhappy all the time away; yet I can't bear to let slip the opportunities that offer to get to the front." While he might fear that she would want to "stay away from home right along," Eva was equally certain that her ambitions would benefit them both. While she suffered from "a bad fit of homesickness," she was "all right when [she kept] moving or [had] a crowd listening to [her] eloquence." But, as she admitted frankly, "I don't want any breathing spaces."[70] Tensions between her career and personal life continued to strain her marriage, even as she continued to write and lecture on the labor reform circuit.

By this time, Eva Valesh's role in the Minnesota Populist movement had effectively ended, even though she continued to write for the Populist press.[71] In his speech before the Farmers' Alliance in 1892, Donnelly blamed her for the decline in Alliance membership. With some rhetorical flourish, he explained, "I have no desire to reflect upon any one, but I think it will be conceded that the work of our Lecture Bureau has not been as efficient during this past year as we could have hoped; and the work has fallen largely upon the shoulders of volunteers, who have traversed the whole state in their efforts to keep alive the alliance sentiment." The long-suffering Everett Fish reluctantly assumed the position.[72] Now with an infant and a husband to care for, eased out of her position as state lecturer and temporarily an invalid with only small writing assignments to account for her time, Valesh did not know and could not have planned for the future. The People's party and its industrial army still shone out as possibilities for political change, and Eva Valesh believed she could rise again to take her place as a comet on its horizon.

Women on the Stump; or, What I Learned at the People's Party

Eva McDonald Valesh's life as a labor organizer, Populist reformer, and journalist followed the path of many prominent women in the late nineteenth century. While social movements recruited and mobilized vast numbers of women in the cause of temperance, monetary reform, and social justice, most women remained on the periphery of reform politics in the electoral realm. During movement-building and movement-politicized phases, women could be found in local and even state offices, speaking on the stump and in the meeting and writing and editing reform newspapers. As movement leaders increasingly sought electoral means to ameliorate their grievances, women became increasingly marginalized, with the exception of such Populist speakers as Mary Elizabeth Lease, Annie Diggs, and Eva Valesh. The transformation of social movements into political parties created new spaces for women to act politically. Once third parties became routinized, women—always disenfranchised but not always excluded—became less important to the political efforts of reform. In effect, one mode of politics was abandoned for another, leaving most women behind.[73]

Despite—or perhaps because of—the powerful influence of women like Valesh, the Farmers' Alliance and the People's party shifted tactics from economic cooperation and education to electoral politics. It is perhaps a historian's conceit to imagine that the Farmers' Alliance could have continued to exist outside the electoral system, acting as a gadfly to political parties and the capitalist economy. Rural producer cooperatives, insurance programs, and purchasing agencies were designed to organize farmers of the South and West into a political movement and did that without permanently establishing links between economic self-activity and political reform. Moreover, while the emphasis on economic and social means to political ends brought women into the Populist movement in large numbers, their integration was effectively halted as social movement culture became institutionalized in electoral form.

Instead, the Populist shift to politics raised the stakes of participation for women as varied in their commitments as Annie Diggs, whose roots were in Prohibition and woman suffrage, and Eva Valesh, whose abiding commitment—in her own words—was to the working people. If these women could assume a partisan role in state and national races but retain a reputation for nonpartisanship—that is, for being aloof from sordid political dealings—they enhanced the chance of reform success. Given the radical nature of proposals for women's suffrage, prohibition, and labor reform, cooperation from allies across the political spectrum was required, which in and of itself served as a break on partisanship. At the same time, if women could remain outside the partisan fray, they might be able to ride out the tides of personal factionalism and ideological conflict that seemed repeatedly to inundate reform movements. But the contradictions of political reform—one sought a place in the system in order to change it—were hardly to be overcome by women who had already crossed the gender divide in partisan political activity. Being an advocate for women and workers was no longer safe from the charge of special interest attached to partisan activity.

McDonald Valesh's short-lived career as a national Populist speaker and writer was built on her experience in and commitment to the cause of working people. The national character of her work and reputation led to greater opportunities, a renewed commitment to journalism and the labor movement, and the abandonment of the regional context in which her star rose. Political opportunities as speaker, writer, and organizer led her farther and farther away from the local arena of the Twin Cities and eventually fueled the controversies that brought an end to that stage of her career. It was her connection to national and state political efforts, her work as a publicist and journalist, and her speaking ability that led to her long-term alliance with Samuel Gompers and the American Federation of Labor—arguably the most public and sustaining work she attempted in a thirty-year career in labor reform.

CHAPTER 5

FROM STRIKES TO STRINGS

The Trade Union Woman as Journalist, 1892–1895

> She has used her tongue in a lively way and taken all the benefit that
> her sex controls when in argument with a man. We have had to listen.
>
> —*St. Paul Trades and Labor Bulletin*, 1893

In 1892, after her son, Frank, was born, Eva McDonald Valesh faced the prospect of retreating from public life, owing to the challenges her personal life now presented—a husband, a newborn child, and recovering after a difficult pregnancy. While she feared her career might end, she found other ways to keep informed of political developments and contribute to debates. The trip to New York presented her with opportunities for which any ambitious woman longed, and it opened up a new field for her writing. Still, the men's world of journalism and politics made no allowances for private life. In labor circles and in newspaper offices, men often seemed to have no family responsibilities at all, although wives and children appeared at social gatherings and surfaced in reports of comings and goings. As Valesh wrote succinctly to Albert Dollenmayer, "I hardly think marriage makes the difference to a man that it does to a woman."[1] To balance her domestic and professional responsibilities, she made a series of compromises that enabled her, like other exemplary women of her time, to integrate the public and private self.

A career in labor reform journalism—occasional editing, freelance writing, and opinion columns—better suited Valesh than most other alternatives. If it paid badly (and it certainly did), there was the compensation of knowing that at least one could make one's own schedule. If fame and fortune eluded occasional writers, it proved little better for most women journalists. The comparative hazards and rewards of the city desk versus the lady's page did not determine her choice. Rather, freelance journalism was one of the few means by which married women could balance the demands of marriage and childcare with those of a career. One could write at home about what one knew, using correspondence, visits, and occasional interviews to eke out enough copy to sustain a career. If the writer, like Valesh, was ingenious enough to solve the childcare problem, she could travel and write investigative reports and essays for news syndicates and national journals. These options enabled Valesh to continue her remarkable work in labor reform despite mounting obstacles and considerable opposition.

With all its flexibility, journalism, especially reform journalism, was not an easy job for women. It entailed long hours, tedious sleuthing, small rewards, and constant competition for resources and visibility, not the least of which came from other reform journalists and women reporters. As writer Brooke Kroeger wrote of Nellie Bly, her chief rivals were not men but other women journalists who traveled around the world in her shadow.[2] Valesh's major obstacles were directly related to the ways that editors, reporters, and working-class readers viewed women. Trade unionists tangled with her over advertising revenues and attitudes toward politics. And sexism, to use the modern term, pervaded the public sphere in which Valesh sought to acquire fame, fortune, and security. Fame was fleeting; fortune was elusive; and security was unlikely, subject to the whims of owners, editors, colleagues, and readers. In newspaper work, as Valesh later learned at the city desk of the *New York Journal*, yesterday's failures—and triumphs—were quickly forgotten.[3] Work in these worlds was about risk, persistence, and adaptability, enlivened only by luck. Valesh had the additional burden of being a woman, and quite possibly an unlucky one, to increase the difficulty of making it in the public worlds of journalism and labor reform.

At a time when the labor movement changed its public identity and mass culture emphasized class experience as central to politics, Valesh was able to find opportunities to do what she did best—to tell new stories of class and translate working-class grievances into concrete political proposals. While she failed with others to significantly alter the course of class politics, she remained on the front lines of a changing working-class world. Politically dividing into the respectable aristocracy of craft unionism and the unorganized and impoverished immigrant masses, the working class at the turn of the century was the subject of Valesh's many reports.

Metropolitan Journalist

A cub reporter for the *St. Paul Globe* in 1888–89, Eva McDonald Valesh had a regular assignment to cover labor news and write a column on workingwomen.

As her career took shape, she left the *Globe* for more lucrative endeavors. While on a speaking tour, she sent to *Tribune* editor Albert Dollenmayer prose sketches of the Populist orators to be used for political articles, adding, "If there is anything of interest, fix it up at your own discretion." Over the next few years, she wrote Dollenmayer regularly with political news, seeking to exchange ideas about what was happening in the lively realm of politics.[4]

After the birth of her son, Valesh sought work again as a reporter, but her options were limited to political reporting and commentary. She did not receive a regular weekly or monthly salary; rather, she wrote articles on "string," being paid by the length of her published stories—an experience common to many writers of the time. Although the late nineteenth century was the heyday of the reporter, a journalist's life was precarious. Copy had to be produced on a daily basis to ensure a regular income. Salaried positions were the rare reward for many years of experience and luck. This was the unstable world in which Eva Valesh made her career. Like many women journalists, she thus took up "space work" rather than find a salaried position. As a journalism expert explained, "As special articles can be written at home and sent by mail to the editor, this is a field in which women have as good a chance as men." It often was one "avenue of access" to salaried positions.[5]

In the 1880s and 1890s, intense competition among urban newspapers prompted changes in their content and appearance. In major cities across the country, newspaper wars over circulation and advertising gave rise to "the new journalism," with its emphasis on sensational news reporting, popular language, and mass readership. The first round of competition began when Joseph Pulitzer took over the *New York World* in 1883. To be successful, he knew he had to supplant the city's leading papers. As he had with his earlier paper, the *St. Louis Post-Dispatch*, Pulitzer employed the best journalists he could find to establish his popular daily. He edged out city competition with sensationalist headlines, new newspaper features like comic strips and women's pages, larger typefaces and graphic illustrations, and more stories per issue. He capitalized on newspaper trends throughout the country to bring to his readers "stunt journalism." Sending undercover reporters out to "investigate" a story—be it one of political chicanery, factory conditions, or urban poverty—was integral to Pulitzer's style. Even star reporter Julian Ralph masqueraded as a mayor's secretary in pursuit of "news."[6]

As important as Pulitzer was in the history of journalism, the changes he implemented in the *World* were not unique. In cities around the country, newspaper owners and editors eager to increase circulation and advertising revenues courted new readers with the same techniques. The *Minneapolis Tribune*, one of the major newspapers in the Twin Cities, underwent similar changes. Valesh described its owner, Alden J. Blethen, as an "able man with a charming personality. However, in his witty contempt for the masses he forgot that they are the people who buy newspapers, who build up circulation."[7] As the fortunes of the newspaper declined against competition, the *Tribune* took on heavy debt and lost subscribers. It suffered more when its local rival, the *Journal*, cut its price to two cents and undersold the *Tribune's* nickel sheet.[8] The *Tribune* fire that year deepened the newspaper's woes. By 1891, it had had six different owners when two partners, W. J. Murphy and Gilbert A. Pierce, bought the newspaper. Two years later, with the aid of streetcar magnate Thomas Lowry, Murphy purchased Pierce's stock and became sole owner. Murphy, who "thought of himself as the Midwestern Pulitzer," sought to update the newspaper and turn it into a profit-making enterprise.[9]

By Valesh's account, Murphy was "quite brilliant intellectually and a keen businessman."[10] Running the *Grand Forks Plain Dealer* had taught him the newspaper business. By 1891, he had learned all he could from it and wanted a new challenge. Taking over as *Tribune* editor-in-chief, Murphy changed fundamentally how the paper operated, looked, and read. It, too, followed the path of news specialization, expansion of size, and shift in content. With expanding political and cultural coverage, Murphy's innovations gradually increased the *Tribune's* Sunday circulation from 21,000 in 1889 to 31,000 in 1894 and 37,400 in 1895. The "modern" look of the newspaper, its increasing circulation, and shifts in advertising made a success of the once-unstable publication.[11]

In the day of the independent newspaper, party politics did not determine newspaper policy, but it did shape coverage. Murphy's political perspective could be summed up in his statement that "it is hardly necessary to say that the paper will be Republican in politics, not from policy but from that conviction which is born from faith in a party whose history is so remarkable and whose mission, they believe, to be not yet completed."[12] He also knew he had to court readers outside traditional Republican strongholds. One of the principal ways he achieved that objective was by connecting to the labor movement in the Twin Cities. He asked Albert Dollenmayer, one of his editors, to recruit Eva Valesh to write for the newspaper. In December 1891, Dollenmayer wrote Valesh that he wanted to "make a business proposition" to her; "business," he said, "pure and simple." Her articles were to be as long as the occasion would warrant "upon timely Alliance subjects." While they were to be written from a "free lance standpoint," she was also to refrain from being "too hard against the dear old Republican party." Knowing the value of Valesh's name, Dollenmayer suggested she "set [her] own price," for they would "pay anything you say." She would "get a better salary if [she] didn't seem too eager."[13] As Valesh remembered, the *Tribune* "had incurred the opposition of working people on account of the fierce hostility it displayed toward them and especially their unions." Murphy now hoped to overcome labor's antagonism. While her husband disapproved of her going back to work, Valesh accepted the new assignment.[14]

Eva Valesh's apprenticeship with *Tribune* editor William Murphy resembled the mentoring relationships she had established with Jack McGaughey and Ignatius Donnelly. Described as "distinguished" and "aloof," Murphy was "relentless," "shrewd," and above all analytical.[15] He appreciated similar talents in Valesh, who later recalled that he had put her "through a course of analysis training that no college would have." She explained, "He let me try everything on the paper—book reviews, dramatic criticism, editorials on economics, the weekly review of current topics—anything but the society news or the daily assignments, which I regarded as plain drudgery."[16] Even after her stint at the *Tribune*, Murphy remained a significant person in Valesh's life. When she needed to borrow money for a business enterprise[17] or sought an intermediary to handle her divorce settlement, she turned to him. He willingly lent the money and supervised custody and child-support arrangements.[18] Their relationship, however, was not like the friendship Valesh had with McGaughey. Murphy was a professional advocate who saw that his protégé survived the obstacle course that professional women often encountered.

In writing for the *Tribune*, Valesh joined the ranks of journalists in the rapidly expanding field of the metropolitan press. City dailies had hired a vast army of reporters, copy editors, proofreaders, and content editors to handle, treat, and report the "news." News became an increasingly valuable commodity, as information about business transactions, court appearances, personal peccadilloes, and urban vice and poverty seemed to attract exponentially larger audiences. To a great degree, this news explosion was less about the quantity of available information than the transformation of the facts and artifacts of daily life into the category of "the newsworthy." At a time when newspapers were looking to attract new readers, every sensational story of murder, mayhem, and skullduggery, as well as heart-warming tales of personal sacrifice, uncommon charity, and heroic endeavor, could be translated into a commodity—the news story—and sold first to a newspaper editor and then to a newspaper audience.

The commodification of information had been under way ever since the Penny Press had taken over old commercial sheets in the 1830s and turned its attention to true stories of crime and sex in the city.[19] As the century drew to an end, the appetite for sensational stories—which is to say their commercial appeal—moved mainstream city journalism to new heights of inventiveness. As historian Christopher Wilson has written, "The reporters' search for the sensational news item, their growing disregard for privacy in favor of the public's right to know, and their exposure to crime all gradually became the hall-

marks of the profession."[20] When tales of domestic disorder and political battles did not engage, international relations and war crowded front pages and
sidebar columns. Still, the bread and butter of city newspapers remained their
ability to capture the local scene, to provide political news and economic information as well as entertainment for the masses. An article might amusingly
speak to how an electric wire from the streetcar lines charged a metal plate,
shocked passersby, and frightened a dog. It could report on the growing number of divorces, recent suicides, and political races in the outraged tones of partisan journalism. Within the evolving standards of journalism, confusion
reigned about what constituted news and what priority each kind of news
should receive. Readers, editors, and advertisers weighed the relative value of
each news story.

The end of the nineteenth century was the age of the reporter.[21] Mass-mar-
ket urban newspapers elevated the role of the heroic news writer, whose first
goal was to present and represent the "truth" by telling stories of urban life.
As newspapers moved from political journalism and editorial to commercialism and "fact," the news-gatherer gained new status. In recognition of their
central role, reporters were given bylines and higher salaries. And as newspapers engaged in an ever-more elaborate division of labor, reporters were assigned to specialized subjects and specific tasks. The leg work of investigation
was separated from the rewrite work, whereby writers edited and revised the
data into the newspaper's style and voice. In his essay "The Reporter's First
Murder Case," Julius Chambers noted that a single murder investigation required the work of five people besides the reporter. With more illustrations
came specialized artists and photographers and more editors. A central editor
assigned reporters to cover specific events, which limited their autonomy, and
copy editors assumed a larger role in the process.[22]

As newspapers became corporate, journalists' working conditions changed
as well. Intense competition not only fueled innovations but also increased the
demand for and salary of front-line journalists, even as thousands flocked into
the profession on less certain wages. Despite rising income and status for a few
"star" reporters, the more common story was of low pay and constant uncertainty. In his memoirs, Julian Ralph emphasized how strenuous the job was:
"The life of every journalist is hard as nails; that of the special correspondent
is even harder." He said that reporters "see their strained, exciting, never-
halting toil through glasses colored by sentiment or through the heat-waves
of excitement. They are forever formulated by competition and freshened by
novelty."[23] Such dramatic prose masked the fact that newspaper reporting was
work. And as the major news dailies became corporate enterprises, reporters
lost their earlier autonomy to choose their subjects and set their own pace.

Along with the reporter's loss of control over the written word came shifts in salary and compensation. Despite an increasing demand for journalism, the labor market for reporters remained glutted. News services such as Associated Press reduced the demand for individual reporting. In the hierarchy of the newsroom, editors were paid the most and cub reporters the least. Daily journalism—the world of the beat reporter—was in many ways "a young person's work." It required endless hours and physical endurance. It also called for persistence through the poverty that accompanied the early years of a career. Beginning writers might receive as little as $4 a week, although experienced reporters averaged from $15 to $25 a week in the 1880s, or from $700 to $1,200 a year. More specialized writers could earn from $40 to $60 a week, copy editors from $35 to $80 a week, and content editors considerably more. Nellie Bly, a star in the world of New York journalism, took home $200 a week in her contracts with a story paper. At the time, that was enough to make her a wealthy woman. As with other famous reporters, her salary was a reflection of how her very name became a commodity in the culture industry.[24]

Still, the role of the reporter was primarily a masculine one. In popular culture, it was the journalist who, without regard for his own safety, sought out the news at the front lines. To bring readers the "real" story, he—and it was almost always a he—pursued every angle and brought the reader "the truth." Women, when they engaged in such escapades, were thought of more as stunt artists than reporters. The rugged image of the journalist remained as the male denizen of "dirty, dingy, tobacco-polluted" newsrooms and press clubs. They wore wrinkled clothing and drank scotch, engaged in "journalistic horseplay" in the city room, and sharpened the hard edge of newspaper prose. A popular correspondence course in journalism proclaimed as both boast and warning that the newspaper office was "not a Sunday school room" but "the barracks of the reportorial corps." A "cold-blooded calling," it nevertheless endowed reporters with the character of "bright young manhood"—"courageous, sharp as a hawk, mentally untiring, physically enduring."[25] According to Wilson, "The reporter became America's first public agent of exposure, the high priest of 'experience,' the expert on 'real life'—all keywords at the heart of American popular discourse."[26]

For all their stunt work, women reporters could not aspire to the position of "priest." Few could "sell" their image and authority as reporter in the sphere beyond domestic and society news. Not even the inestimable Nellie Bly earned the same coinage as a male journalist. Women, according to one expert, were "generally looked on with disfavor as applicants for active newspaper work" for "the same reason as that which would keep a woman, though starving, from getting employment as a coal heaver." The rough-and-tumble public world remained inaccessible to the woman reporter, "so long as she gets no sterner training than that of the girl's boarding school, the parlor, and the ballroom."[27] Other observers at the time assessed that even exceptional work from a woman journalist was undervalued. As one editorial put it, "Her best work will be taken as a matter of course, and anything less than her best as a deliberately planned and personal injury."[28]

Valesh's connection to the labor movement seems to have been crucial to her finding work beyond the women's and society pages. Discontented with work as a space writer, she was eager to find better-paying work on the newspaper. Albert Dollenmayer had been her contact there for the occasional pieces she wrote. Her newspaper work, while not extensive, brought in small amounts of cash.[29] A few months later, she wrote to ask if the *Tribune* had paid her the right amount: "I don't want to enter a very audible protest, but my check for February was only $3.50 and that strikes me as a trifle below the amount." He responded by asking for any information she might give him, but he also added that his new responsibilities made him "a very unreliable string keeper."[30] In April, still trying to square accounts, Valesh recounted what she had published, listing not articles but dates and column inches. At one point, she confessed, she had to rely on headlines, because "that is about all [she] remembered of it, but it may be of some assistance in finding it." She evidently learned her lesson, for she told Dollenmayer, "I have kept my string for March."[31] While she regularly published material beginning in late February, only when she took up editorial work did her pay significantly increase.[32]

Friends of Yore

Dollenmayer was not only Valesh's *Tribune* agent but a trusted friend. Their strong personal connection was richly played out in letters that dissected politics and personages and paid homage to friends and family. He believed in land and tax reform and had some sympathy with labor. She felt she could reveal her views to him without restraint. They had started in journalism at about the same time and married within a few weeks of each other.[33] They shared as well a certain sensibility about the profession, revealed in ironic and skeptical references. They even had similar reactions to the *Tribune* staff. As Valesh wrote to Dollenmayer, "There has been no change in my position since you left. Bartram and Hamblin love me as of old; but I'm not at all sensitive about it."[34] There was at times a humorous cast to Valesh's reaction to him. On his marriage, she wrote, "I am sure that Mrs. A. Dollenmayer has a model husband and I've no doubt you would certify that A. Dollenmayer has the sweetest and best wife in the world." Afterward she teased that he must have been comparing notes with her newlywed husband: "It must be as good as a comic paper to hear two newly made Benedicts exchange views."[35] Dollenmayer responded that he had not had the chance to speak with Frank since the marriage: "I saw him only once at the coffee house and meant to talk an arm off him, but he escaped while I was eating, not even so much as coming up and allowing me to take his hand but then again bride grooms are very shy and modest. I have been there and I know."[36] Interspersed in all of the surviving correspondence is a genuine affection for each other. In fact, when Dollenmayer married, Valesh told him that she hoped "marriage won't make either one of us despise or forget the friend of yore."[37]

Over time, their spouses became a part of the relationship. Dollenmayer and his wife, Claribel, socialized with the Valeshes when they were in town, and Frank contributed to the correspondence. When Eva was recovering from the difficult birth, Frank wrote Dollenmayer to ask if he would postpone the visit a week to let Eva recuperate. There was an advantage to waiting. By then, Frank wrote, "Things will be in better shape, and the baby being then considerably older will appear more intelligent and hence will be more of a credit to his family."[38] More often, however, Eva wrote to Dollenmayer about the family and set up exchanges of photographs. In another letter, she wrote of her son that "his papa regards him as a most remarkable young man. He walks and climbs and talks so that the whole household is full occupied in looking after him." After asking for a photograph of Dollenmayer's young children, she added, "I suppose you are firmly convinced of [your son's] superiority to all other boys. I hope he will fully justify your expectations."[39]

In her letters to Dollenmayer, Valesh revealed some of her frustrations and fears about marriage and motherhood. Writing home from her trip to New York, she told of discovering new ambitions. At the same time, she confessed, she was "wretched" without Frank.[40] Conflicting desires now caused friction in the marriage. Physically and emotionally, the birth of what would be Valesh's first and only child took an even greater toll. Still, by the following year, her work on the *Tribune* expanded. With Dollenmayer's help, she became the paper's labor editor. As she wrote to another friend, she had "a very nice position and a satisfactory salary."[41] Motherhood and marriage may have slowed her down; but as Dollenmayer foretold, Valesh refused to allow them to be barriers to her work.

Still, the demands of marriage and motherhood posed major obstacles to Valesh's career. After their marriage in 1891, Frank served as assistant labor commissioner. He spent most of his time on the road conducting state factory inspections and performing other public duties. He was often only home on

Sundays. About this time, Eva wrote to Dollenmayer, "Frank is still in the Bureau and traveling about the country, leaving me a widow part of the time."[42] No letters between the couple survive, so it is difficult to even speculate about the tenor of their relationship as lovers, parents, or co-workers. That he continued to be active must have worn on Eva, especially after her son's birth. It must have become worse when Dollenmayer, her "friend of yore," was appointed Washington correspondent for the *Tribune*. She confessed that "we often speak of you and envy you being where people live and are not vegetating like the inhabitants up here. I'm dreadfully weary of this section and spend more time planning to get away from it than I do at work."[43]

Valesh's work on the *Tribune*, her increasingly frequent speaking engagements, and her other editorial work meant that she had to find someone to take care of her son. She wondered to Dollenmayer whether housekeeping in Washington was easier than in Minnesota, since she thought there were "unlimited" domestic servants available.[44] At first, Eva's teenage sister-in-law, Julia, babysat young Frank. As Julia grew progressively weaker from tuberculosis, someone else had to be found. Frank's mother probably stepped in from time to time. Luckily, Eva's younger sister Blanche was able to care for the child when Eva's career was beginning to make greater demands on her.[45]

In the Realm of Labor

As the newly appointed labor editor of the *Tribune*, Valesh was able to pursue both a career in writing and to maintain a publicly visible role in the local labor movement. The labor column she edited appeared in the Sunday paper. Variously called "In the Realm of Labor," "In the Industrial World," and simply "Labor," the column published local and national labor news, labor meetings, and reviews of political economy, new novels, and political tracts. In it, Valesh discussed the principal labor issues of the day, state legislation and local government, legal cases of interest, labor leaders, and conflicts over organization and politics. While Valesh culled most of her material from national publications, local labor newspapers, and the minutes of meetings, many of her columns had editorial asides expressing her perspective on labor developments. Her partisan support for certain labor leaders, particularly Samuel Gompers, gave her page a definite trade-union bias. She also captured the precipitous decline of Knights of Labor and working-class party leaders who were losing out in local labor circles. At the same time, however, she strove for an objective editorial voice. Even as she addressed a particular labor constituency, she sought to claim the labor page as the voice of the working classes.

Eva McDonald Valesh as a journalist, ca. 1890s. She used this photograph in sketch form as a column head during her years with the *New York Journal*. Photo courtesy of Dolores Lautman.

In this respect, Valesh engaged in a journalism of advocacy—one directed toward a specific political audience. If the *Tribune*, like other major metropolitan dailies, was a business enterprise, it was still dependent enough on working-class readers and institutions to be influenced by their expectations. Under her editorship, the labor page addressed the unemployment crisis of the 1890s, the horrific gap in public relief and public works, and legal and political battles over the anti–iron-clad law barring blacklists, prison labor, the right to strike, and arbitration.[46] The creation and progress of a state card and label league to promote union-made products, of which Frank Valesh was secretary-treasurer, was a major topic, as were elections of officers and labor celebrations.[47] Valesh also chronicled the progress of labor organizing among such varied groups as the waiters, Scandinavian boardinghouse keepers, and women laundry workers. Sometimes, with the acknowledged contributions of other labor figures such as Gompers, she provided news coverage of the major issues of the day.[48]

Valesh's work for the *Tribune* neither paid as well as she wanted nor provided her with the only venue for writing and speaking. In December 1891, just before being hired by the newspaper, she accepted the job of editing the *St. Paul Trades and Labor Bulletin*, a monthly news journal.[49] Her talents as writer and speaker in local and labor circles had opened the door for the hire. Being married to Frank Valesh, the first president of the Minnesota State Federation of Labor and assistant labor commissioner, undoubtedly helped. The editorial work was probably not onerous, and it kept Eva connected to the labor scene. Under Eva Valesh's leadership, the *Bulletin* also paid particular attention to the organization of women workers. As she wrote in an editorial comment on one campaign, "The organization of the laundry workers is proof that the spirit of unionism is constantly growing in St. Paul, not only among the wage earners themselves, but the employers are beginning to see that a union may have reciprocal interests with their own if approached in a spirit of friendliness and fairness." She continued, "Women are proverbially hard to organize. Yet this union of more than a hundred women wage workers would encourage the veriest pessimist that ever lived."[50]

The most important story during her tenure as labor editor, however, was the economic depression of 1893 and the growing ranks of the unemployed. Even as the struggle between the trade unions and the Knights of Labor raged, the plight of unemployed workers began to preoccupy all forces involved. As she recorded in her column,[51] the crisis left many workers, especially those in the building trades, without resources. Moreover, a "stream of unemployed mechanics poured in from the West to the East." While labor unions met to discuss the problem, "the depression which is everywhere felt [made] the problem a perplexing one." Trade unionists predicted that there would be "an immense amount of suffering during the coming winter." Already more than 6,000 people in Minneapolis were idled that month. While the Central Trades Council put into place employment bureaus and sought to give relief to its unemployed members, the numbers made it difficult. It would be more than two years before Valesh could write that "the Minneapolis unions withstood the season of depression wonderfully well. They are already in a condition to profit by good times."[52]

Valesh's connections to the Populist press continued to pay dividends. Late in 1892, she wrote an article for the reform journal *Arena* on the sweating system in the tenement district of New York. She took up the assignment with typical enthusiasm. As she wrote Dollenmayer in December, "I am up to my ears in investigating the sweating system and am getting good stuff."[53] The themes she explored—immigration, labor organization, gender, and the uses of the state—would surface again in her later work. Following a pattern set during the Eva Gay series, Valesh took her reader on a sensory journey through the tenements. Led by an experienced guide who "spoke the dialect of the quarter," Valesh traveled through Mulberry Bend, supposedly in search of a missing tailor.[54]

The contrast between Mulberry Bend and Valesh's earlier tour of Minneapolis shops and factories was striking. In her adopted city, she had seen native-born and Scandinavian immigrant women at work, but she observed in Mulberry Bend "the lowest class of immigrant." Her studies in Midwestern factories had revealed women who needed time for reading and churchgoing; the thousands she saw in the tenements were, in Valesh's words, "as oblivious to the civilization typified by Broadway and Fifth Avenue as if they had remained in some Russian village." Minneapolis had poorly ventilated workplaces and dust; New York workers not only worked among the dank tenements, but they lived there, too. The sanitary provisions were primitive; "heaps of rags and clothing hanging from fire escapes were eloquent of the poverty that despaired"; and the buildings were dark and crowded. A cholera scare heightened the sense of danger.[55]

On the December morning she visited Mulberry Bend, Valesh wrote, "grim tenements seemed to wall the street in." She spoke with horror of inhabitants who "even burrow in the ground in their frantic attempt to find shelter" and of "babies with that pallid, haggard expression characteristic of the quarter."[56] She described in detail a two-room tenement with only two windows that served as workplace for twelve to eighteen men, women, and children. It served as dwelling place as well, and the evidence remained in the room—finished clothing mixed with rubbish and food. The result of this system of production, Valesh contended, could only be despair and illness. As she wrote, the tenement district "had a desolate weirdness, as if these were the shades of departed victims of poverty condemned to wander up and down, carrying on a ghastly semblance of the transactions of life. Alas! They were not even shade but flesh and blood, out of which a profit could yet be wrung."[57]

To an audience that included middle-class reformers, Valesh wrote of these conditions as hazardous to the general community. She played to the fears that contagious diseases could spread quickly in the dirty and cramped environment of the tenements, that it could "filter out in the clothing made there to all parts of the country." She suggested that even in a cholera epidemic, sweatshops could exist and thrive as they did "when diphtheria, scarlet fever, and nameless contagious diseases claim their percentage and leave their germs in the clothing manufactured in their midst."[58]

Like many labor advocates of her time, Valesh located the cause of the poverty she found in the government's unrestricted immigration policies.[59] Although Valesh did not doubt that industrialists and landlords profited from the sweating system, she argued that it was the character of the immigrant population that made sweatshops possible.[60] Her race-based thinking established those she wrote about as fundamentally different from the native-born working class. As she wrote, immigrants, "always inured to toil," accepted these appalling conditions without protest. "Having come from country villages," the denizens of the tenements did not even know how to judge their environment. "Accustomed," she wrote, "to the habits of country villages and plenty of fresh air, they endure the many hardships and still maintain their health." She imagined that the tenement poor were capable of enduring the "cunningly devised slavery" of sweatshop labor in ways that native-born workers could not. Ironically, only a few years before, Valesh had condemned similar conditions. As she noted, simply "getting used to the work" might have convinced workers to tolerate the dangers of industrial work. Workplace hazards in many industries caused frequent injuries and even deaths among factory operatives. Immigrants working in tenements were no better equipped to tolerate bad working conditions than were the workingwomen of Minneapolis. Yet she wrote, immigrants "come from generations of hardy peasants who have toiled in the fields, and they really bring with them a sturdy health and vigor that takes more than one generation of factory life to bleach into impotence."[61]

As in much of her advocacy writing, Valesh presented solutions to these problems informed by the labor thinking of the time. First, she suggested labels for the clothing trade, similar to those of the cigar trade, to assure customers not just of an honestly made product but one free from disease. Second, she supported current efforts to restrict "pauper and ignorant immigration," a remedy that would exclude certain groups without closing the borders. Finally, Valesh reiterated the demands of earlier New York reformers for state or municipal regulation of tenement housing, "to improve the general health."[62] These policy proposals echoed much of the political program of labor in the 1890s, just as trade unions began to dominate labor politics. The article marked a turning point in Valesh's career, as she increasingly, despite the voluntarist tone of labor politics, accepted the need for both private and state intervention in labor relations. Labor organization could not do it all. With a foot each in the worlds of labor and journalism, Valesh increasingly looked toward the realm of public opinion, rather than labor politics, to obtain results.

Trade-Union Ascendancy

Valesh's journalistic endeavors revealed that she had abandoned her support of Knights of Labor ideals for the path of craft unionism. Eva McDonald and Frank Valesh decided to shift their allegiance to trade unions when they became involved in the Eight-Hour League. The leagues served as a halfway house for many Knights and trade unionists before they entered the insurgent trade unions of the American Federation of Labor (AFL). Focused on educational work among employers and the public, the leagues had neither the mission to serve as unions nor the legitimacy needed in terms of a union charter. The need for a stronger central body seemed clear. On July 7, 1890, more than forty delegates representing the Eight-Hour League, the state Farmers' Alliance, the Minneapolis and St. Paul trade and labor assemblies, and the Knights of Labor clubs gathered in St. Paul to form a state labor federation.[63] For the year following its founding, Valesh had worked for the Farmers' Alliance, but her work both in local circles and nationally soon brought her to the forefront of labor reform.

In 1891, Valesh took another step by speaking on "Women and Labor" at the AFL's national convention.[64] Characterized as "a very interesting and instructive lecture on the evils connected with the working women of America and the necessity for organization among them," Valesh's speech was published first as a pamphlet and later as an article. Her ideas echoed attitudes shared by many trade unionists about the necessity of organizing women, and they were instrumental in convincing the AFL to hire organizer Mary Kenney that year.[65]

Whatever impact sexism had on the labor movement, Valesh developed a personal friendship with AFL President Samuel Gompers, which was reflected in her work as a labor editor. That friendship also entangled her in what would become the most heated conflict of her tenure as editor, when a small war broke out between local trade unions and the remaining Knights of Labor assemblies.[66] The motivating force was the search for legitimacy in working-class politics. The relationship of local unions to the national organizations— the rapidly weakening Knights and the emergent trade unions affiliated with the AFL—further intensified local conflict. While declining in number, the Knights of Labor still strongly influenced local politics. Sensing their own growing power, trade unionists were less tolerant of what they considered to be interference. The depression that began in 1893 only made matters worse.

In the Twin Cities, Eva and Frank Valesh were among the best known labor figures of their generation. They were better connected nationally than many of their peers. Frank had already climbed the ladder of local labor success by serving as officer in the Cigar Makers Union local in St. Paul, president of the new Minnesota State Federation of Labor, and deputy labor commissioner, a political appointment. Eva's connection to the national AFL was equally compelling. She and Frank joined in the effort to strengthen the hand of trade unions locally. The result was constant conflict with those Knights of Labor assemblies that still held power.

Strategic and principled debates were at the heart of the conflict—the first over the Knights' perceived antagonism to trade unions and the second between those who embraced "practical politics" as a solution for working-class woes and those who wanted the economic weapons of trade unionism to have priority. The disputes hinged on widely divergent interpretations of the class conflict of the "great upheaval" of the late nineteenth century. Massive strikes locally—the Haymarket riot in 1886, the Homestead strike in 1892, the Pullman strike in 1894—and the wave of court injunctions raised the fundamental issues of the day: the role of the law and the courts, the relation of the state, the constitution and content of the labor movement, the place of political organization, and the definition of class, solidarity, and union.

As labor editor, Eva Valesh emerged as a partisan player in these debates. She owed much of her early career and loyalty to the Knights of Labor, but just as she had disagreed with older Populists, so now she found herself on the opposite side of the fight between them and the trade unions. Fundamentally, Valesh rejected labor strategies that emphasized politics at the expense of economic action. It was not that she abandoned legislation or party politics but that she had little use for third-party politics after 1892. Even in her Populist writing, Valesh criticized those who gave production issues greater priority than redistribution. The wage system, she argued, was a permanent fixture, and the question was how to make it more just.[67] This perspective shaped how she approached labor politics and the direction of labor organization. Not surprisingly, Valesh backed the increasingly trade-union–dominated AFL as the voice of the working class.

The choice of trade union organization made both Frank and Eva Valesh early allies of Gompers. Nationally, the increasingly powerful AFL needed to win over local labor assemblies and state federations individually. Connections—both political and personal—between Gompers and local trade unionists brought the labor unions into the AFL one by one. In the Twin Cities, the Valeshes became key players in the transition of labor to a more prudential and conservative trade unionism, but they were not alone. As Gompers wrote in 1893, "I am obliged to you for your description of the conditions prevailing in the labor movement of Minneapolis although I heard considerable of them both in letters from there as well as the press. It seems strange that there are still some of our trade union which allow themselves to be hoodwinked and diverted from their proper course either by an enemy or pretend friend."[68] The Valeshes understood exactly who were labor's friends.

While much of the conflict centered on where workers ought to be organized, the Knights of Labor, according to Gompers, were "not wage-workers at all and . . . should have absolutely no standing in the labor movement." They were associated with secrecy and mystery and stood apart from trades unionists in their heterogeneity as well as their "trickery." In trade union campaigns across the country, Gompers and his trade union allies sought to edge out the Knights from both local labor politics and labor organization. At the same time, Gompers was seeking to establish his own leadership over the AFL. His biographer, Bernard Mandel, wrote, "Gompers recognized the importance of personal contacts and as a result did an immense amount of traveling. He spent about a third of his time on the road, averaging 30,000 miles a year." In effect, Gompers recruited "local shock troops of trade unionism." Through his ability to appoint organizers and commission articles for the *American Federationist*, he built a network of labor activists loyal to him alone. The allegiance of talented young trade unionists such as Frank and Eva Valesh contributed to the ascendancy of both Gompers and the AFL.[69]

The Valeshes were early converts to the political style and organizational savvy of the trade unions. At a fairly young age, Frank had become an assistant labor commissioner in the state on the basis of his political ties, and yet both he and Eva viewed labor's political involvements with skepticism. They knew the local personnel and their history. In working out her strategy, Eva wrote Gompers to find out where he stood on the political question. He replied, "Let me say that as a matter of fact our organization has been in politics since its inception, but as you are well aware they are different kinds of politics." For some, politics meant lobbying, and for others it meant seeking any political office, whether "President of the United States or . . . town constable."[70]

In this letter, Gompers outlined his view of party politics as a venue for labor's efforts. Rather than party allegiance, the AFL, Gompers thought, should emphasize state legislation on such matters as government employees, contract and prison labor, immigration, and the eight-hour day. Trade unionists preferred to limit political action to where it might be most effective—in local and state federations. If labor was to engage in politics at all, it should use the party system on a nonpartisan basis. The evolving stance of the AFL was not pure-and-simple trade unionism, nor was it simple voluntarism in the way that labor historians have understood it. Labor politics in the late nineteenth century undertook limited efforts to regulate labor where it came into contact with the state—in prisons, in immigration, in government employment. Other choices were made impractical by the judicial regulation of labor, to use Victoria Hattam's words, and by the division of power among federal, state, and local government. It was this style of political action—not its ab-negation—that attracted like-minded trade unionists like Eva and Frank Valesh to the AFL.[71]

Valesh's term as labor leader and editor on the local scene soon became as conflict- ridden as her time as a lecturer for the Farmers' Alliance. Gompers's letter to Valesh indicated that the amicable relations that initially brought local Knights of Labor and trade unionists into alliance was rapidly deteriorating. Furthermore, the local trade assemblies fought to maintain their dominance in labor affairs. Conflicts now surfaced in the relationship of Eva Valesh to the St. Paul Trades and Labor Assembly over her control of the *Bulletin*. As its edi-tor, she was expected to carry out their policy in the publication, but there were evident disagreements. By April of 1893, the St. Paul Assembly had had enough of John McDonald's daughter. In what might have been simple disagreement over policy or personal conflict over control of the journal, the Assembly de-manded that Eva Valesh resign as *Bulletin* editor.

Given the gender politics of the time, it is no wonder that the St. Paul As-sembly responded with a certain hysteria to Valesh's actions as editor. The split between her and the Assembly, however, had its source in the factional fight-ing of the labor movement, in which Valesh undoubtedly played a role. In their public statements, the St. Paul assembly attributed Valesh's departure to argu-ments over revenues from advertising in the *Bulletin*. Specifically, the former advertising solicitor of the journal accused Valesh of defaulting on his contract. Accepting his word, the St. Paul Assembly immediately demanded Valesh's res-ignation. There were, it seems, conflicts over revenue and ownership of the paper. Running the paper for "selfish benefit" was not its purpose. Rather, the assembly insisted, the *Bulletin* "was founded for the sole aim and object of being an instructor and educator in the labor cause and not an advertising fake to fill the pocket of an editor and manager." Valesh's response, they added, was to "throw every obstacle in [their] way to try to kill the paper."[72]

Trade-union resentments went beyond accusations of personal greed or dis-honesty to condemn Valesh's ambition. To quote the *Bulletin*, Valesh had "used her tongue in a lively way and taken all the benefit her sex controls when in argument with a man." Insisting that Valesh would not respond to either their objections or corrections, they had determined that "plain actions call for plain words."[73] In the months ahead, the battle between the St. Paul Assembly and Valesh continued. While she had only quietly noted her resignation in the *Tri-bune* labor column, the Assembly leaders found excuses to attack. In August 1893, the *Journal* chimed in when its labor editor reported that Valesh "and her style of labor agitation" had come under the scrutiny of the Trades and Labor

Assembly of Minneapolis.[74] One month later, the *Bulletin* commented, "In the last issue of the *Eight Hour Herald* appeared an article entitled, 'From High Authority.' . . . Perhaps as far distant as Chicago Mrs. McD-Valesh might be considered a 'high authority,' but we have no hesitation in saying that she is not so regarded in the immediate vicinity of the Twin Cities. An examination of the records . . . will readily convince any right-thinking man beyond a shadow of a doubt. The *Herald* should not be so liberal with its 'taffy.'"[75]

The dispute in which Eva Valesh was involved was not merely one of advertising revenues—an issue for all reform papers—or the "liveliness" of her tongue. An ambitious woman, perceived as aggressive and cunning, was never trusted much. More important, Valesh belonged to the "pure and simple trade unionists" who were the growing force within the local labor movement.[76] Conflict broke out into the open only months after her resignation, when the election in the Minneapolis Trades and Labor Assembly turned into "a spirited contest." The "sometimes humorously dubbed 'political section'" of the Knights of Labor faced down trade union opponents and won the election. Trade unionists, led by former Knights like Tom Clark and Mike Mogan, took "little stock in practical politics" and sought to change the direction of local organization. The question was, Would the dwindling number of Knights of Labor-Populist reformers like H. B. Martin and his allies continue to lead the local labor movement with grumbling from the trades, or would the trades take over the organization and oust the "political seekers" and "embryo statesmen" from the local councils, the state federations, and the national movement as well? As many acknowledged, the national conflict between the Knights and the ascendant AFL had "crept into local labor circles."[77]

The widening gulf between the Knights of Labor and the trade unions surfaced after the assembly election. The newly elected officers so alienated trade unionists with their politics that they threatened to secede from the organization. A month later, five major craft unions, among the largest in the assembly, had withdrawn to form their own organization, the Central Trades Council. They had two specific grievances. First, they believed that the assembly no longer assisted trade unions. Second, they insisted that "a political ring controlled the body and the cigar makers did not propose to be made a stepping stone for any man's political ambition." The Cigar Makers led other crafts in the formation of the Central Trades Council.[78]

W. C. Krueger of the Cigar Makers Union summarized the problem. While trade unions had long cooperated with the Knights and "there [were] members of that order still who are among our best workers and for whom every trade unionist has the greatest respect . . . the order [was] practically dead." Despite the Knights' decline, they "saddled" the Minneapolis Trades and

Labor Assembly "with a ring who use the ghost of that order to conjure with." Moreover, apart from the North Star Labor Club, the Knights had no active assemblies. It was only politically motivated Populists who sought to "revive" the dead locals. Such men wanted control over the Trades and Labor Assembly "so they [could] outvote the representatives of trade unions having hundreds of members and make it appear that organized labor throughout the city support their plans." Krueger warned, "The trades unions are tired of it, and if they continue to withdraw at the present rate, there will be nothing left but the Populist faction and their alleged organizations."[79]

Although the situation was reminiscent of trade-union struggles to edge out the Knights nationally, the personal aspects gave a sharp edge to disagreements. H. B. Martin, who personally benefited from the withdrawal of trade unionists, took the offensive when he charged Valesh of violating rules about publishing proceedings. The assembly held a hearing on the case even as she continued to serve on its press committee.[80] While trade unionists publicly asserted that they had no wish to antagonize the Knights, they effectively sought to usurp power in local labor politics. As one trade unionist argued, "We have been roundly abused for withdrawing from the Trades Assembly. Yet in reality we have been very generous. We have left the K of L in possession of the Trades Assembly and all the prestige it may have gained by the united efforts of the trades unions and the Knights of Labor in the past. When we felt that the best interests of the unions demanded a separation, we simply went out and did all the hard work incident to forming a new organization."[81]

By this time, the conflict between the Knights and the new Central Trades Council made news on a regular basis. Cross-fired resolutions were passed and repealed in the local labor bodies in repeated attempts to set the record straight. The Minneapolis Trades and Labor Assembly accused Eva Valesh of disregarding its instructions about the secrecy of assembly meetings and reporting dissension in its ranks. They further charged her with trying to establish a rival organization in the Central Trades Council.[82] In September 1893, the St. Paul Trades and Labor Assembly passed a resolution implicitly labeling "the so-called Minneapolis TRIBUNE-McDonald-Valesh-North Star Labor Club-Trades Council" an attempt to "disrupt organizations by a few disgruntled office seekers" rather than "furthering the interests and cause of organized labor." The Central Trades Council "did not relish" being called "disgruntled office seekers" and wanted an explanation for the new attack. The assembly concluded that they were in the wrong and apologized.[83]

The situation worsened after the downfall of Martin in the Minneapolis Assembly. It was, Valesh explained to her readers, his "treachery to [Terence] Powderly" that caused him to lose his influence at a time when the Knights in

Minneapolis remained "mostly Powderly men." As Valesh reported, "The local Knights of Labor deplore the factional troubles which are rending the once powerful order, but there is no prospect of peace so long as the warring factions exist." As expressed in her labor column, the Knights' traditions of secrecy and political action contributed to their troubles. Valesh referred to the "veil" or "mantle" of secrecy that "worked downright mischief" in labor organization. It had, she wrote, "shielded a class of people who desired to work the movement for their own advantage."[84] Within weeks, the Minneapolis Assembly had passed resolutions accusing her of misrepresenting the situation and printing "malicious statements" and "deliberate falsehoods." They further argued that Valesh had striven to "bring about a fight between the trade unions and the Knights of Labor." While the resolution called for the assembly to refrain from sending news to the *Tribune*, their response seemed evidence of the very "dry rot" of which Valesh accused them. Once that more was known about the Knights nationally, labor readers would realize that her columns focused on "facts, not fictions."[85]

Valesh's role in the local feud between the Knights of Labor and trade unionists made her a woman to be known nationally. As a result of this growing reputation, she was asked to join Gompers, Morgan, and others on the podium of the Labor Congress at the World Columbian Exposition in Chicago in 1893. In the days preceding the event, the unemployed had staged massive demonstrations.[86] The morning the Labor Congress opened, Valesh was on the program as a lecturer on tenements and sweatshops. The size of the crowd outside, however, convinced organizers to move the Labor Congress to the lakefront. There the crowd of 25,000 could listen to labor speakers from the six wagons that served as platforms. On her wagon, Valesh joined George McNeill and Elizabeth Morgan as speakers. After McNeill's speech, Valesh added her voice to those who saw the depression as a result of faulty government policies. She told the crowd that the state from which she had come had granaries that overflowed: "Some of them contained the accumulated products of three years, but the people were poor, many of them in absolute want." Overproduction, she argued, "glutted the markets and caused the employers to discharge their workmen and leave them to starve." And yet, while this economic system was the source of much misery, it was "the Nation, State and city [that were] responsible for this state of affairs. If the workmen starve[d]," it was, she argued, "the fault of the government." And if, as had happened a few days before, the unemployed resorted to violence, it was "the responsibility of government."[87]

Appearing at the Columbian Exposition assured that Valesh's bold assertions about the economic crisis were circulated nationally. Her friendship with Gompers and other labor leaders reinforced her desire to leave the limited scope of local labor movement politics. What followed were articles for the newly founded *American Federationist*, some of which were syndicated nationally. Valesh became moderately successful in the effort of syndicating some labor columns and contributed essays to the *Railway Times*.[88] With each new invitation, the world seemed to open up possibilities for her, especially as she met and got to know the national and international labor scene. She had grown tired of working at the *Tribune*, where the daily grind and poor pay of editorial work simply did not match her ambitions. By 1895, Eva Valesh was eager to move on to new challenges. Whatever the consequences for her marriage and her career, she longed to move from the confines of Minneapolis labor politics to a wider world.

CHAPTER 6

"A Slim Chance of Making Good"

Labor Journalism, Yellow Journalism, and the New Woman

Mrs Valesh is conspicuous largely because of her nerve and frequently uttered disbeliefs in the truth of anything that is said by any one but herself.

——*Fall River Herald*, February 10, 1898

Chafing under the routine of married life and the monotony of editing, Eva Valesh ran up against the limits of what it was possible for her to accomplish in the Midwest. Lecturing at the 1893 Labor Congress had been the highlight of her life to that point. The invitations that followed might have led to new horizons, but two years later she was still in Minneapolis. The acrimony attending the split between the Knights of Labor and the trade unions soured labor politics in the city. More than that, the local labor movement had come to a standstill. With the economic crisis hampering trade, there was little to do but watch the events unfold. Just as the labor movement found its organizing drives stymied, so, too, did Valesh feel her career stall. It did not help that old friends left her circle. Both Timothy Brosnan and John Lamb moved west, where they were elected to political office. Jack McGaughey increasingly withdrew from labor politics. When Albert Dollenmayer finally returned from Washington, D.C., he opened his own advertising agency. Valesh's enterprise as literary editor and political reporter did not make up for lacking the chance to make good in the same way.

Local labor journalism simply was not enough for Eva Valesh. She might have become reconciled to the state of things, but a family crisis intervened. When Frank suffered the loss of his brother and sister, he, too, became ill. In response, Eva made a decision for both of them. Not content to be on the prairies any longer, she insisted that they take time off to travel to Europe. With her connections, she could help put together enough funds to sustain them. She reasoned that it would advance their careers to make connections abroad, and the holiday would do Frank good.

At this point in their married life, the tensions and conflicts around ambition and decision-making had become familiar. Because Frank feared his ill health and wanted to renew ties with his Czech family, he agreed to the European journey. He had not seen his grandmother since he had emigrated to the United States in 1877. He could not have known that the trip would only fuel Eva's ambitions to enter the national labor scene. For her, the trip to Europe opened new career possibilities. Perhaps after they returned, she also reasoned, Frank could be persuaded to move to the East Coast, where they could engage in a wider world of political and labor activism.

When Eva Valesh finally arrived in the East a few years later, she came as a single mother and worked not for the labor movement but for Hearst's *New York Journal*. As she brought to bear her skills in investigative reporting and political analysis, she became a new woman in the new journalism—a transformation with far-reaching effects on her career. Not only the style and language of the sensationalist press but also the complex role of mass-circulation newspapers as entertainment, advocacy, and business provided Eva Valesh future opportunities to translate her knowledge into new approaches for labor's cause.

The Working-Class Grand Tour

In the fall of 1895, Eva and Frank Valesh were preparing to take a trip to Europe. The personal reason was Frank's declining health. As Eva later recalled, "My husband suffered a great shock during his second term as Deputy Labor Commissioner. His only brother and sister died within a few hours of each other of tuberculosis. Investigation revealed that his father had died young of the same disease."[1] Frank feared that he, too, would die of consumption. His doctors advised him to take a trip to Europe as a way of recovering his health. Both he and Eva took a leave of absence from their jobs and prepared for the journey. Although Eva wrote to her friend Samuel Gompers that Frank's appetite and sleeping had improved, there was still worry.[2] His work as assistant labor commissioner had been physically demanding, and his continued union activity further drained his strength. He needed to regain his health, and a holiday seemed the surest way.

A grand tour of the labor capitals of Europe provided other advantages to the couple. As Gompers's protégés, they could expect a strong welcome from their European counterparts. The trip would complete their education in political terms and lay the foundation of their future careers. At the same time, the Valeshes visited Europe at a time when European trade unions were facing many of the same challenges as the American labor movement. They, too, battled over the fate of independent political action and the role of trade unions. The 1890s saw the entry of French Socialists into national politics, the emergence of Syndicalist unions, the struggle of German Socialists against Otto von Bismarck's repressive government, and the victory of Italian Socialists. While these trends stood in stark contrast to the trade-union repudiation of independent party politics in the United States, making connections to trade unionists in Europe was a clear sign that Frank and Eva Valesh were on their way to national prominence.

Financing a trip to Europe on the meager salary of a junior state employee might have been difficult, but Eva Valesh worked her press connections to write for the Bacheller and Johnson syndicate when she was abroad. As she wrote to Dollenmayer, "I think I told you Bacheller & Johnson will take my European letters. The *Federationist* . . . is arranging to pay some cold cash for correspondence. We have some expectations with the American Press Association and I am getting excellent column rates for some 'stories' for the New York papers. So our prospects are very good."[3] Later, Valesh recalled that "all through the trip my husband had shown a perfect phobia on the subject of lack of money. It was unfounded. We had enough to make the trip comfortably." She continued, "I recalled that a New York syndicate had said they would take several articles of a kind I could do easily, so I wrote several."[4]

The Valeshes were prominent speakers at the AFL meeting in December of 1895. Newspaper accounts of the AFL convention reported that "Mrs Eva McDonald Valesh, of Detroit [sic]" and her husband, "Deputy Labor Commissioner for the State of Michigan [sic], were about to make a trip to Europe to study the conditions of laboring people there. They will travel through Europe on bicycles, living among the workers, and Mrs. Valesh said that she would send regular contributions to the *American Federationist*." The convention resolved to pay her for the articles.[5] Like the other editors, Gompers saw an opportunity to capitalize on Valesh's trip by hiring her to write for his journal, thus making ties with European labor and aiding his friends with monetary support.

Within a few days after the convention, the Valeshes boarded a French steamer for Paris, taking a second-class cabin on the journey. They landed at

Le Havre and took their bicycles with them. In Paris, the young couple met several labor leaders, and Frank made some Czech connections. The first day, he found a café of Bohemian expatriates. He subjected Eva to an evening in a "beer 'cave,'" drinking Pilsener, speaking Czech, and listening to folk music.[6] Eva was not enthusiastic and soon found other things to occupy her. While she studied perfume, pottery, and French cooking, Frank spent his time doing research in libraries.[7]

From Paris, the couple bicycled across parts of southern France. When it proved too tiring, they sent the bicycles back and journeyed by train to Marseilles. In both Cannes and Marseilles, the Valeshes made connections with French labor leaders. They began to study industry, working-class organization, and the conditions of European workers. Then, as now, there was a belief in the peculiarity and uniqueness of the American situation. The battles over the role of political action were on the minds of most trade unionists, so Eva spent time comparing the French and American labor movements. She sent back a corrective to those who argued that the labor movement in France had rightly chosen political over economic action: "An impression prevails throughout the United States that France has no labor movement at all similar to ours, and that whatever does exist is purely political in nature." To the contrary, she wrote, "France has a flourishing trade union movement. It is conducted as openly as our own, and the idea of trade autonomy fully carried out." Like their American counterparts, French workers were organized in trade unions, which they called syndicates or corporations, and they devoted as much time to economic struggle as to political organizing. "The masses," she wrote, were "evidently tired of secret, semi-political organization, and every year witnesses large accessions to the ranks of the trade union pure and simple. There is a strong labor party in politics; but the two phases of the movement are kept distinct and separate."[8]

Much of the differences between the two movements could be attributed to what Valesh called "a unity of race." Unlike in the United States, where workers came from diverse racial and ethnic backgrounds, she argued, the French were unified in their national traits and attitudes. In particular, she noted, that "In any condition I describe, the reader must take into account the French temperament—the quick intelligence, the restless, emotional nature, and yet the stoical patience, born of long struggle with hard conditions."[9] As in her writings on immigrants, ethnic stereotypes and race-based explanations informed her perspective. Different traditions, environments, and—she might have added—nationalities determined how working people responded to an unfair wage system and an unjust government.

Valesh's articles for the *American Federationist* were filled with graphic physical descriptions of working-class lives. As sensory tableaus, her stories contrasted with the middle-class press's milder, more antiseptic reports of workers. They were essentially ethnographic in character. As she once masqueraded to discover the secret lives of working girls, so now she demonstrated her skill in eliciting the concrete details of workers' diets, housing, and culture. She listed foods eaten and prices paid. In a sense, she invited readers to examine the boiled meat at the charcuterie, a French delicatessen, and decide between it and cheaper sausage or hash. She devoted paragraphs to workers who refused to admit that they ate horsemeat and yet relished rooster combs. "Chicken feet, beef bones, fat meat and all sorts of odds and ends are saved up for the national dish, 'bouillon,'" she wrote. "As a matter of duty, I sampled every kind of meat I saw, but must confess that I should not like many of the compounds for a regular diet."[10] And yet most workers did not eat meat more than two or three times a week. Vegetables, cheese, and bread made up the vast part of their diet: "You often see a street laborer make his whole dinner on half a loaf of bread and a radish." Far from being picturesque, the thin soup and black bread marked European workers as more impoverished than their counterparts in the United States.[11]

Clothing also caught her eye. In speaking of wages and cost of living, she used the example of a printer she met. The young man, who once had been a teacher, was dressed in "a cheap, ready-made suit, a bear-skin cap, a loose cape, and wooden shoes." "Imagine," she asked, "an American printer wearing wooden shoes!"[12] Similarly, when she reported on the Union des Chambres Syndicales Ouvrières, the central labor union in Marseilles, she reflected on the deputies' fluency of speech and inadequacy of dress. They were, she noted, "not as well dressed as American workmen. The question of clothing is a rather serious one." Taking on this issue, she explained, "The mild climate makes light and cheap garments permissible, but both cotton and woolen goods are fully as expensive as in the United States." While luxury goods were less expensive than at home, the "ready-made suit, the outing flannel shirt and working blouse" were just as costly, and French workers earned less.[13] The reader became a witness through the detail and texture of Valesh's descriptions, which invite her/him to feel the cut of clothes and hear the sound of working shoes.

One of her major concerns was the impact of and reaction to women working outside the home. She noted that in France, Austria, and Italy it was common for married women to work outside the home. Moreover, in rural areas, women "work[ed] in the fields at the roughest kind of labor." The consequence was the failure of family life: "The absence of home life strikes a foreigner forcibly. It is merely stating a self-evident fact, to say that the industrial system has crowded out the home. Husband and wife each go out to their daily labors. It is absolutely necessary for the wife to add her earnings to the family fund."[14]

A long trip around Italy by boat brought the couple to Trieste, but not before they had had a chance to observe Italian workers and meet with Captain Volani, a self-proclaimed Socialist agent. Valesh marveled at his facility with language and his ability to analyze and describe national traits, which shaped her impressions. Seeing not the tourist attractions but the city streets and small villages enabled her, she wrote, to see the "real" Italy. She described it in words that resembled her earlier essay on the tenements of New York: "Just behind the street of palaces is a labyrinth of narrow, dark streets; the tall houses crowded from top to bottom with people, who have scarcely clothes to cover their nakedness or food to stay the pangs of hunger. The labyrinth of narrow streets is the real city. It is where the people work and live."[15]

It was in order to understand the places "where the people work and live" that Valesh had undertaken the journey. The poverty of first France, then Italy, and later Austria and Germany shocked her. In Italy, she reported, in "the very shadow" of churches, "the people [bought] a handful of roasted chestnuts or pumpkin seeds, or macaroni. Any one of three articles . . . furnish[ed] the one meal of the day." When she questioned one workman whether he ate meat, he replied, "I have eaten a small piece, several times in my life, on great feast days, . . . but I hardly remember how it tasted." Nothing, not even the sod houses of the Dakota prairies, compared to the lives of the European poor.[16]

In Italy, Valesh asked questions about conditions that brought thousands of Italian immigrants to American shores. Addressing the anti-immigration sentiment in the AFL, she pointed out that "we, in the United States, see only the Italian laborer; the poor, ignorant fellow, who comes from some inland country village. It should not be forgotten, that there are plenty of highly skilled and intelligent workmen in the cities." While she did not think the "skilled workmen lack[ed] brains," she thought their "intelligence is sadly hampered by the environment." Still, she admitted, "one cannot help noticing that the skilled Italian workman is clever, shrewd, and an adept at his trade."[17] In contrast to France, where the workers were "so attached to their customs and amusements that they cannot endure the idea of a foreign country," Italian workers had positive incentive to emigrate. Yet, Valesh added, even the "bare animal existence" of the Italian poor could not convince her to approve emigration as a means of escape. She wrote, "I have no desire to transfer the wretched people to the U.S. Emigration from the mother country put off the solution of the problem, instead of aiding the formation of the better order."[18]

In Austria, the couple had a chance to observe a powerful labor movement strongly allied with the Socialist movement and the liberal press. Austria was, Eva Valesh wrote, "a loose confederacy of nations, having no particular love for one another." Yet, she wrote, "strange to say, the labor movement [was] causing these people to lay aside national prejudices and work for economic freedom." "Thoroughly despotic," the government's extensive use of censorship and police surveillance worked to suppress working people. The Austrian state, she declared, "had saddled two armies on the people—one of soldiery and the other of state officials." Moreover, there were heavy restrictions on public meetings and political organizations.[19] A compulsory program for sick insurance and strict apprenticeship rules gave trade unions some leeway. Workingmen elected sympathetic members to the Boards of Control. Valesh added, "The government is . . . much chagrined to see its pet paternal institution turned into an instrument for trade union propaganda."[20]

Conditions in Austria exhibited the same poverty that had characterized France. High levels of taxation and slow industrialization meant that the standard of living was low and the cost of living high. Women worked after marriage, and "the combined earnings of husband and wife will hardly equal that of a day laborer in the United States." Breakfast, lunch, and dinner were often coffee, potatoes or soup or meat, and bread, with a glass of wine or beer supplementing the evening meal. The meagerness of the fare, supplemented for American tastes with an occasional dessert or omelet, captured Valesh's attention. As she declared, "The Austrians look robust and well kept, but I am sure an American craftsman would be hungry all the time if they lived as frugally as they." And yet, she reminded her readers, "those who live so poorly and have such a constant struggle for a bare existence are not an ignorant, uncultured people. On the contrary they are well-educated and skillful workers who have a keen appreciation for the good things of life."[21]

In Germany, Valesh found much the same story. She and Frank attended a trade-union congress there, and she had to limit her observations to the trade unionists she met. Focusing on the trade union–Socialist alliance, she argued that German Socialists "know the value of trade unions, and will not permit any interference from the narrow and prejudiced element, which believes that political action is the panacea for all evils." Their brand of socialism she attributed to the national temperament. "With all due respect to Karl Marx," she argued, he "would have written things differently if he had lived in other countries."[22] Ignorant that Marx had in fact lived abroad, she thought she brought home her point when she added that "the war of self-styled socialists on the trade union movement of America loses much of its force when they must admit that the Germany which they are so fond of holding up as an example has a trade union movement much like our own."[23] What escaped her was that European labor movements were rapidly moving away from the strict trade-union model and stood on the threshold of their heroic period.

Valesh much later recalled the other Europe she had seen. The coastal journey from Marseilles to Malta and Trieste, the sightseeing in Italy, and the coffee and sweet cakes on Vienna's Ringstrasse came to mind; so, too, did the journey to Frank's home village of Lisov. There, surrounded by "patriotic Czechs" in what was old Bohemia, Eva was silenced, because she could not even use her limited German. What she remembered later was the music and gossip in neighboring homes. She thought, too, of souvenirs she bought while surveying the social conditions of European workers. While she wrote of poverty, she observed fine craft work in Italy—designs in filigree, tortoise shell, and coral. In her later years, she recalled the small paintings she had bought from a young Italian artist and the pottery that, years before, had been lost in a warehouse fire.[24] As a student of political economy she could not see anything picturesque in Europe's poverty, but as a tourist she could.

Gompers and Friends

On their return from Europe, the Valeshes searched for employment in the Twin Cities and were unsettled by the difficulties of picking up old work. While they were in Paris, Gompers wrote to ask if Frank and Eva would settle in the East. Existing evidence suggests that that possibility would have been in accordance with Eva's wishes. Still, the couple returned to Minneapolis by June of 1896, and Frank looked for work in a cigar factory. Despite her ambivalence, Eva returned to the *Tribune*. Given this state of affairs, Gompers wrote them that it was "a pleasure for [him] to learn that though like Micawber [in Dickens's *David Copperfield*], [they] had been waiting for 'something to turn up,' they were somewhat more fortunate than he." When Frank returned to his position at the Bureau of Labor Statistics, Gompers practically responded that "it goes without saying that I am glad that Frank has been recalled to his old position. I suppose his advancement in the Bureau is now out of the question, but this is far better for him than to attempt working in the cigar factory." When Eva expressed discontent, Gompers responded that "you will be able to do good work on the *Tribune*, even though it may be difficult for you to go back to the old position."[25] As to her suggestion that she apply to be an AFL organizer, he advised, "I doubt though that it will be advantageous to you since the recommendation provides that the organizers or lecturers shall receive . . . $3.50 per day and expenses. Of course, that would be very little for you when

Samuel Gompers, 1901. He was president of the American Federation of Labor from 1886 to 1924 and Eva Valesh's boss. Photo courtesy of the George Meany Memorial Archives.

you could do so much better at your own home." A few months later, he told her to take advantage of a new *Tribune* assignment to cover the proceedings of the state Senate. Although it "may not be as lucrative as you might wish," he advised, "it is an additional experience to you which will unquestionably prove valuable." At the same time, he did promise to submit her application for a position as organizer, if she wished.[26]

Gompers's relationship with Eva and Frank remained cordial, even familial. While neither Frank's nor Eva's letters to Gompers survive, Gompers's letter-books reveal a steady, if sometimes irregular, correspondence with the Valeshes during this crucial period. His support for their careers was a product of their close friendship. When Eva was promoted to literary editor, Gompers wrote to her, "To me it is something more than the mere desire to convey a perfunctory congratulatory message, for in it I see the advancement of a friend and the appreciation of merit. I have no doubt that higher things as well as more advantageous positions are in store for you." He took a personal interest in their careers. In the same letter, he hinted at his discomfort at Frank's decision to study law, which Gompers thought might weaken not just their careers but their marriage: "If he succeeds . . . is it not likely that the studies of both of you lying in different directions may in a measure divert the bond of sympathy now existing between you?" As Eva's "desire for more knowledge" would lead her naturally to more "literary work," Frank's study would "lie in an entirely different direction." "For my own part," Gompers added, "I should prefer to see you united rather than divided in your labors."[27]

Gompers's liking for the young labor reformers had its basis in similar origins and interests. As we have seen, Frank Valesh was an immigrant who spent his early years in the cigar trade, much as Gompers had. Gompers apparently appreciated Frank's quiet and scholarly demeanor as well as his talents as an organizer. Still, after Frank's sister and brother died, Gompers advised Eva to tell Frank "that he should not overtask his strength. It is all very good one's being active, but he is not as strong as we would all like him to be, and he is too good a fellow to wear himself out, by getting up too much steam."[28] During their European trip, which it was hoped would improve the couple's health, Gompers's letters evoke his primary concern for Frank's recovery, wishing that he come back a "'typical British beef eater.'"

On the couple's return, Gompers wrote to Eva, "It is gratifying for me to hear that you and Frank and Frank, Jr., are feeling well. I should much prefer hearing though that Frank is strong and robust. . . . I do not want to think of him in any other way but as a well and strong man."[29] Later, Gompers professed that he "should be delighted to learn that [Frank] had become robust and rugged."[30] Associating good health with the ability to "do much excellent work"—indeed, to be manly—Gompers longed for Frank's recovery while fearing his physical weakness. Throughout the fall of 1896, Gompers expressed dismay that Frank and Eva would not be at the Detroit convention: "It is a great pity when we need good advice and staunch defenders of trade unionism."[31] His comradely, even fatherly, regard for Frank was tinged with fraternal feeling and concern that Frank would not survive the tests he faced.

Gompers's response to Eva was quite the opposite. In letters to her, Gompers asserted an absolute faith in her talents and ability to succeed as writer and political worker with a certainty that is astounding in view of the odds against women both in the labor movement and the newspaper profession. To another labor leader, Gompers described Valesh as "a most excellent public speaker, as well as a good writer, and her heart [was] in accord with pure Trade Unionism." He frequently complimented her writing and speaking abilities, and he continually hinted of greater opportunities.[32] There was, however, no offer from the AFL.

Sometime in 1897, Frank Valesh's health grew worse. His regular factory inspection tours as assistant labor commissioner and Eva's frequent public speaking engagements troubled their relationship. As Eva had once joked to Dollenmayer, "The powers that be kindly let [Frank] come home on Saturdays occasionally."[33] By March 1897, the situation had become dire. In a letter to Eva, Gompers implied that Frank was not yet "strong and robust" and "ought to give a little more attention to himself and to his health." "I do not want," Gompers continued, "to think of him in any other way but as a well and strong man. He can do considerable towards it if he wills it."[34] Less than two months later, Frank resigned from the Bureau of Labor Statistics and retired to Graceville, Minnesota, to start a small cigar factory. A well-known small businessman, he produced a popular item, "the King of Trails," for consumers who appreciated the value of a hand-rolled black-twisted cigar. Gompers, who received a regular Christmas gift of the cigars from Frank, was a fan. Apart from business excursions, Frank would live in Graceville for the rest of his life.[35]

At the time of Frank's illness, Eva Valesh made a difficult decision. In an era in which women were expected to follow their husbands wherever they went, she went her own way. Despite an increase in divorce in the late nineteenth century, it was uncommon for married men and women to seek separations, formal or informal, and even more rare for couples to divorce. That the decision to separate from Frank was in many ways a career decision added to how risky even this step was for both her personal and professional reputation. But, as Eva must have realized, accompanying Frank to Graceville would have been a career-ending choice. At the top of her marketability as a writer and reporter, Eva had no desire to abandon her work for life in a small town. She departed for the East Coast in April 1897 and never resided in Minnesota again. Afterwards, both she and Frank maintained the fiction that her departure was only a temporary situation. Perhaps they thought that if Frank could regain his health, things might improve between them. Either way, the public story was that she had left him to earn money for the family in a more lucrative East Coast newspaper.[36]

When the rising labor journalist Eva McDonald and the up-and-coming labor leader Frank Valesh married in 1891, observers predicted personal and political success for them both. The hazards of public life then were no easier to clear than the hazards in this century. Married couples who followed the nontraditional path of engaging jointly in public life had to endure the pull of ambition and the constant stress of travel, writing and speaking commitments, and personal conflict. Eva McDonald and Frank Valesh were among the best-known couples in labor reform—partners who emerged as public activists at a time when the labor movement endorsed both the public equality of women and their activism. The realities of family life, however, and the stress of careers in the public eye took a toll on marriages. In most instances, men could sustain public activism while their wives retreated. Faced with a similar situation, Leonora Barry Lake of the Knights retreated from public life. Eva, however, made the opposite choice.

Sensationally Clever

With neither the possibility nor the desire for a compromise, Eva Valesh left Minnesota for Washington, D.C., in the spring of 1897. She stayed with Gompers and his wife, Sophie, in their modest house. While she later asserted that she resisted his attempt to recruit her—she wanted newspaper work, not a labor job—Valesh was now a single mother who needed to support herself and her son. She remembered that Gompers "took a dim view of my getting newspaper work in New York."[37] Whatever his views, she had to find some kind of position. She met with Herbert Browne, the editor for William Hearst's Washington paper. In a tactic familiar to newspapermen, he disposed of her queries by suggesting an impossible assignment. To earn a place on a big newspaper, she should interview the president. With a typical disregard for convention, Valesh met William F. McKinley through Minnesota Senator Knute Nelson and published her interview in Hearst's *New York Journal*.[38] The tactic had a certain boldness. Custom had it that reporters were not supposed to publish private interviews with the president; she laid claim to be the first.[39]

At this point, William Murphy intervened to parlay Valesh's coup into a full-time position. He asked Charles Edwards, a former business manager for the *Tribune*, to find her a job at the *New York Journal*. Somewhat prickly about women reporters, Edwards told Valesh that she could report to the city room. Still, he added, that "a reporter would have to be 'sensationally clever' to stay."[40] The competitive newspaper world made it unlikely that a newcomer to New York could succeed. Valesh took the position despite his warnings. In the summer of 1897 she moved to New York.

What Valesh was offered would have been discouraging to most journalists with her experience. As a regular reporter, if the *New York Journal* editors didn't like or have room for her work, she simply was not paid. Earlier, when she had worked on the *Globe* and the *Tribune*, she had had the security of her father's or husband's wages. Now, she had only what Frank was willing to send for her son's upkeep. "Still," Valesh later recalled, "I made more money on the Hearst *American*[41] that year than I had ever earned any year in my life before."[42]

Determined to make it work, she struggled through bad assignments to put something into print.

Years on Minneapolis's Newspaper Row, with its two blocks of low buildings,[43] could not have prepared Valesh for the world she was entering. The size and scale of Park Row in New York dwarfed its Midwestern cousin. The massive skyscrapers and hurried crowds were both intimidating and exhilarating. Working for the *Journal* meant joining one of the largest and best-paid corps of journalists in the country. Among the fifty to seventy regular reporters were some of the best-known writers of the time, as Hearst had "fairly raked the country for journalistic talent and applied to the upbuilding of his newspaper a genius never equaled for sensationalism and advertisement."[44] The city room's atmosphere reflected the brawny enthusiasm of the newspapermen's world. The horseplay in the *Journal* office was memorable enough for one veteran reporter to write, "My own reaction was expressed in a letter to a Chicago friend to whom I ruefully wrote that I had secured very remunerative employment in a lunatic asylum."[45]

For women, the world of William Randolph Hearst's *Journal* was even more daunting. They faced hostility from fellow reporters and editors, most of whom came from an older, more traditional generation. Prejudice against women journalists made life more difficult for them specifically because their own editors did not want them in that world. As historian Ishbel Ross wrote, hundreds of women journalists had "passed through his [Hearst's] doorways, some to lose their jobs with staggering swiftness; others to build up big syndicate names and draw down the highest salaries in the profession. From the moment he entered newspaper work he dramatized them; he got them to make news." Making news became immeasurably harder if the newspaper restricted its women reporters to society news or the women's page.[46]

It was not only that women reporters had to battle traditional views of their sex. Rather, Hearst's newspapers were fiercely competitive and therefore harsh and quick in their judgment. Hearst himself was often shy, considerate to his writers, and tolerant of their failings. But while he "never commit[ed] an act or [spoke] a word to those whom he [knew] that would be wounding," his editors had no such qualms. Editor Willis Abbot recalled, "Incredibly brutal things were done by Hearst's lieutenants in his name. No man, even when protected by a contract, could feel any certainty of his employment or of financial security in it."[47] Circulation wars—the most heated between Joseph Pulitzer's *World* and Hearst's *Journal*—kept everyone on edge.

Working as one of the army of journalists at the *New York Journal* was very different from the newspaper world in which Eva Valesh had apprenticed.

Physically, both the office and the terrain of reporting were larger than the beats she had known and covered in Minneapolis and St. Paul. Unfamiliar with Manhattan, Valesh took along a map on every assignment and asked police-men for directions. She seemed to have received many leads from unassuming and curious women and children. Her sex, in this regard, might have been a positive advantage, as she interviewed those people whom male reporters ig-nored. Along the way, she received assignments far removed from covering labor meetings or legislative sessions. Instead, she was sent to identify run-aways and corpses, interview businessmen, and occasionally solve mysteries, all of which made surprisingly good copy. City editor Charles Edwards, how-ever, had Valesh convinced that she was not long for the position. He simply did not like women on newspapers, she recalled. The "trifling assignments" that Valesh received seemed to promise failure.[48] Minor stories meant she just scraped by financially and, worse yet, was in danger of losing her place.

After some weeks of working, Eva Valesh was handed an impossible assign-ment. If she failed, she'd probably lose her position on the newspaper. The trick was that she had to identify a young woman who committed suicide a few days before.[49] No one had so far had any luck, and it was no longer current as a story. Still, Valesh went to view the body. After she left the morgue, she explained her problem to a boy in the neighborhood. He sent her to a neighborhood drug-gist. Following that trail, Valesh discovered that he had refused to sell the young woman poison. He did not know where she lived but knew someone who did.[50] She was sent to the Florence Crittenden mission, a rescue home for "fallen women." Valesh spoke to an assistant matron, Mrs. Van Norman, also known as Sister Mary, herself a former prostitute, to tell her what happened. Mamie Donahue,[51] the young victim, was a member of a club of "street girls" who had pledged themselves to commit suicide at age twenty-five rather than live to "the last dregs of life." The talkative matron provided Valesh with many of the de-tails she needed. The members of the club, "such women as the Florence Mis-sion strives to regenerate," were "inspired by a common horror of life as it un-folds itself to such as they, after the first unwholesome glitter has been tarnished. They are inspired by the same terror of work, the same monotony, of subjec-tion to authority, of the hospital, of waning beauty, of hunger, of contempt." As she took down the facts, Valesh accompanied the matron to the morgue and convinced her to postpone identifying the body until the following day.[52]

Valesh reconstructed the story from the facts she had compiled. "Since the fantastic imagination of Robert Louis Stevenson gave birth to the suicide club in 'The New Arabian Nights,'" she wrote, "there had been countless attempts to exploit duplicates of that weird organization in real life." The suicide club at the Florence Mission was a real life version of the fantasy. The women "demonstrated their loyalty to the club by leaving it and the world in one desperate act." The root of the problem was what Valesh defined as "a kind of hysterical sentimentality on the subject of early death, of newspaper notoriety, of a sympathetic funeral, of flowers, of tears." Mamie Donahue, the third such suicide, "possessed the wistful, heavily lashed, dark blue eyes characteristic of a certain type of Irish beauty. Her figure was graceful, her manner discreet." The twenty-two-year-old woman with the "lovely soprano voice" came to New York from an Illinois town "in search of a faithless lover and fell into bad habits after wandering vainly about the streets in the hope of meeting him." After learning of two other suicides, Mamie considered her own wasted life. "Heartsick and penniless," with only ragged clothes to her name, she purchased fifteen cents of whiskey "to brace her courage for an encounter with death" and ten cents of carbolic acid. That afternoon, she committed suicide on the street before a crowd of passers by.[53]

When Valesh turned in her story at the newspaper, a city editor, Casey, "didn't even look up" as she began to talk. She relayed to him that the club involved more than a dozen girls and that the young woman was only the latest in a series. As Valesh detailed the story, Casey's "black pompadour crest gradually came up," and he ran for the managing editor. Only as he hurriedly arranged space did she tell him it was an exclusive. He retorted, "'Oh, you would wait until the last minute for that. Any other reporter would have yelled that word as he came in the door.'" Cast as it was in the melodrama of the fallen innocent and the wages of sin, the article made the evening edition and was later reprinted.[54]

After the suicide club story, Valesh received more and better assignments. Gompers had already written to express his delight "at the success attending you in your newspaper work in New York, but I am not astonished for I am confident that with a fair field you will make your mark." He had hoped that the newspaper would assign her to "special work" so that she could avoid what "the ordinary rut of newspaper drudgery entails."[55] Instead, Valesh was "given all the mysterious suicides after that." Worse, for a while, she was "dubbed the 'suicide editor.'" Still, even without a byline, she had cracked her first big story, which led to a new kind of acceptance in the frantic city room. Valesh recalled, "The city editors and reporters nicknamed me 'Blackie' because I wore a black astrakhan coat and that fur was not in style at the moment in New York."[56]

Journal Woman

Surprisingly, Eva Valesh had been working at the *Journal* for nearly nine months before she received her first labor byline. Although there were many labor disputes reported, including a major strike among tailors and garment workers in New York, Valesh's name and experience was simply not tapped. While she might have written stories without a byline, she had no special labor assignment. This was to change. On January 17, 1898, as the country stirred with news from Cuba, nearly 9,000 textile workers in New Bedford, Massachusetts, went on strike to protest wage cuts and the fining system. Led by Harriet Pickering, the "Joan of Arc" of the strike, the 4,000 women weavers became a focus for newspaper coverage and union political battles.[57]

Taking on the Arkwright Club, a trade association of textile manufacturers, the striking workers had few resources. Club members knew that the weak link in the strike was the women weavers. Much poorer than its counterpart among mule-spinners, the weavers' union could not manage to pay out a dollar-a-day benefit to its own members, let alone the nonunion workers who joined the strike. The conflict between wealthy mill owners in New Bedford and neighboring Fall River and the textile workers was prime material for the *New York Journal*. This strike and its coverage allowed Eva Valesh to use her expertise.

Valesh joined the small army of journalists who descended on New Bedford in January 1898. Sent by Hearst himself to the scene, she was eager to impress the boss. In the preface to her first article, the *Journal* ran a short biographical sketch that portrayed her as a forthright advocate of labor's interests. Asserting that she had been one of the workers in the 1888 strike, the story recounted her successes covering European labor and speaking in front of the Labor Congress at the 1893 World Columbian Exposition.[58] Like other star reporters, Valesh needed not only a byline but an identifiable history and persona that captured readers' attention. It wasn't simply that a strike occurred or that the president acted, but that she—and thus her readers—met the strikers and shook the president's hand. What was being sold was not simply the commodity of news but the reporter herself.

To make a sensation in New Bedford, and hence draw the attention of Hearst and his readers, Valesh had not simply to report news but to make it. After initially covering Harriet Pickering and the poverty of strikers, Eva Valesh changed tactics. As she explained in an interview decades later, "I thought, 'Here these people have real grievances. The employers show no disposition to meet them. Why not go to the legislature which is in session in Boston to get them to pass a resolution to appoint a committee to hold hearings of both the workers and the employers, and see if the strike can be settled'?[59] She hoped the legislature also would provide remedies for "the disturbance" in the cotton textile industry, including an anti-fine bill presented to the legislature.[60] Public opinion was pivotal. It was not sufficient for workers to rely on their own resources to bring strikes to a successful close. As had been driven home to her in every strike Valesh had witnessed since 1888, public support for strikers played an essential role in their ability to win any benefit from collective action.

Area newspapers ridiculed the *Journal*'s and *World*'s crusading women reporters. In editorials deploring how yellow journalism "descended" on their town, editors lampooned the outsiders interfering in local affairs. They claimed that women reporters exaggerated or fabricated stories of misery among strikers. They found the comparison of millwork to slavery particularly galling. For many locals, the "bad publicity" about slumlike conditions, dire poverty, and tubercular workers only heightened class conflict and antagonism. Writers complained that "real sensational journalism" simply lied about the conditions of the city and its workers. In one case, two women had, a writer charged, said the city was "at the mercy of a mob" and that "neither prosperity nor life was safe" in New Bedford. The only violence, an editorial retorted, were boys throwing stones and the breaking of windows the first day of the strike. As one writer asserted, "The wickedness of the articles comes in the bitter feeling which has been intensified by the printing of threats against the personal safety of the mill treasurers on the one hand and alleged flippant remarks from the manufacturers." There were harsh words as well about the reporters' "mission"—to make sensational headlines. "The leading newspapers of New York," one article noted, "know how to profit by the troubles here by making sensational news, and increasing their circulation." Sent with instructions to "make sensations every day," the reporters "car[ed] little for the truth" and did not "even respect the greatest good sense."[61]

Ignoring the critics, Valesh brought public authorities to bear on the question. In what was her second interview with President McKinley, she asked him what he thought of the strike, the possibility of hearings, and the condition of wageworkers. In each case, she prefaced McKinley's abbreviated replies with descriptions of the situation from the *Journal*'s perspective. As reported, his answers seemed to endorse obliquely the hearings and the "living wage" for workers. A further issue was raised when Valesh told the president—and her readers—that "the mill operatives of New England are practically all foreign born, and that still others are coming in search of work." She urged "that agents of the mill owners are about to visit England for the purpose of bringing over here Russian Jews who have learned the weaving trade there and are willing to work even more cheaply than the French Canadians now in Massachusetts." Foreign competition for jobs, she wrote, had a negative effect on the thousands of native-born workers in New Bedford as well as other cities. Resonating with her earlier writings on immigration, Valesh's analysis opened the door for another favorite remedy of labor—a bill to restrict immigration then before the U.S. Senate. This, too, she represented as eliciting McKinley's support. In a similar vein, Valesh sought out Joseph Flynn, a state senator and former weaver, and Samuel Ross, a state representative and secretary of the national Spinners' union, on behalf of the *Journal*'s call for public investigation. Letters and quotations from the two legislators were used to bolster local support for the weaver's bill. In contrast, Valesh's interview with Maine Senator Nelson Dingley, Jr., author of a protectionist tariff, highlighted the *Journal*'s free-trade policy.[62]

In the New Bedford case, Valesh saw that the women workers in particular had few weapons to contend with the harsh fines and low wages of the textile companies. Their vulnerability to the fining system and its abuses—because of their comparatively weaker bargaining power and the employer blacklist—was the focal point of much public reaction.[63] In his testimony at the hearings, Gompers stressed that "the wage-earners by virtue of their numbers, by reasons of their comparatively helpless condition, are not in a condition to enter into [contracts], and they have not attained that status where they have the freedom of contract contemplated by the law."[64] Heightening her own visibility in both making and reporting the news, Valesh served as counsel for the *Journal* in lobbying for legislative hearings. She helped to write the Weavers' Fines bill to replace an older, ineffective, and unenforced law. In her campaign against the fine system, she relied on sympathetic state legislators such as Ross and Flynn, who had similar ideas about how to resolve the conflict. While the bill in no way addressed the 10 percent reduction in wages that had sparked the strike in the wider industry, it was in fact the fine system that had brought about the inquiry.

In hearings before the labor committee of the Massachusetts legislature, labor unions and cotton textile manufacturers detailed their cases. Eva Valesh was at her grandstanding best. She interrogated the witnesses, including weaver Harriet Pickering, who now appeared to testify against the bill. She made legislators aware of her presence by alternatively cajoling and encouraging the witnesses. Choosing workers to testify from among the "throngs of petitioners," she allowed them to tell their own stories about fines. Valesh's wit served her well, as she was able to turn the tables on one textile lawyer, who grilled a worker by questioning whether he understood how textile prices were set or the intricacies of management. She took her turn when a management witness was on the stand and asked if he knew how to weave cloth or support a family on a weaver's wages.[65]

In three days of hearings, Valesh made both the supporters of her Weavers' Fines bill and its opponents uncomfortable. Her summation passed over "the sarcastic compliments to the New York *Journal* by the opposing counsel," because, she asserted, "ridicule is always resorted to when there is no argument." While the counsel for the Arkwright Club sought to emphasize Valesh's ignorance of weaving, she argued that she was rather an expert in economics. She declared, "I admit I am not a weaver, but an expert in economics does not need to have been an operative in order to understand these abuses. And, for that matter, I don't think my learned friend, the counsel on the other side, is a weaver either." Some textile employers tried to maintain a fair and just system, but others unjustly imposed arbitrary fines. Valesh continued, "I have worked in a factory and so have some members of your honorable committee. Do you suppose that the weaver who leaves her little children at home to go late into the mill has anything to say about the justice or injustice of the grading system? She simply has to accept it because the employers have put it there." The *Journal*'s bill made a strategic intervention by allowing the workers to see the reasons for fines and to have an option of grieving them.[66]

The opposing counsel did not refute the fine system or offer solutions. In fact, as Valesh reported, the textile lawyers played on how the *Journal* illegitimately had interfered in a local matter. Reed, the counsel, asked how a "sensational journal coming into this Commonwealth in order to enhance its circulation and notoriety, can come before you as members of the general court, to ask for a change in an established law of the Commonwealth, making a general aspersion upon the integrity of the employing classes, that they have been negligent in their duty." In her article, Valesh retorted, "Having paid this tribute to journalism that acts," Reed argued that no legislation was needed. Not surprisingly, textile lawyers denounced the *Journal*'s bill as "confusing, spongy and fungous."[67] The labor committee had additional hearings in New Bedford, Lowell, and Fall River, but it discussed its findings in a closed session. In those deliberations, the success of Eva Valesh's campaign might be determined.

As the *New York Journal*'s "special commissioner," Eva Valesh became the special target of local newspapers and later of the men who headed the textile workers' union. Newspaper reporters charged that her interview with McKinley and letters from Ross and Flynn were fakes.[68] Journalists further showed their palpable dislike of Valesh in articles such as "They Want Sensation" and "Worried Labor Men" as they chronicled the hearings and heaped scorn on her performance. After supposedly dismissing the male leaders of the strike, local reporters asserted, Valesh had sought out "some labor leaders with disordered ideas, with speeches scattering dynamite, and with revolutionary tendencies."[69] While she failed, the writer continued, she still sought to inflame her readers' passions with distorted images of crushing poverty and unbearable misery.

By the time of the legislative hearings, Valesh's opponents, both in the press and in the State House, had had enough of her. A reporter argued that she was "a new woman," one who used both her maiden name and her married one, "the understanding being," the writer teased, "that Valesh married her and then died." Hinting at her divorce, ridiculing her manner, or simply impugning her sexual reputation, the article then found fault with her actions in the legislature: "The counsel, is a 'she,' a new woman, as some of the spectators call her. It is quite manifest that she is different from anything else seen at the Massachusetts State House." Indignantly, one writer announced, "She assumes to be the representative of the honest working people of New Bedford . . . but if her claim be true, it had better be said at once that the real representatives of the honest working people have washed their hands of her." Reporters insisted that union officers asked for Valesh's silence at the hearings. Concluding that her whole effort was fraudulent and subversive, one declared that "Mrs Valesh is conspicuous largely because of her nerve and frequently uttered disbeliefs in the truth of anything that is said by any one but herself." Her performance at the hearings was only fodder for the prurient readers of Hearst's papers.[70]

The textile strike had a prolonged and unsuccessful course. While some stalwarts held out until mid-May, the New Bedford strike effectively ended in mid-February, when those workers without resources slowly returned to the mills. The hearings produced no bill in the state legislature, and interest in the strike dwindled as international events began to claim the attention of New Bedford and the nation. What had happened during the strike, however, was that Eva Valesh, who had served as a New York City reporter for more than six months, reconnected with her roots in labor reporting. As time would prove, her thinking during the strike on the importance of arbitration, autonomous interventions, and public opinion clarified the lessons of the past decade. The New Bedford strike marked a turning point in Valesh's continually changing views.

The Cuban Crisis

During the Massachusetts hearings on the textile industry, another event captured the attention of the country. As readers were to learn in blazing headlines, the U.S.S. *Maine* exploded and sank in Havana harbor, killing 266 crewmen. The long-anticipated war with Spain threatened on the horizon, and the Hearst machine sought to keep up the pressure. Valesh was recalled to New York and then Washington. Herbert Browne quickly recruited her to join the *Journal*'s special commission to investigate conditions in Cuba. International relations was certainly not her beat, and she feared she would lose her position on the city desk. Still, Valesh went on the trip, and as she admitted, "It wasn't lacking in exciting and totally unexpected incidents."[71] As Willis Abbot recalled of the newspaper's atmosphere, "about every one on the editorial staff of the *Journal* who had influence became a war correspondent."[72] Eva Valesh was no exception.

In the history of American journalism, the Cuban conflict stands out as one of the high points for the influence and excesses of what was called "yellow" or "sensationalist" journalism. From the time that William Hearst bought the *New York Journal* in 1895, he engaged in cutthroat competition with Joseph Pulitzer's *World*, on which he had, ironically, modeled his own newspaper. Hearst took no prisoners in the war with Pulitzer. He had hijacked most of the *World* staff by paying the highest salaries in the country, and he kept the pressure on the *World* with ever more sensational coverage of murders, strikes, and scandals. As Hearst once claimed, his reporters constituted "a detective force" whose efficiency was at least as great as the public police.[73] From stunt reporting to the social investigations that served as precedent to the more respectable muckraking exposés, the *Journal* and *World* tried to outdo each other as both entertainers and shapers of public opinion.

The New York newspaper war did not reach its height, however, until the Cuban crisis in 1897–98. Competing with each other in the speed and fury with which they responded to events unfolding in that country, the *Journal* and *World* spent and lost hundreds of thousands of dollars in the process. In 1897, the attention was focused on the rescue of Evangelina Cisneros, detained without cause by the Spanish authorities; her story occupied the front page of the *Journal* for months. Other gambits, such as the stolen De Lôme diplomatic letter or the plight of American citizens in Cuba, heated up the rhetoric. When the United States finally declared war on Spain, the two New York newspapers printed 750,000 copies of dailies and extras and put a million copies of the Sunday edition on the street. At one point, the *Journal* spent $3,000 a day to provide every possible angle on the crisis. By the time war broke out, its staff in Cuba numbered 39 of its star reporters and illustrators—nearly 10 percent of the 500 journalists who eventually covered the war.[74]

For three decades, Cuba had been the scene of social strife as domestic rebels sought to overthrow Spanish colonial government. After ten years in exile, rebel leader José Martí returned to the island in 1895 to take up arms again. While he was killed, his compatriots Maximo Gomez and Antonio Maceo led the rebel army in a guerrilla campaign to undermine colonial rule. The stirrings of revolt provoked stronger government measures to maintain control over Cuba. The newly appointed Spanish governor, General Valeriano Weyler, adopted a policy of forced resettlement of Cuban peasants in guarded detention camps, called *reconcentrados*, to undermine rebel resistance. Known for poverty, brutality, and lack of sanitation, the camps became an embarrassment to the Spanish government and the focal point of arguments for American intervention. Each step of the way, interested parties in the United States, many of whom had long hoped for annexation of Cuba, took the opportunity to pressure their government. Threats to American lives, and to American investments, had the attention of newly elected President McKinley, but he hesitated to act until April 1898. In the interim, American aid poured into Cuba. As part of the response, the *Maine*, anchored off Havana in order to protect American citizens. When it inexplicably exploded in the harbor, newspapers like the *World* and the *Journal* increased the pressure on the government to act.[75]

After his early attempts to intervene, Hearst organized his own congressional junket to investigate the conditions of the camps and the situation in Havana. Hastily assembling a fleet of dispatch boats for his reporters, he borrowed a yacht, the *Anita*, from Standard Oil. Hearst then recruited his own "special commission," which included Senators Hernando Money of Mississippi, John Thurston of Nebraska, and J. H. Gallinger of New Hampshire and Representatives William Alden Smith of Michigan and Amos Cunningham of New York, along with their wives and *Journal* reporters. Most of the politicians were already committed to intervention.[76]

It was this commission that Eva Valesh joined. As the only woman journalist on board, she not only wrote articles on their findings but also served as the newspaper's hostess. The voyage would have need of her organizing talents. Not long after their departure they encountered a storm off Cape Hatteras. The hastily prepared *Anita* tossed and turned through turbulent seas and at one point almost capsized. Most of the passengers, including Valesh, were seasick from the storm. Surveying the damage the next morning, she commandeered crew to take care of the passengers, providing them with chicken sandwiches, champagne, and blankets.[77] The next day, headlines announced that brave congressmen had faced death in their mission of mercy. After the engines were repaired, the *Anita* continued on its way to Cuba.[78] A few days later, its passengers gathered with others from the *Journal* dispatch boats in Key West. Celebrating the "new journalism that acts for the betterment of mankind," the commission members made one toast after another to the president, to William Hearst, and finally to "the new woman in journalism," Eva Valesh. "Devoting its energies to patriotic ends," the commission sailed for Havana the next morning.[79]

Once there, the commission toured Havana, including the cathedral where the bones of Columbus were interred, and the *reconcentrado* camps. The members sent back reports that elicited much sympathy for the cause of Cuban liberation. Just as the newspapers had reported, the congressmen declared that those in the camps were slowly starving. The stories were illustrated with drawings of emaciated, skeletonlike figures dressed in rags, barefoot or with worn boots, staring vacantly at the artist.[80] Describing her experiences in an article, Valesh took the reader along to visit the hospital that Red Cross head Clara Barton had established. Children of the camps were being cared for with the limited foods and medicines made available by American relief. Wandering around Sagua La Grande on the following day, Valesh recalled later, she noticed something "like piles of clothing scattered on an embankment." They were victims of starvation who "were left lying out there and no attempt made to give them a decent burial." These stronger impressions were put aside in her reports and surfaced instead in articles under the names of senators and congressmen.[81]

Cast in tones of moral outrage, the *Journal* coverage focused on the question of how a civilized nation could permit the conditions of starvation and brutality that undermined Cubans' will to live. Given pollution taboos for the treatment of the dead, the commission members were, as was Eva, horrified by what they saw. Congressman William Alden Smith said that he didn't need to "to see the unburied dead being eaten by vultures to convince me that the slow starvation of these innocent and helpless people is one of the greatest crimes against humanity that could be perpetrated by an allegedly civilized country."[82] Seeing *reconcentrados* in Havana begging for alms was "an object lesson in Cuban conditions." Indeed, the "thousand agonies of starvation's slow death inflicted by the Spanish on women and children" called for retribution and redress.[83]

When Valesh remembered her experiences later, she described little of Cuba itself. Instead, she shifted her focus to the personal aspects of the trip, especially the death of Senator Thurston's wife. In one report, Mrs. Thurston appeared to have been the only passenger aboard the *Anita* who did not become seasick in the turbulent seas. She took a leadership role during their stay in Cuba and acted with an arrogance born of wealth. Her death from a heart attack, after having toured the *reconcentrados* in Havana and Sagua La Grande, shocked everyone. Afterward, Mrs. Thurston became a newspaper martyr to the cause of Cuba. When her husband spoke before Congress, the *Journal* claimed that his eloquence had come "at the command of silent lips." Mrs. Thurston, another headline proclaimed, had died "pitying Cuba" as a "tenderhearted wife" shocked by Spanish atrocities against women and children.[84] Her "Appeal to American Mothers" became a kind of deathbed injunction for the country to spring to action: "Oh! Mothers of the Northland, who tenderly grasp your little ones to your loving hearts! Think of the black despair that filled each Cuban Mother's heart as she felt her life blood ebb away, and knew that she had left her little ones to perish from the pain of starvation and disease."[85] In a newspaper culture in which heroes and saints, villains and dupes, were created instantaneously, Mrs. Thurston's self-sacrifice made her a martyr for the cause.

Over the Hump

The Hearst-sponsored commission read their findings in Congress, gave speeches, and wrote—or had written—numerous articles pleading with the public for the swift intervention that was soon to follow. For Valesh, however, both her Cuban venture and her newspaper career in New York came to an abrupt end. Back in the city, she hurt her back on a streetcar running board. A few weeks in the hospital and she found she had lost her place at the *Journal*. Moreover, she concluded that "my job had required an awful lot of footwork. The *American* paid good wages, but the physical exertion was too much for me. You were just one of the crowd." A senior editor, Charles Russell, advised Valesh to quit while she was still healthy. "'You know,'" she recalled him saying, "'the kind of sensational reporting you've been doing is all right for a short time, but in two or three years you'd be thrown aside like a squeezed-out lemon. You've got all the experience out of it that will be of any value to you.'" She could take the knowledge she had acquired and put it to use in her own work.[86]

At odds about what to do, Valesh went to Washington, D.C. After turning down a position in the AFL, she went to see Herbert Browne, the same editor who recruited her for the Cuban excursion. He proposed editing a syndicated political newsletter with her. As a well-paid editor for the *Journal*, Browne had the ready cash to invest in the enterprise. Valesh borrowed a thousand dollars from her old editor, William Murphy, and she and Browne went into business. She later recalled that they had more than two hundred newspapers subscribing. In addition to their syndicated newsletter, the partners established themselves as advertising agents in what was essentially the new profession of public relations. As she later recalled, she performed public-relations chores that ranged from gathering news from Capitol Hill and Washington receptions to ghostwriting articles that congressmen and other political figures marketed to magazines and newspapers. By providing telegraphic news service to twenty newspapers, Valesh also became a member of the press gallery in Congress.[87] Under the name Industrial Publishing Company, Valesh's syndicated newsletter also provided dispatches to the labor press. Samuel Gompers recommended it to unionists such as August Gansser, a local union secretary, who sought a source for "the latest authentic labor news."[88]

These were heady days for Valesh. As she later described them, her letters were liberal-Democratic in tone. With the Republicans in power, she said, they figured the newsletter would be lucky to break even. Neither she nor Browne received salary that first year. While he worked his job in the Hearst Washington bureau, she raised money by freelancing. The syndicated newsletter, however, was the passion of her life. She enjoyed listening to sessions of Congress and discovered a favorite hangout in the Marble Room off the Senate chamber. There she took up a seat on one of the windows and watched the senators talking to their "home folks." "It wasn't," she said, "that I got any definite amount of news there, but that was the place where I could put my mind together."[89] She attended the receptions of official Washington and appreciated its broad-mindedness. As she told an interviewer, "If you had anything to offer intellectually, you were well received in Washington. It doesn't make any difference if you've got a dollar to your name or not, and no one is critical of your dress." Her three evening dresses—"a white, a black, and a pastel-colored one"—got her through most doors. Moreover, because members of Congress realized that her syndicated newsletters gave them free publicity, "this led to invitations to more select affairs and to dinners where very important persons might be met." It was no wonder that she told an interviewer that the syndicated newsletters were "the happiest work I ever did in my life."[90] When Browne showed his disinterest in continuing, Valesh bought him out. The connections she made gave her the life she had long sought.[91]

During William Jennings Bryan's presidential campaign of 1900, Valesh served as an expert on labor affairs and was, she later asserted, "the only woman in the country who was on salary with the National Committee."[92] At the end of the election, she returned to her offices. Located across from the New Willard Hotel, a watering hole for the Washington press corps, the business, still called "Herbert J. Browne and E. McDonald Valesh, Advertising Agents," was located on the third floor at the rear of an old-fashioned building. She recalled, "They had no elevator, and you had to walk across the 'Camel's Hump' to get to them—this was a short corridor, three steps up and three steps down, that connected my building to an earlier front." The rent was low, and one of Valesh's friends told her that the "ancient shabbiness" gave her "class." She worked there putting out her mimeographed syndicated newsletters with the assistance of a young African-American secretary and an office boy. Because "not many people climbed 'the Hump,'" Valesh had the freedom to work on her newsletters in peace.[93]

Without many prospects, however, Valesh was "a bit at loose ends." The Democratic National Committee had given her exposure; but with Bryan's defeat, there was no further work to be done. One day when she was sitting at her desk, Gompers came for a visit. Because he rarely called on anyone, he obviously had a purpose, but he came to it indirectly. He talked first about the work at his office. There was, he said, "a lot of letters piled up at the AFL office." While his secretary was competent, she had "no knowledge of the labor movement." He wanted someone who knew enough about labor to handle the queries. Furthermore, "little by little, he began to say what a poor, bedraggled thing his official magazine was. He didn't know what to do."[94]

To convince Valesh to join the staff, Gompers commented on the shabbiness of her office and her seeming lack of prosperity. A position with the AFL was regular income. There was no reason, he added, that she had to give up her syndicated newsletter or freelancing.[95] She agreed to his offer. In 1901, Valesh began working for a national labor organization in a position that she had sought for more than a decade. The AFL had at last brought on board a woman schooled in labor organizing and the techniques of mass communications, politics, and public relations work. Valesh had learned not just a new style from the *Journal*, with a simpler and more melodramatic language, but she acquired a different approach to reporting and to the business of information.[96] While Gompers may have preferred a more genuinely enthusiastic supporter, he knew he had hired someone whose loyalty and skill would serve him well. As he wrote to Thomas Tracy, a general organizer, "It is true that Mrs. Valesh has consented to assist me, and I am very glad of it. At least, if she cannot say anything good of the A.F. of L and of me, she will revile neither."[97]

CHAPTER 7

Samuel Gompers's "Right-Hand Man"

Eva Valesh and the Gender of Labor's Political Culture

> That is Eva McDonald Valesh. She was a factory girl herself, and
> now is a leader of the hosts of workingwomen. She is "the right-
> hand man" of Samuel Gompers.
>
> —Ada Patterson, *Human Life* (December 1908)

In his essay "Women as Bread Winners—the Error of the Age," Boston
labor leader Edward O'Donnell captured the moral outrage of many craftsmen of his era. Fearing widespread displacement of skilled workingmen,
O'Donnell decried "the invasion of the crafts by women" that was causing "ir-
ritation and injury to the workman." Women doing men's work undermined
not only men's ability to find employment but also the ability of the family and
civilization to survive. Wage work unsexed women, demoralized them, and
stripped them of modesty while it "unmercifully strengthen[ed] the multi-
tudinous army of loafers, paupers, tramps and policemen." Fostering "the dis-
ruption, ruin or abolition of the home," the employment of women in craft
work cost manhood "its dignity, its backbone, its aspirations."[1]

As increasing numbers of women entered the industrial labor force, they
became the objects of social observation and political debate among labor
unionists and social reformers. They, like O'Donnell, argued about the place
of wage work and its potential threat to morality, family, and the natural or
God-given relationship between the sexes. In this debate, craft unionists most
often advocated control of the labor force through exclusion—by craft custom or rule, the regulation of women's and children's labor, and restrictive
immigration laws. Faced with competition from the machinery of mass pro-

duction and the immigrant workers hired to operate it, craft unionists argued that only native-born and naturalized tradesmen possessed the right of access to skilled positions. Believing that skill was a masculine virtue and wage work its proving ground, trade unionists resisted opening their ranks to women workers and to those socially and politically defined as "Other," whether new immigrants from Eastern and Southern Europe or African-American and Asian workers. The AFL's ideology assumed "manly work" was by definition the domain of the citizen worker.

How did Eva McDonald Valesh, an anomaly among the men of organized labor, address a labor movement that cast her and the women workers she claimed to represent outside the bonds of solidarity? As a woman printer, journalist, public speaker, and trade unionist, she repeatedly had crossed the boundaries of restrictive craft unionism. In the decade in which she worked for the AFL, dramatic changes in the labor force and labor's political stance offered opportunities to enlarge labor's field of vision. But as Samuel Gompers's "right-hand man," Valesh did little to extend the privileges and rights of union membership—citizenship in the working class—to native-born workingwomen or immigrants of either sex. In her writings on women workers, immigrants in the labor force, and child labor, she became one of the authors of an exclusionary unionism that restricted her own participation. Her language and imagery, and her politics within the labor movement, required the double consciousness of those excluded from the arrangements of power but fully enmeshed within them. Bringing to labor her own skills as journalist and politician, she became an unacknowledged contributor to a labor politics that did not know her name.

Entering the House of Labor

At its December 1900 convention, the AFL endorsed the appointment of McDonald Valesh as a general organizer. Introduced by Gompers himself, Valesh addressed the necessity of the AFL's drive to organize women workers. As the proceedings recorded, she spoke "on the benefits of organization and made an eloquent appeal for the organization of women into trade unions, so that in time, they might, through organization, emancipate themselves from the industrial field back to the home, and the man would take up her work in the factory and store as the breadwinner."[2] Such rhetoric, balanced between the reality of workingwomen's lives and the AFL's conservative gender ideology, made her invaluable to the organization.

The year that Eva Valesh joined the staff, the AFL was in the midst of an unprecedented expansion. In 1898, it had 278,000 members; by 1903, its ranks had grown to 1,500,000. As the organization grew, its national headquarters expanded to meet new demand for services. In his autobiography, Gompers recalled how, in his first year as AFL president, he had a small office rent-free from a local, with a used table as desk, a box for a chair, and empty grocery store boxes for filing his papers. Within a few years, these modest arrangements had improved. Moving first to Washington, D.C., in 1895, the AFL took up temporary headquarters in three rooms at 14th Street, N.W., where the president and four members of his staff worked.[3] By 1900, it relocated in the Typographical Temple on G Street, where AFL offices occupied the entire building. Seven hundred volunteer organizers sent in reports from the field on the activities of local and international unions. Fifty full-time organizers helped coordinate union drives and arbitrate disputes across the country, and a clerical staff of from twenty-five to forty-two handled correspondence, financial reports, and the preparation of the AFL's journal, the *American Federationist*.

With few specifically assigned duties and the need to report only to president Gompers, Valesh held an ill-defined position on the AFL staff. Listed variously on reports as clerk, typographer, and organizer, she earned a salary comparable to newspaper reporters of the day. Her salary ran from $16 a week in 1901 to about $30 a week in 1909. While her salary was in the middle range for organizers and significantly below those of Gompers and Frank Morrison, it was the third highest regular salary on the payroll. She was being paid, in large part, for her professional credentials as journalist and publicist and for her work experience—a practice consonant with the AFL's own craft-union ideology.[4]

As Valesh sometimes managed to record in the *American Federationist*, her primary responsibility was as assistant and effectively managing editor of the journal. The little surviving correspondence between Gompers and Valesh in these years primarily concerned the journal. Gompers sent her material for it and inquired about paper quality and costs; Valesh handled business details, such as investigating paper and printing costs or fielding copy for publication.[5] In an interview, Valesh recounted, "I found that I had to write most of the material that appeared in the first issues I edited. I tried to say something in a constructive, educational way to keep up with the current economics."[6] While she managed to write a series of articles under her own name, much of her work remained unsigned. In addition to her editorial duties, she worked on miscellaneous publications, including the AFL pamphlet, *Labor Aroused*.[7]

As Gompers's principal aide, Valesh had relationships with office staff and labor heads that were congenial but distant. Few official visitors and no congressmen or senators passed through the office. Although Gompers regularly met with union presidents who sought advice and favors, Valesh and his secretary kept these hours to a minimum. Soon after Valesh's hiring, union leaders surmised that she had special access to the president and stopped by her desk on their visits. In exchange for her insights, they gave her information about the member unions that was helpful in editing the *Federationist* and, more important, in steering clear of controversy.[8]

Despite her role as Gompers's aide, Valesh had few—if any—friends on the AFL staff, and she particularly did not get along with AFL secretary Frank Morrison. As she later told an interviewer, "Morrison and I were not on good terms because I wouldn't let him give me any orders. President Gompers was my boss, if I had any."[9] As a condition of working for the AFL, Valesh demanded autonomy, and she received it. Her own sense of privileged access had other repercussions. Unlike other of his employees, Valesh "never idolized" Gompers. She displayed a certain cool distance toward a man who had been a personal friend: "In fact, personally I was a bit allergic to him. I just didn't like him so very well at times."[10]

After a decade of friendship with Gompers, Valesh had now become his employee, and the tenor of their relationship changed. In her oral history, she praised him and their friendship, but she also knew his faults. Years later, she admitted that "I always felt that Mr. Gompers had a streak of true greatness in his character, but the rest of the man was just earthy." At the same time, she argued, "this streak of greatness was always in regards to economics."[11] Evasive with his instructions, Valesh related, "he was what the Scotch call a 'sneeper'— they pick at you with this or that thing after the event."[12] In editing the *Federationist*, Valesh received little direction and often had to guess at policy. She had no specific duties and only a moderate salary. She chose to stay with the AFL, one suspects, both out of security and from her own conviction that the *Federationist* offered the opportunity to serve as an authority on economic matters.[13]

As Valesh recalled years later, she "came down from her daydreams quickly enough." The *American Federationist* in 1901 had little reputation and a bundle of problems from a lack of profitability to a dearth of publishable material. While Valesh wrote unsigned articles summarizing union campaigns and labor legislation, she was not allowed to set the editorial direction of the journal. In keeping with his view of the *Federationist* as his personal publication, Gompers wrote most of the editorials. He did not want Valesh to edit anything he wrote. The problem was, it was difficult to get him to prepare material in time, and, moreover, "he liked to write editorials, but he wrote them badly." As a self-educated man, Gompers had a love of long words, and, Valesh added, "he had such a stilted manner. He knew his economics and the labor question all right, but he wouldn't put it in simple language."[14] She argued with him constantly over the use of words that not even labor leaders could "swallow." Because Valesh had been tutored in public speaking and wrote for mass newspapers, she knew the value of simple words and clear presentation. Labor editor John Swinton once wrote of Gompers that he "seemed to do his editing with an axe."[15] Years later, Gompers was not a more giving author. His predilections kept the editorials from acquiring the popular touch Valesh thought they required.

The *American Federationist* had a particularly important place in Gompers's vision of what the AFL ought to be. While in its infancy, the AFL had withdrawn its support from its original journal, the *Union Advocate*. Gompers made sure his next effort was given its due. After a rocky beginning in 1894, he commissioned interesting articles from up-and-coming trade unionists, including Valesh's letters from Europe, but the journal remained "poor and bedraggled." Recruiting her as assistant editor was his first step in remaking the *Federationist* into a flagship journal worthy of the AFL. As Valesh explained, "The idea of the official magazine was that there was so much prejudice against the unions in the newspapers that they couldn't get a hearing. If they had a central magazine where they could express their own ideas, explain their own ideals, and have an interchange of thought, it would be educational."[16] Sharing the belief that public opinion was a major arbiter in labor matters, Gompers decided that the *Federationist* had to provide the best labor information possible in a world in which the facts of labor organization were distorted. His understanding of the importance of the magazine made him jealous of its reputation and the credit for it. Throughout Valesh's time on the journal, the only time she claimed the title "assistant editor" was when Gompers was out of the country. Unacknowledged except as his aide, Valesh served as Gompers's right-hand man only as long as she tolerated the anonymity required of women in a men's organization.

Valesh's exact contribution to the *American Federationist* is impossible to discern. Because much of her copy was unsigned, there remains the difficulty of distinguishing it from the material that Gompers submitted and the information sent by union secretaries around the country. During her tenure as assistant editor, Valesh expanded the content of the *Federationist*. In 1905–1906, for example, the journal published a series of articles on women workers, including her essay "Wage-Earning Women," and reports on women in trade unions in meat-packing, waitressing, and shirtwaist manufacture.[17] In addition, the journal published a special issue in 1901 on "The History of Labor by Those Who Made It" and forums on issues before the AFL. For the 1903 Child Labor Symposium, Irene Ashby-Fadden, an AFL lobbyist, wrote an article, as did Valesh.[18] Over the decade, the journal published more advertisements, mostly for union-label goods in food, beer, clothing, and even medicinal remedies. In doing so, the *American Federationist* began to resemble other advocacy journals with its blend of serious articles, organizational matters, and features of the popular press.[19]

In addition to acting as managing editor, Valesh served more irregularly as an AFL general organizer in union and political campaigns. Overturning its customary rejection of party politics, the AFL assumed a much more aggressive political stance after 1900. In the congressional election of 1906, it sought to reward its friends and punish its enemies. More than 1,300 volunteers and 42 paid organizers raised labor's visibility in the campaign and mobilized working-class voters to support labor-friendly candidates.[20] Two years later, in the presidential campaign, the AFL distributed more than five million pieces of campaign literature and put more than one hundred political organizers in the field. Extending its political clout, it brought to the campaign an army of what it called "minute men of labor" to the field in support of Democratic candidate William Jennings Bryan and labor-friendly congressional candidates. These efforts engaged not only AFL field organizers but also the headquarters staff.[21] Complementing campaign literature, the *American Federationist* devoted its pages to the campaign as labor's political turn absorbed the energies of Eva Valesh. As she wrote to Gertrude Beeks, secretary of the National Civic Federation, she was "rushed to death since [we] laborites have gone into politics, but I'm very enthusiastic over the work." Two years later, she similarly recorded that "I'm so deadly tired since the campaign closed."[22] Her political experience undoubtedly paid off in campaigns to mobilize working-class voters.

The Making Not of Paupers but of Men

The political campaigns of the AFL signaled shifts in the labor world that Valesh entered as a young woman. Where the labor movement had earlier embraced a vision of a cooperative community among those who toiled, the AFL saw itself as an organization of wage-earners only. That identity served to restrict the meaning of class, community, and union solidarity. Where Knights of Labor and Populist activists found ways to integrate women in the vision of community, the AFL and its constituent unions saw the workplace as the focal point of working-class solidarity and envisioned class struggle as masculine labor grappling with powerful, and even tyrannical, employers.

Rooting their politics in an ethic of class respectability and the American standard of living,[23] craft unionism associated union brotherhood with manly forthrightness, independence, and physical strength. As citizen workers, men were made—craft unionists believed—by testing their masculinity in public acts of work, political activism, and protest. This merging of gendered republican rhetoric, liberal politics, and class-informed collective identity made the AFL the prototype of twentieth-century unionism and labor reform.[24] Like other political forces of the time, the AFL moved beyond the individualism of early liberal theory to an acceptance of group interests as legitimate in the realm of the state. Labor leaders imagined that their organization expressed the unity and the common interests of all wageworkers.

At the turn of the twentieth century, the AFL and its constituent craft unions faced new and pressing challenges from organized political and economic interests in the country. What many historians have called "the employers' offensive" began as corporations and small businesses organized themselves into groups to combat the growing bargaining power of unions in the workplace. The National Association of Manufacturers, the American Anti-Boycott Association, the National Metal Trades Association, and the National Civic Federation were all products of the general impulse to restrain trade unionism, either by limiting its capacities to contest wages or by allying with more conservative trade unions against the threat of a wider industrial unionism among factory operatives. The period saw the widespread use of the private and public police, labor spies, and court injunctions in labor disputes. Not surprisingly, when two important court decisions, *Danbury Hatters* and *Bucks' Stove*, supported employer injunctions against union boycotts, the AFL turned to politics to seek an anti-injunction law and to revise the antitrust laws to exclude labor unions. Equally as important, the AFL reiterated its support for immigration restriction.[25]

In pursuing its political and economic aims, the Progressive Era AFL drew on the republican language of opposition and the new liberal language of citizenship.[26] In framing political claims and demanding rights, labor advocates drew on the union brother, tradesman, and citizen worker[27] as important icons for a craft-union movement that saw social solidarity as masculine. Culturally, such language served to exclude from membership those who were neither brothers nor citizens; and it reinforced the association of craft privilege with white workingmen of native birth or Northern European origin. Not yet enfranchised nor trusted within the workplace, women workers remained outside the boundaries of labor struggle. Perceived as weak, volatile, and unreliable, immigrant workers—male or female—presented problems for a unionism that viewed them with the same ambivalence and hostility tendered to women.

The AFL's craft unionism celebrated first and foremost the craft traditions that underwrote the collective power and identity of skilled tradesmen. From older trades such as printer to the relatively newer occupations of mule-spinner and machinist, workingmen understood skill as a masculine trait—the outcome of apprenticeship, common work experience, and shared work ethic. Pride in workmanship, individual and craft independence, and manly bearing were at the heart of the social codes of skilled trades. As a machinist wrote, "Principle is the foundation of our trade and the cornerstone is workmanship. Without principle we have no manhood. To have manhood we must have both of these as they go hand in hand."[28] Nineteenth-century craft ideology, historian Patricia Cooper wrote, "stressed autonomy, collective identity, and mutual aid, a fierce independence, pride, and self worth, control over work, respect for manliness, a sense of both adventure and humor, duty to the trade, and loyalty to each other." David Montgomery similarly noted that machinists measured manliness in terms of class solidarity, craft identity, and ability to control work. For tailors, cigar-makers, shoemakers, iron-molders, and other trades, the work they did defined who they were as workers and as men.[29]

While masculinity defined skilled labor in craft union ideology, wage work in general was seen as a masculine trait; and its absence could suck the very marrow of a man's masculinity. Describing the effects of unemployment and deskilling, Samuel Gompers wrote that a man without a job, without a craft, was not a man. In his autobiography, *Seventy Years of Life and Labor*, he sketched an imagined meeting with a former trade union brother on the street. Since the craft worker "fell out of his job," the man "lost in self-respect, for he feels every hour that men may speak of him as not having made good. He has lost flesh and even strength." If the brother can only find work, "[the worker] who quailed in fear lest he might be relegated to the human scrap-heap may become a man again." Tragically, Gompers intoned, "if his chance hangs off too long, the worker's fate is to 'lay down.' He is 'gone.' . . . The real man having passed away, the poor body remains only to succumb, in its weakness, to one of the hundred forms of illness."[30] Such words echoed the fears that Gompers had for his friend Frank Valesh—that illness was a sign of weakness. Gompers's "dissertation" on the unemployed man expressed labor's belief in the relationship between the body, work, manliness, and citizenship.

Remembering his own traumatic unemployment after a cigar-makers' strike, Gompers believed that the burden of unemployment sat most heavily on men, forcing them to forego necessities of life, including decent food, doctors, and the self-reliance so fundamental to a man's identity. The anger he harbored over his own powerlessness while unemployed is apparent when he describes his inability to get a doctor to wait on his wife during labor: "Once I was ready to commit murder."[31] Because he had cast his grandfather as prone to "manifestations of savage outbursts of uncontrollable rage" and he avoided showing anger toward his family,[32] Gompers retold the doctor's tale as a sign of how devastating unemployment—and by extension dependence born of poverty—was for craft workers. Resonating with Valesh's earlier rhetoric that many feared labor as "a Frankenstein born of hard times and unrestricted immigration," the general view of unemployment was that it yielded both monstrous and violent progeny.[33]

As a citizen, the working man, labor unions argued, had the right to work at a calling that gave him independence, respect, and the ability to support his family. Gompers wrote that "man, by his physical condition, is the natural breadwinner of the family, and it is his duty to work; not only is it his duty, but he has the right to work, the right to the opportunity to work. When that right is denied him, society does him and his an injustice."[34] This emphasis on the "natural" breadwinning norm for men was mirrored by a similar acceptance that women's work was unnatural, or at least undesirable. Typographical union leader George McNeill further argued that "woman is not qualified for the condition of wage labor. The mental and physical make-up of women is in revolt against wage service. She is competing with the man, who is her father or her husband, or who is to become her husband."[35] Wage work, many unionists believed, further thwarted women's role as mothers.

Consequently, women were unmade and undone in proximity to wage work, especially in trades and occupations unsuited to their capacities. While some women might have to accept wage work temporarily for economic reasons, the outcome of public work for women was a change in physiognomy, bodily strength, and the capacity for motherhood. As a product of late Victorian culture, labor ideology exhibited increasing—even obsessive—concern with the physical, mental, and political consequences of work and work organization. Thus, men's bodies, as Gompers wrote, were susceptible to unemployment and destroyed by it, and work invaded women's bodies in ways that confirmed their differential relationship to labor.

Sexual difference between men and women workers surfaced in Valesh's articles on workingwomen as well. As her writings attest, she—with others of her time—saw a direct correlation between the kind of work one did and one's face, demeanor, posture, and health. As she wrote, work "frightfully ravages our women" with the strain of employment diminishing their vitality.[36] Low wages that put some women into moral trouble led others to rapidly declining health, disease, physical disfigurement, and even death. A working girl wanting to conceal her occupation from the crowd could hide her lunch pail, but "stooping shoulders, the head bent forward, hair unkempt, even dull and lifeless"[37] gave her away. The issue was not hygiene so much as the toll that work took on women's bodies—an idea that emerged repeatedly in the writings of both labor and Progressive reformers. Working girls acquired "pinched faces and hollow eyes," looked feeble, and aged decades before their time.[38]

Workingwomen in a Movement for Workingmen

Despite its history of excluding women, the AFL's policy toward organizing them was a work-in-progress to which Eva Valesh contributed significantly. As both a cultural worker for labor and a trade unionist, her writings straddled the fine line between the AFL's restrictive policies and its capacity to aid women workers through trade unionism. Only a few years after the organization's founding, Valesh addressed its convention on "Women and Labor." She argued that it was the AFL, not the rival Knights of Labor, that was "the body best fitted to investigate woman's work and apply the proper remedy for existing abuses." She added that "no class of people can understand and sympathize with working women like those who stand side by side with them in the factory."[39] The heart of her talk addressed the causes and conditions of women's labor. Valesh rejected what she defined as the middle-class assumption that women worked for economic advancement. Most women did not work as a matter of free choice. She then established what she considered the "basic facts" of women's recent entrance into the labor force. Improved technology and economic need led the way for women's displacement of men in the workplace. As she argued, "The prejudice of the employing class, and the idle and surplus labor in the market" threatened reform. Moreover, a man seeking work confronted neither "foreigners" nor "denizens of another race" but his own wife and children as competition. The only solution was to organize women, "making them valuable allies instead of a source of danger."[40]

As members of the committee on organizing women workers, Valesh and her compatriot Ida Van Etten urged the AFL to hire a woman organizer who would have a seat on the executive board. While the convention declined to put a woman on the board, they appointed Mary Kenney, a Chicago trade unionist, to be the AFL's first woman organizer. Given an annual salary of $1,200, Kenney traveled widely through her four months of active organizing. Despite having organized in a variety of trades, Kenney's appointment was not renewed at the 1892 meeting.[41] Over the course of the next eight years, a few women organizers were brought in on a temporary basis. Ardent trade unionists for men, the board simply argued that hiring women to organize was not cost-effective. Most women organizers were unpaid volunteers.[42]

Trade unionists for the most part insisted that "the normal place for women is in the home."[43] In their worldview, men were the "natural" breadwinners whose role was to defend wives and daughters against the ravages of employment. Defining wage work as male duty and privilege, they actively discouraged women from working. Fundamentally, labor leaders believed employers to be at fault. And despite a public defense of women's right to work, Gompers

voiced the position of craft unions in arguing that "it is not for any real preference for their labor that the unscrupulous employer gives work to girls and boys
and women but because of his guilty knowledge that he can easily compel them
to work longer hours and at a lower wage than men." It was "the so-called competition of the defenseless woman worker, the girl and the wife," he noted, that
lowered "the wages of the father and the husband."[44]

Unionists simultaneously insisted that the AFL alone had the ability, right,
and strategy to organize women and that women were, by nature, impossible to
organize. So it was that when women workers organized and sought union charters for their locals, they instead were assigned to federal locals, which came to
serve as a kind of holding company for nascent unions. These locals were then
either raided for members by existing craft unions or left without services and
equal representation in the AFL. The belief that women workers were inher-
ently unable to be organized thus became a self-fulfilling prophecy—one that
would remain central to union lore. No resources were devoted to organizing
women, and no women were organized. Women were, the story went, only temporary workers. Most were bent on matrimony, and they had no incentive to
join unions. They also lacked the self-assertiveness necessary for union membership. As Valesh claimed, organizing women was "the more arduous because
the individual working woman is prone to suffer in silence where conditions are
bad instead of seeking energetically to establish her rights."[45] These contradictory messages impeded women workers who sought to join the ranks of labor
and frustrated the few who saw unions as necessary for women's progress.

Valesh expressed the same contradictions in her writing. "Wage-Working
Women," for instance, highlighted the tension between the need of workingwomen to organize and craft unions' desire that women refrain from working.
Still, while labor unions argued that women should remain in the home, Valesh
contended that "for some generations to come, the wage working woman is likely
to be in evidence in even greater numbers in the industrial world than today."
Women continued to work in unsanitary conditions for low wages and for long
hours. Poor health, shortened education, and lack of opportunity kept them from
challenging their station in the labor force. The "evils of industrialism" thus ag-
gravated women's physical weakness and undermined their potential for motherhood. Industry exhibited "criminal negligence" in its employment of women for
profit.[46] Delicately balanced between the traditional beliefs of her trade union
readers and her own insistence on women's place in the House of Labor, Valesh's
words reflected her ambiguous position with the AFL.

Valesh's message to women workers, however, was neither as negative nor
as hysterical as those who saw workingwomen as "the error of the age." The
labor movement, she argued, had a vested interest in organizing women. It

also served as "an abject lesson in the equality of women" by their admission of women as equal members with the right to both vote and hold office.[47] The question that remained was whether those who stood with them side by side would ever open the doors of the union hall.

The Industrial Slaughter of Innocents

Whatever their ambivalence toward women workers, unions expressed a nearly unanimous condemnation of child labor. On grounds that ranged from viewing child laborers as competition to the Victorian cult of the child, the AFL pursued child labor legislation at both the state and federal level. The fear that work undermined or destroyed bodily strength, physical prowess, and reproductive capacity, along with the sensibility required of future citizens, gave unions a politics of reproduction that they did not otherwise articulate. Descriptions of the physical effects of child labor on future men and women mirrored what unemployment would do to a skilled worker. If unemployment broke the will and physical constitution of a trade-union man, employment destroyed the mental and physical abilities of women and children. As Eva Valesh wrote in "Child Labor," hiring children potentially destroyed "their adult productiveness and reproductiveness." "Early put to confining and unhealthy work," working children grew up "such stunted and degenerated specimens of humanity that their children [were] still more enfeebled than themselves."[48]

By 1890, labor's desire to save children from sweatshop labor, unstable families, and juvenile delinquency could be heard in a variety of contexts. To eliminate child labor and thus end "the industrial slaughter of innocents" was one of the AFL's principal goals. It sought "to make the labor of man so remunerative that it will enable the bread-winner to maintain his loved ones as becomes a man and a citizen."[49] The rhetoric of child-saving bolstered arguments about controlling child labor for economic reasons and resonated with fear of foreigners. Child labor was characterized as "the exploitation of the tender and young, drawn into the factory, into the shop, into the mill, into the mine and the stores by the drag-net of modern capitalism." Because children frequently "supplant[ed] the labor of their parents," they were "robbed in their infancy of the means of an education" and "dwarfed both in mind and body." As Valesh proclaimed, "humanity and patriotism cry aloud against this great wrong of our time."[50]

The AFL argued that the evil of child labor was directly due to the "commercial spirit" of industry, as employers "deliberately [sought] the labor of children because it [was] cheap and easily exploited." In Valesh's words, "commercialism overrode moral law" when employers engaged in "the wickedness of coining young flesh and blood and energy into dollars." The rapacity of employers was not the only issue. Reflecting the general hostility toward new immigrants, unionists blamed them for preventing their sons and daughters from getting an education and driving them into the factory out of their own greed and laziness. The same race-based beliefs that pervaded labor union policies toward immigration shaped their view of parents who would send their children out to work. Sharing these prejudices, Valesh asserted, "naturally, the newer and needier the immigrant, the easier to enslave his children." Immigrant parents "lack[ed] the capacity for self-sacrifice and unselfishness which would make them suffer rather than send their children out to work."[51]

Valesh described child labor in tones familiar to trade unionists: "Our centers of industry with their mills, factories, and workshops, are teeming with young and innocent children, bending their weary forms with long hours of daily drudgery, with pinched and wan cheeks, emaciated frames, dwarfed both physically and mentally, and frequently driven to premature decay and death."[52] Coupling her analysis of work's harmful effects on the body with an image of the greed-driven employer, she wrote that "every buyer and dealer should know when his 'bargain' is purchased at the cost of worn, torn childish fingers; of cramped, withered little muscles that ought to be free and easy in play; of bleared, strained child eyes; lungs that are compressed for want of air."[53] Labor demanded protection of children. The state, "with its power, should step in and see to it that its future citizens, men and women alike, should not become mental or physical deformities or derelicts in the body politic."[54]

For years, the AFL had been agitating for legislation to regulate child labor. It worked to educate public opinion on the conditions and consequences of child labor, introduced legislation at the state level, and aroused the public for its passage and enforcement. By 1907, labor unions believed it was time for federal legislation to be enacted. Like Samuel Gompers, Valesh wanted to use the limited powers of the state to address the very real needs of child laborers. As she wrote a few years later, "If we allow the children of the tenements and mountains to work their little lives away in a sweatshop and mill, we are building up for ourselves a Frankenstein that will topple down our very civilization. That is the reason of the unceasing effort to abolish child labor."[55] It was time, she argued, to eliminate child labor wherever possible.

Voluntarism and the Citizen Worker

In contrast to the perceived weakness of women and child wage-earners, American craft unionists embraced ideas of working-class men's vitality and independence. In public discourse, they had an aversion to state interference in labor relations, for their experience had taught them that the courts and legislatures were unreliable allies. As a result, they fought against any state action as an impediment to men's autonomy and self-respect. In its policies, the AFL criticized those who argued for state intervention in labor relations. Rather, its advocates asserted that voluntary association, or voluntarism, was the appropriate and natural model of citizenship for the labor movement. Compulsory legislation constrained citizens, whereas voluntary associations were, in Gompers's view, "the natural growth of natural laws, and from the very nature of their being have stood the test of time and experience."[56]

This argument recognized both the potential and the damage that state police powers could inflict on the labor movement. Craft-union autonomy and independent manhood seemed better bets. In an essay written in the 1890s, Frank Valesh expressed skepticism shared by many in the labor movement. Legislation intended to regulate tenement sweatshops, shorten working hours for women, prohibit trusts, or outlaw blacklists all failed to live up to their promises to alleviate labor's condition. The recently overturned Illinois eight-hour law for women, Frank Valesh wrote, demonstrated "how limited the practical good that trade unions attain through legislation." He declared that "much of the sentimental legislation passed in the name of labor either failed to obtain its object, or has, in fact, been used to the detriment of labor unions." The use of the antitrust law in the Pullman strike was yet another case in point. According to Valesh, trade unions should not "divert" their resources "from the legitimate and natural channels in the direction of legislative bogs." Only "more freedom and a better conception of their rights" could bring about constructive change.[57]

As a result, the labor movement viewed any proposals for protective labor legislation and social insurance with suspicion. Writing against social insurance, Gompers argued that "there must necessarily be a weakening of independence and virility when compulsory insurance is provided for so large a number of citizens of the state." Unemployment insurance, old-age pensions, and welfare were all seen as "soften[ing] the moral fiber of the people" and entailed "the loss of red-blooded, rugged independence."[58] Social insurance funded by compulsory programs touched on the fear of state police powers that runs throughout the autobiographies and public writings of many Progressive unionists. As Gompers wrote, "Compulsory social insurance cannot be administered without exercising some control over wage-earners. . . . [It] is in its essence undemocratic."[59] This was also the case for compulsory arbitration, which was thought to put the worker at the mercy of employers and an employer-run state.[60] To be compelled in any way was not to engage in independent action or thinking but to be dependent on the state for guidance, support, and protection—grounds on which one could be denied equal citizenship.[61]

Protective legislation for women and children was another matter. As dependents and not wage-earners, they could be compelled. According to Gompers, however, unionism could only succeed if workingwomen understood that "though their individual connection with employment may be temporary . . . the employment of women is not temporary."[62] Only if they had union protection could they address their problems. Absent the protections of political equality and trade-union bargaining power, workingwomen were disadvantaged in the market economy. Only the state had the capacity to even the odds.

Citizen Workers and Immigrant Idlers

The growing presence of immigrant workers presented another aspect of unionized labor's contradictory stands. Controlling access to employment, especially in the skilled trades, had long been a goal of craft unions in the late nineteenth and early twentieth century. Still, access to the specific entry points for the trades did not stop the continual erosion of skilled workers' power in the labor force, and for this, AFL-affiliated labor unions looked to the state for aid. Seeking eight-hour days for government employees, regulating labor among seamen and longshoremen, cutting back on state use of prison-made goods, and restricting immigration were high on the AFL's political agenda in these years. Many of labor's grievances were, in fact, directed toward those areas in which political control of the labor supply and conditions would be possible without incurring opposition from the courts. The AFL devoted ever-increasing resources to this agenda.[63]

One of labor's most absorbing concerns was the growing number of immigrant workers. For the most part, the labor movement recognized only the rights, claims, and needs of native-born American workmen and their naturalized trade-union brothers. As historian Catherine Collomp has argued, the AFL sought political integration for its craft-union members through a new ideology of citizenship that brought together wage-earning, skill, and union participation with national identity. Thus AFL ideology defined who was the ideal trade-union member by its support for restrictive immigration policies, exclusionary rules, and the equation of Americanism with traditional work and the American standard of living.[64] To a great extent, the language of labor, highly refined in racial and ethnic terms, was gendered from its origins in fraternalism and the republican ideology. Following cultural trends in celebrating the male wage-earning role and the family wage as the basis of equal citizenship, the AFL's language rooted the political rights and claims of craft workers in working-class respectability. Thus, the labor movement defined the trade unionist in narrow cultural terms and put into place the legal, political, and educational foundations for labor's new citizenship in the twentieth century.

Still, the entrance of unskilled immigrant labor into industry occasionally forced the labor movement's hand. Reporting on the 1909 Pressed Steel Car Strike in McKeesport Rocks, Pennsylvania, Valesh decried the "crude outbreak of violence" of nonunionized immigrant workers. While employers, she noted, had "assumed it safe to deal with unskilled and recently arrived immigrants of the Slav race," they were mistaken. The "ignorance" and "inherited patience under bad treatment," which employers attributed to immigrant laborers, did not make them "incapable of resenting the very low wages and oppressive treatment" they received. The contempt, brutality, and injustice of which the company had shown its employees led to their "blind revolt." Yet, as Valesh wrote, "many employers forget that you cannot injure or degrade any portion of the body politic without injuring all, even to the remotest edge of the circle."[65]

As Valesh's writing revealed, the long-standing ambivalence of labor unions toward the new immigration surfaced even in the promise of union democracy. Her writings expressed labor's broader fear of foreign competition and alien customs and echoed the attitudes she had first cultivated in Mulberry Bend and in the streets of Europe. Defending labor's stance, she wrote, "Labor unions are not prejudiced against immigration, but they believe that if the immigrant has a sound body and clean mind and can read and write when he arrives, he is better material for a good citizen than the criminal, the ignorant, the pauper, or the defective." Only labor-union involvement, Valesh wrote unselfconsciously, could replace "class limitations and narrow prejudices" with patriotism. In reaching out to workers, unions were a constant education in self-government, self-reliance, honesty, integrity, and self-control.[66] In her analysis of immigration, as in her writing on women workers, Valesh visibly struggled to balance the need for class unity against the rhetoric of a labor movement suspicious of and hostile toward the new immigrant workers.

Despite the increased presence of immigrant workers, unions kept the new workers at bay. They strictly created and enforced exclusionary rules, long apprenticeships, and citizenship requirements that maintained the native-born or naturalized character of their membership. High dues also served to exclude unskilled workers who otherwise might have made common cause with a more broadly defined labor movement.[67] At the same time, however, in equating trade-union participation with citizenship, the AFL asserted political claims in a language that spoke not of private interest but of common welfare. Labor unionists claimed universal (albeit white-male citizenship) rights, not particular needs. They publicly claimed to speak for all workers. Yet seeing themselves as fundamentally different from "ignorant" foreign workmen, trade unionists based their claims on their status as respectable citizen workers. As the means to integrate workers into the polity and wider society, the exclusionary definition of labor citizenship stood in contradiction to its rhetoric of universality.

The emergence of the citizen-worker ideal in the late nineteenth century underwrote what British sociologist Jeff Hearn has described as "the whole conceptualization and understanding of the proletariat . . . [as] male."[68] It was also, as we have seen, racially and ethnically specific. Skilled trade unionists saw much of the new U.S. labor force as women and immigrant "others" thought incapable of the kind of solidarity and discipline that would make them good union members. For Gompers and many craft unionists of his generation, the stance toward immigrant labor was an implicit denial of their own status as once "foreign" workers and now naturalized citizens. Trying to define themselves in a political culture that saw both physical labor and workingmen and women as ignorant, dangerous, immoral, and greedy, labor unionists set up their own mirror image in the uncouth immigrant radical. While labor unions did not have a blanket policy of immigrant exclusion, in practice they, too, looked down on the masses who possessed neither recognized skills nor citizenship papers. The consequences of their willful fragmentation of the working class were decades of disharmony and the division of workers in their political and economic striving.

Hearth and Home for a Union Woman

Battles for union solidarity and political influence occupied center stage during this period of Eva Valesh's life. Her life in Washington and New York, however, continued much as it had in her *Journal* and freelance days. She lived during that decade at a range of residences, from the comfortable shabbiness of the F Street address to the Plaza on Pennsylvania Avenue.[69] From the time her son, Frank, was six, she sent him to the Xavier Brothers Boarding School, Mt. St. Joseph, near Baltimore.[70] With her son away, her life was devoid of most of the domestic concerns of middle-class women. She went to work, attended receptions on a regular basis, and traveled frequently for work and pleasure. Like AFL leaders, she ate out frequently and lived in hotels on the road. An interview with Valesh in *Human Life* magazine in 1908 includes a photograph of her with her son in front of the AFL offices. Another family photograph captured Frank with the family servant, a young African American woman.[71] It is this photograph that seems to capture the essence of her domestic life, and she was not in it.

Eva McDonald Valesh and her son, Frank Morgan Valesh, in front of the AFL
offices, Washington, D.C., 1908. Although Valesh spent little time with her son, this
photograph reveals their affection for each other. Photo from *Human Work* (1908),
courtesy of the Library of Congress.

European tour: Eva Valesh, Blanche McDonald, and British labor leader John Burns. In Britain, Valesh poses with her sister and Burns, whose work she had written of with admiration throughout her career. Photo from *Human Work* (1908), courtesy of the Library of Congress.

Valesh's surviving private correspondence reveals the daily routine of this "new woman." She rose sometime between 10:30 a.m. and noon.[72] As she recalled, "I used to do my work at any hour I chose. I spent a great many evenings until midnight at home on magazine work and on confidential research for [Samuel Gompers]." When Gompers complained, she told him frankly that she'd resign if he mentioned it again.[73] Her rigidity extended to her relationship with her son. She would not see him except on planned visits from school, and once she sent him back angrily when he appeared one day uninvited. Frank spent summers in Graceville with his father, so that Valesh's time was relatively unencumbered with the need to look after her son, even on holiday. Despite being the eldest child, Eva Valesh appears to have had little contact with her remaining family. In contrast to her other siblings, she forged close ties to her younger sister Blanche, who resided in the household at various points. At age seventeen, Blanche accompanied Eva to New York during the early months of her separation and took care of young Frank.[74] Blanche also worked temporarily for Eva at the AFL and later at a magazine. Although she thought her sister "the most selfish and self-absorbed woman [she had] known,"[75] Blanche cooperated in Eva's ventures. In 1907, the sisters went together to Europe on an extended tour.[76]

One senses from Eva Valesh's life that she was difficult to know and hard to have as a sister, friend, or co-worker. A "thriftless person" by her own admission, Valesh depended on the speaking engagements and writing assignments to supplement her AFL salary. She had no compunction with charging expense bills to those who employed her services, even when it caused them inconvenience and provoked resentment.[77] Pleading that she needed money to entertain her son over the holidays, she pressured one friend to pay money owed. In 1907, she asked friends for the money to go to Europe again. She was, she admitted to National Civic Federation secretary Gertrude Beeks, "always hard up." She always asked for, and usually received, money for needs and expenses.[78]

During her time at the AFL, Valesh resolved the crisis of her marriage by finally divorcing Frank. Separated for nearly a decade, she returned in 1906 to file for divorce in Minnesota. The proceedings were brief and the divorce uncontested. Having accepted separation from Eva, Frank Valesh now accepted the legal responsibility for "deserting" her. The divorce complaint charged him with nonsupport, although those who knew the story probably felt the injustice of the charge. The state district court granted the divorce in 1907. After that time, Frank Valesh regularly paid child support and boarding-school tuition for his son. Until young Frank reached age twenty-one (he was fifteen when his parents were divorced), *Tribune* editor W. J. Murphy administered the stock trust set up for the boy's education and support. While he upbraided the father for insufficient payments and for spending money on extravagances for the boy, Murphy discharged his duties in a distant and businesslike manner.[79] For her part, Eva remained aloof.

Eva Valesh's life thus bore little resemblance to the lives of most women of her time. Neither married nor publicly a divorcee or spinster (she was always "Mrs. Valesh"), she became a member of the small minority who chose separation and divorce, career and work, over domestic life. Boarding schools for her son, domestic servants, meals at restaurants, and frequent travels relieved her of the responsibilities socially assigned to women. Any woman who wanted a career in the early twentieth century had to make similar compromises and arrangements. What strikes one forcibly is how her life increasingly resembled not the lives of women of the working class but of women from the upper middle and upper classes. It was among these women that Valesh increasingly found common cause and shared politics, as we shall see in the next chapter.

Eva Valesh had brought her skills and experience to the AFL in her decade of work there. Yet her assigned duties were almost always performed in the shadow of the great man, Samuel Gompers. As in the past, she sought an arena in which she had more control and more recognition. The door to greater involvement and responsibility was still ahead of her, but she would be entering it not as a trade unionist but as a workingwoman representing other women workers. It was not to the organization of women workers that she was called, but to the organization of their allies, patrons, and benefactors, and Gompers once again provided the key.

CHAPTER 8

"JOAN OF ARC OF THE WOMEN OF THE LABORING CLASSES"

Authentic Experience, Publicity, and Women's Cross-Class Alliances

> In the more colorful chapters of my life, it was always good to feel that I had a real trade to fall back on, and, when accused sometimes of being a working woman only in theory, I could point out that I was a member of one of the best paid and most skilled unions in the country.[1]
>
> —Eva McDonald Valesh, 1952

Throughout her life, Eva McDonald Valesh told the story of her life as "the daughter of a working man and as a working girl herself"—from printers' apprentice to a career in labor reform. Her claim that she was a union woman was at least as important as her class origins in receiving the sympathy and support of audiences. In capsule summaries of her life, offered on the Populist stump or in front of "the daughters of plenty," Valesh "spoke with the tongue of experience" about workingwomen. Just as the Pygmalion myth of her "discovery"[2] by the Knights of Labor masked her own ambitions, so, too, did her working-class origins obscure a career spent more on the podium and the newspaper office than in a workshop setting type.[3]

In 1908, journalist Ada Patterson vividly captured Eva Valesh's speech as "the daughter of toil" before the "gowned women" of the Colony Club in New York City. Among the silks and feathers, Eva's dress was a modest brown. It is doubtful, however, that her apparel was made of sackcloth. Valesh understood the importance of dressing at the level of one's audience. In her reminiscences, she recalled how she and Samuel Gompers's secretary persuaded him to wear a tuxedo to a social gathering.[4] Valesh herself liked to dress well. In matching her lifestyle to that of wealthy clubwomen and patrons, she openly sought their friendship and support in transforming women's working conditions. As she once proclaimed, "To have the wife . . . sister or daughter of the employer going into the factory or the shop and seeing for herself what the conditions are, and if they are not just what they should be, persuading the head of the firm to see that proper reforms are instituted . . . is one of the dreams I have longed cherished."[5] To do that, one needed not merely to dress like the elite but to learn their language, emulate their manners, and retain at the same time an "authentic" workingwoman's identity.[6]

The women of the Colony Club created the Women's Committee of the National Civic Federation and through it carried on welfare work in New York, Chicago, and Washington, D.C. In their concern for workingwomen and their coalition-building, they were joined by other elite and middle-class women in broad-based campaigns for social reform and suffrage. They redirected their energies to the educational, legislative, and organizing efforts of the Women's Trade Union League (WTUL) and later to the Democratic and Republican parties. Their commitment to cross-class alliances brought these women to focus on improving working conditions and mobilizing workingwomen in a range of causes. Valesh's story, therefore, involved the "wedlock of brains and work," as was once said of her, but also the marriage of true minds, the blend of silk and wool, and the search for legitimacy. In effect the search for a Progressive Era alliance among elite and working-class women was the result of the political reconfiguration. In her desire to mobilize and integrate these circles, Valesh helped pave the way for the new generation of women activists to enter the realm of welfare capitalism and party politics.

The Beast of Prey

At the turn of the century, political fissures between various elite and business groups and the continual instability of the trade-union movement provided the context for a unique coalition of emergent labor and corporate capital known as the National Civic Federation (NCF). Socialist leader Eugene Debs once described the NCF as "a beast of prey, which always tells its victims, 'our interests are one,' and then devours them,"[7] but conservative trade unionists like Gompers and John Mitchell saw it as a prime opportunity to legitimize labor as a political force. The pragmatic realities of a renewed employer offensive against labor, the structural limitations of American politics, and judicial obstacles to collective bargaining required that labor pursue a coalition with a sympathetic corporate elite. The alliance would help stabilize union ranks against incursions from the Left and Right and add to its political arsenal, while finance and monopoly capital gained insulation from the threat of socialist agitation and corporatist politics.[8]

The NCF was the brainchild of newspaperman Ralph Easley.[9] In founding its predecessor, the Civic Federation of Chicago, he had sought common ground between the respectable skilled workers and employers after the Pullman strike. By 1900, the idea of creating a national organization had supporters not only among business and trade-union groups but also among reformers known for their Progressive leanings. In alliance with such men as banker August Belmont, politician Marcus Hanna, and Gompers, Easley established the NCF to work for labor-management cooperation, improved welfare, and regulation of workplace conditions through private means.[10] For Gompers and Mitchell, unprecedented access to corporate offices and their support of labor in the legal and political arenas offered some hope of finally establishing trade-union legitimacy and of quelling dissent in their own party.[11] Under the NCF, the labor movement sought not only arbitration for labor disputes but also the righting of wrongs through such tools as reformed employer liability laws and workmen's compensation.

As a member of AFL staff, Valesh met Easley and Gertrude Beeks, the head of the NCF welfare department, in 1903. It was a friendship that opened doors for Valesh to a new network of organized elite women and introduced her to their political ambitions and activities. At first, she stepped in primarily as an occasional lecturer on contemporary labor issues. Welfare Department head Beeks coordinated Valesh's public addresses for the General Federation of Women's Clubs, a press club meeting, and a Pilgrim Mother's dinner. In return, Valesh proved willing to fulfill Beeks's requests and broaden the reach of NCF interests. By 1906, although Valesh was "rushed to death since we laborites have gone into politics," she remained "enthusiastic over the work" of the NCF. Small sums of money in terms of speaker's fees and expenses exchanged hands, and the familiarity with which Valesh asked for money or apologized for taking Beeks's taxicab spoke of a personal as well as a political alliance.[12]

Correspondence between Beeks and Valesh revealed a marked collegiality within the confines of their professional relationship. In familiar tones, Valesh occasionally confessed to being a "little short" or needing extra cash for her son's holiday visit or spoke about "thriftless people," a label she admitted applied to herself.[13] These letters provide glimpses of Valesh as a private person that are difficult to find anywhere else in her surviving correspondence. While this familiarity was tested by Valesh's lack of attention to accounts, she and Beeks formed a strong working relationship that reinforced the connection between the AFL and the NCF. By 1908, Valesh was actively involved in the movement of elite women into NCF's welfare work. As the women's interests moved, as historian Elizabeth Payne argues, "from charity to reform, from paupers to workers,"[14] Valesh became an important link between organized working-class women and upper-class women activists.

Madame Society

The NCF Woman's Committee had its genesis in the founding of the first woman's social club in New York, the Colony Club. At the turn of the century, when elite men were reentering the political fray, their female relatives participated in similar efforts. They transferred energies previously used for private and anonymous charity to activism in the public sphere. No longer satisfied with social engagements and aesthetic pursuits, elite women increasingly chose to become active politically. These efforts required an organizational base—a club or group that could raise money, consciousness, and supporters. What the women needed was a social club that paralleled the elite Metropolitan, Union League, and Century clubs for men.

The first public effort of such figures as Elisabeth "Bessie" Marbury, Florence "Daisy" Harriman, and Alva Belmont was to establish a women's club. In *From Pinafores to Politics*, Florence Harriman described efforts that "wedded the Newport gang together" to form a club. The network linked together both old and new money, both respectable and slightly scandalous. Despite being a theatrical agent, Marbury had little to fear socially. She was a descendent of the litigant in *Marbury v. Madison* and a childhood friend of Anne Morgan and Harriman. Her companion, interior designer Elsie de Wolfe, was readily accepted. Morgan was above reproach, as was Harriman. Belmont, a divorcee, had become a major force in the world of New York society.[15] From this nucleus, the Colony Club arose.

The idea to establish the Colony Club had been around since 1902, the same year the NCF was founded. Harriman reported that the club moved along quickly, as "Anne Morgan sent word she was keen, especially if we included a running track in our plans." The daughter of the banker J. P. Morgan, Anne had only recently become interested in activism on social issues. Her involvement in the Colony Club proved to be only one step toward a more public presence in philanthropy and reform. Once she joined, the club's organizing committee grew to forty women, all engaged in the effort to raise capital for the building. According to Harriman, Marbury "worked like a steam engine and brought all her business experience." The most important problem they faced was that liquor was "the keystone of men's club economics." They did not know if the club could survive without a liquor license, but their fears were unfounded. Club organizers commissioned popular architect Stanford White to design the building, and Elsie de Wolfe decorated the interior. The club opened in March 1907, and its membership reached more than two thousand by 1923.[16]

From the precincts of the Colony Club, the women of the elite classes could plan political coalitions and reform campaigns. Not surprisingly, given the history of women's clubs, their first efforts were specifically for public and self-education. John Mitchell, the president of the United Mine Workers, was a frequent guest, along with other trade unionists and reformers. It was this club that first invited Gertrude Beeks and then Eva Valesh to address them on the plight of workingwomen. Answering a request for more material on unemployment, Valesh sent along a copy of a statement on women's wages. She then wrote, "I am glad the women show a disposition to take up such matters as this, for it tends to ground them accurately in economics and will keep them from being led astray by fads and delusions."[17]

The connection between women of the elite and working classes *and* their alliance with the labor movement is important to understand for both its symbolic and pragmatic values. What elite women were looking for—and this was why Valesh became such a central figure on the NCF Women's Committee—was a political model. Ward organizations and working-class trade unions most closely resembled their efforts. They were not, after all, unfamiliar with politics. Marbury's father was a member of Tammany Hall; Ruth McCormick was the daughter of Marcus Hanna, President McKinley's closest advisor. They shared with settlement-house workers an understanding of politics rooted in friendship and patronage. The women of the NCF wanted a means of intervention into the political order of the day, to wield power for a social purpose but also to fit their own conceptions of the importance of merit or "social distinction" and loyalty.[18] In some ways, they sought to reinvigorate political organization along lines that permitted their participation.

In March 1908, Morgan asked Beeks to arrange for Valesh to speak to the Colony Club as a representative of "women in industry." Valesh was to discuss "the value of welfare work for girls in factories per your own experience." Before the Colony Club meeting, Valesh was to meet Morgan and other women she liked and admired in Morgan's home.[19] In particular, Valesh was drawn to Marbury, whose own reputation for activism preceded her. While Morgan was only just beginning to step into the public realm, Marbury had been quite at home there. "What Elisabeth Marbury didn't know about life," Valesh declared, "you didn't need to bother about."[20]

Apart from members of the Colony Club, the NCF woman's committee came to include elite women from New York, Chicago, and Washington, D.C.—the wives and daughters of industrialists, politicians, and financiers. Eventually, the committee membership included Maud Wetmore, the daughter of a senator, and McCormick.[21] "At close range they were no different from other women,"[22] Valesh remembered. In their company, she finally acquired something she had lacked throughout her career—a network of women patrons, whose friendship, influence, and wealth presented an attractive and powerful alternative to the male-dominated world of labor. The "friendship" of such women meant increased access to the political world as well as the resources to sustain Valesh and extend her public career outside the bureaucratic confines of the AFL.

As a woman expert in political economy, Valesh had knowledge and skills that elite women needed if they were to become active in reform. First and foremost, her talent for publicity and her firsthand experience as a workingwoman in organized labor placed her in demand. As Beeks instructed Valesh, she was to "explain the value of welfare work for girls in factories per your own experience" to women poorly educated in practical economy. Her ability to communicate new ideas to an audience and—in the way Jack McGaughey taught her—to combine social criticism with positive stories of political action made her invaluable. To women who did not "understand the difference between socialists and trade unionists,"[23] Valesh's presence was reassuring. An experienced labor leader, she represented an authentic voice from the working class. At the same time, she spoke to elite women in their own language, respected their station, and deferred to their status as workingwomen.[24] Her choice of topics from welfare work to equal wages for women caught their imagination and freed up their pocketbooks. Moreover, in ways that pleased both Valesh and the elite women with whom she worked, "the newspapers seem to be inclined to give the new departure the widest kind of advertising."[25]

The Government Treadmill

In the spring of 1908, the NCF Woman's Committee chose to focus on welfare work among federal employees. Labor had long placed the working conditions and hours of federal employees high on its agenda, but the NCF Woman's Committee had more than limits on hours in mind. It wanted to improve the government workplace and federal employee morale. Apart from its publicity value, government employment was one arena in which the uses of state power were not contested. It offered one setting in which private individuals might intervene politically and gain access to federal agencies as well as encroach on the patronage system. NCF women could thus mediate between employer and worker in workplaces insulated from the market economy in which both men and women of the NCF had vested interests. Finally, welfare work among government employees was an extension of the traditions of paternalist reform.

The focus of NCF women on improving the conditions of government employees led to investigations of federal departments and agencies by committees of women in the New York and Washington, D.C., branches.[26] In general, such efforts garnered publicity for the NCF and for Morgan in particular. Whenever she visited the Brooklyn Navy Shipyard or had tea with the street-car men in New York, coverage of her meetings with workingmen hit the front page of the *Washington Post*. The *National Civic Federation Review* devoted long articles to the positive effects of such welfare work.[27] "Jeers Turned to Cheers" was the theme of articles describing how "Madame Society" met with the sons and daughters of toil.

In March 1909, the grievances of women workers at the Bureau of Printing and Engraving came to Morgan's attention. As Valesh recalled years later, she contacted the women as a favor to Morgan, who was interested in their plight. Valesh already had experience with the bureau. In 1904, Gompers had asked her to substitute for him and speak before its employees.[28] Four years later, Louise Dangler, one of the bureau's employees, approached Valesh as an AFL general organizer about organizing her co-workers. While the NCF Woman's Committee was engaged in establishing lunchrooms for government shipyard workers, there was a group of young women employed in the government's printing office who wanted the NCF's assistance in improving working conditions. It was a situation well-suited to the welfare-work campaign, and Valesh again provided the bridge between labor and the NCF.

About one thousand women worked in the bureau, many of them sheet feeders to the big presses or in the bookbindery. The women were not direct government employees. As printers' helpers, they received only twenty-five cents of their pay from the government treasury. Plate printers paid the remainder. Not coincidentally, many women working at the bureau were wives, sisters, and daughters of the printing men.[29] Still, as Valesh recalled, "abuses had crept in. These girls couldn't transfer to any other government department. There was nothing for them. Someone—not I—began to talk unionism to them."[30]

At an open meeting that Valesh arranged at the public library, two hundred women from the bureau gave an enthusiastic reception to a series of speakers from the NCF and a women's bookbinders' union. Valesh recalled that "The girls kept popping up spontaneously. Anne Morgan said she had never seen any thing like it. Girl after girl would jump up and say, 'This is what they did to me. Can we have a union?' "[31] In presenting their grievances, the women argued that "no young woman should be obligated in a sense to a male employe for the larger part of her earnings." They sought more formal employment status within the government. They had other issues as well—the lack of dining facilities, the failure to provide either aprons to protect clothing from press ink and oil or locker rooms for changing into work clothes, the absence of sick leave, and the discrepancy between men's and women's pay.[32]

At the meeting that evening, the NCF women took the stage. Marbury, an impresario with a flamboyant style, was the major speaker. Talking on "Organization the Remedy," she declared, "While I am not what you might call a working woman, belong to no union, and know but little about bookbinding, I work from twelve to sixteen hours a day and regard myself a producer." From this authority, Marbury spoke of the accomplishments of women and the continual need for their organization in society. According to the *Washington Post*, she offered "a deep and knowing insight into feminine character and conditions obtaining among the laboring classes. [Her speech] was filled with interesting statistics complimentary to the weaker sex, and real witticism, which provoked many peals of laughter."[33] At a time when the woman suffrage movement was gathering momentum, Marbury could not avoid the subject of suffrage. "There is some agitation going on about the question of woman's right to vote," she declared, "but the right to work is of far greater importance. The will to work and the wish to organize is women's best equipment. . . . Be producers, breadwinners, workers whether you are married or single. Keep up your union."[34]

The efforts of Morgan, Marbury, and Valesh struck a crucial chord with the women employed. Even among African Americans in the bureau, there was hope that the campaign would succeed. At the same time that the bureau's white women organized, more than one hundred African-American workingwomen met at African Methodist Episcopal Church to discuss forming a union of their own.[35] With AFL support, they could significantly improve their working conditions. Unfortunately, the union drive ran into obstacles.

The publicity generated by the drive to organize workingwomen in the Bureau of Printing brought to the surface resentment that they were already paid better than most workingwomen. The bureau director announced to the newspapers that "the present pay is higher than the average paid women in department stores and manufacturing concerns and with efficiency there is an excellent chance for promotion. When both sides of this salary question are looked into, it is plain that the women workers in the bureau are well off." Adding to the charges, reporters publicized the willingness of other women to take their places, should the agitation continue. The *Washington Post* declared that "many women and girls not now in government employ are fostering the hope that there may be vacancies in the money mill by the malcontents resigning or otherwise leaving the service." The paper reported that a record number of women and girls were taking the civil service exams as a result. Labor unions, the *Post* insisted, were not appropriate or desirable in government employment.[36] The union drive to organize the women thus met both opposition to a proposed pay increase and administrative constraints. No pay raise could be forthcoming, the director informed the press, because Congress had not appropriated the money. While the women might form a "fair invasion" of Capitol Hill to lobby for a change in the pay structure, it was a legislative imperative and not within the power of his office.[37]

The personal foibles and follies of bureau employees were on daily parade in the newspapers. Married to a bureau woman, Alfred G. Masius, a hapless young statistician for the Department of Agriculture, took poison after his wife sought to keep their marriage secret in order to protect her job. He swallowed bi-chloride of mercury tablets in front of her co-workers but survived. His wife, Josephine Harwood, refused to talk to reporters. Another bureau employee, C. A. Hall, saw his divorce from his wife, Emma, headlined in the *Post*. "Addicted to liquor" and madly adulterous, Emma Hall seemed less an aberration from the morally uplifted bureau employees and more a case in point about the "unwholesome conditions" in the government printing office.[38]

During the first public meeting of women in the bookbindery, one speaker, Mrs. Hopkins, referred to the "unwholesome conditions" of the government workplace. She told the women gathered that night that "if the working girl shows plainly that she will brook no familiarity from men, they will soon desist. The Civic Federation or no other organization cannot assist you unless you do this."[39] Buried in an article that highlighted the inspirational words of Marbury, the remark went virtually unnoticed. After a month of activism among the women, and the refusal of Congress either to increase women's pay or make them direct employees, the campaign's focus had shifted to issues that could be more easily remedied—a lunchroom for workingwomen, aprons to keep their garments from being soiled, and moral uplift through contact with society's best. Yet, while Emily Tuckerman, a young socialite in Washington circles, began to plan for fortnightly teas with the bureau women, a Washington dispatch in the *New York Tribune* reported that investigations at the Printing Bureau examined more than working conditions. Reportedly, the women workers were the target of a morals charge stemming from the promiscuous social arrangements of the workplace.[40]

The news report was something of an embarrassment to Valesh, a careful publicist and union representative. She worked to try to correct the problem by intervening on both sides. In a newspaper interview, Valesh insisted that "such a statement is an insult to every woman employed in the bureau. No matter how definite the denial, the gossip started by such a statement will persist, and every girl who leaves the bureau for any reason will be branded by some people as 'discharged for immorality.'" She described the bookbinders as "a remarkably fine lot of women, bright, well mannered, upright in conduct, and many of them devout church members." For all the talk of immorality, Valesh added, she thought it would be difficult to find "several hundred women in any walk of life where the average of morality and genuine good conduct would be any righter than among these women."[41]

In a letter to Valesh, NCF head Ralph Easley called the conflict a "tempest in a teapot." In a more hopeful vein, she replied that "the girls said the Civic Federation ladies were lovely to them, and I hear equally nice things about the girls from the other side." She also confided that she knew where the article had originated and "underst[ood] that the present moral standard of the [newspaper] manager in question would furnish more salacious reading than anything that ever happened in a government department."[42] In any case, the NCF women's interventions in the bookbindery rapidly came to an end. Their short-lived campaign to improve the working conditions of women in government employment served only as a preface for a more widespread campaign. Diverting attention away from the realm of government employees, the NCF women began to focus on general welfare work among private employers, especially, as we shall see, in New York's garment trade.

Shortly after Samuel Gompers returned from Europe in November 1909, Valesh quietly exited the Washington office of the AFL. According to the financial statements, that was the last month she was paid as a member of the AFL staff. The reasons and time of her leaving were unclear. As she recalled, "I never did have my name on the official magazine as managing editor, and I never thought about it until I knew Anne Morgan." It was Morgan who first asked her why her name was not on the *American Federationist*. Valesh's work with the NCF women had provided her with a new understanding of her role in the AFL and the possibility of leaving. Finally, Valesh confronted Gompers about the issue. He simply asserted that the magazine was his "personal organ" that represented him in the AFL; he could not put her name on it. While Valesh "kept [her] peace," she "couldn't have imagined that he would take [her] ideas, use them and not even give [her] credit on the magazine." It was not, she admitted, "part of his streak of greatness" to recognize her efforts. When Valesh resigned, she lashed out at Gompers, "The truth is I'm tired of your picking my brains and not giving me any credit." Despite her anger, Valesh's leave-taking was ambiguous. Gompers could not tell someone who inquired whether or not she was on a leave of absence. The coolness of his subsequent letters to her suggests that her departure caused friction, and Gompers probably took her resignation as a personal betrayal. Valesh seems to have borne no ill will toward him and continued to write intermittently for years. Gompers remained cordial in response to Valesh's letters but never reengaged the friendship.[43]

Sleek Go-Betweens, Smooth-Tongued Spiders, and the Temptress Eve

That fall, as Valesh departed from the AFL, the broad-based labor militancy called "the New Unionism" sparked new life into organizing drives in the garment industry. In New York, a series of shop strikes eventually culminated in the walkout of 30,000 shirtwaist-makers. After a short and successful garment strike that summer, workers in the Leiserson shirtwaist shop walked out in September. Within weeks, the Triangle Shirtwaist Company locked out its workers to try to stave off union demands and sparked another strike. Striking workers refused to return to work, and the strikes dragged on through the fall. On the picket lines, strikers faced company thugs and the city police as violence escalated. When the union, Local 25 of the International Ladies Garment Workers Union, sought the aid of the WTUL, the mainstream press began to pay attention to the strike. Following the arrest of hundreds of striking workers and their public supporters, thousands of shirtwaist-makers in New York exhibited growing interest in striking the entire industry. Publicity, both positive and negative, stirred the political imaginations of women workers in particular, who came to see the possibilities of going on strike and winning better conditions.[44]

On November 22, at a now-famous Coopers' Union meeting, garment worker Clara Lemlich took the stage to argue for a general strike of the industry. With this call for action, the massive walkout began. The next morning, more than 30,000 shirtwaist-makers were on strike, hitting more than 300 shops in the industry. Within a few days, 100 small shops settled with the union and reopened their doors, and 10,000 strikers returned to work. During the next eleven weeks, the remaining shops held out against the demands of striking workers. Caught in the bind between oppressive workplace conditions and their own new sense of collective solidarity, the shirtwaist strikers refused to concede their demands. While each shop filed separate grievances, the strike in general focused on shortening the workweek to fifty-two hours, improving working conditions, raising piecework rates, and abolishing fines. Another demand was to improve the treatment of women in the shops.[45]

The garment strike brought into sharp focus the poverty, danger, and powerlessness of the urban working classes and their intent to alter their conditions through collective action. By December, a vast array of social and political organizations publicly supported the strikers, including their union, the WTUL, the AFL, and the NCF Women's Committee. Set in the context of widespread socialist agitation, burgeoning suffrage activism, and labor unrest on a massive scale, the strike mobilized men and women from across the class spectrum in a new progressive alliance. Focused on the passage of protective labor legislation, social insurance, and woman suffrage, this social ferment provided the context for Valesh to emerge as a champion of the elite women who sought to acquire power and influence during the labor crisis.

When Valesh arrived in New York during the uprising, the WTUL viewed her appearance on the scene as a sign that the AFL was willing to back the strike with their considerable clout.[46] Valesh's friend Anne Morgan called on her to join the strike effort. When Valesh did offer her services to the WTUL, she found herself in the company of friends from the women's club movement and the NCF. Once on board, Valesh was put in charge of pickets and later served on the legal and publicity committees.[47] It was in the last role she proved most valuable. Public opinion was crucial to the strike, because women in competitive secondary industries like garment manufacture had little leverage in individual shops. The publicity generated by Valesh served to bolster not only the claims of the workingwomen but also their leverage against employers in marshaling public opinion to their side. Once stories of police brutality and harassment of workingwomen surfaced, elite women chose to intervene between pickets and the authorities. When police brought in prostitutes and strikebreakers to provoke strikers and rationalize their arrest, the society women publicly protested to the mayor and the newspapers.[48]

The New York Branch of the WTUL coordinated these efforts. WTUL allies brought to the strike the capacity to translate specific grievances into general condemnation of the role of employers in impoverishing and endangering workingwomen. Much like the earlier strikes that Valesh covered as a labor journalist, the shirtwaist strike aroused significant public support, because it spoke to the common welfare—public health, police harassment, poverty, and women's particular vulnerability in the workplace. The strategy proved effective for the WTUL, as it had for the NCF, in such campaigns as the Kalamazoo corsetmakers strike and the Chicago garment strikes.[49] Publicity—and the role of Valesh in the strike was crucial here—was the primary way not simply to air the "facts" of the strike but to communicate to the public the appropriate interpretation of words and actions. In this sense, the WTUL, like the NCF, was engaged in publicity as politics. As national WTUL president Margaret Dreier Robins claimed, "Securing publicity has always been the one great service we [the WTUL] have been able to render—presenting the facts to the public."[50]

That the strike depended on these publicity efforts was seen in the response of both workers and public to the strike call in November 1909. As Helen Marot reported, the arrest of pickets, including that of New York state WTUL president Mary Dreier, broadcast the struggle to workers of New York's garment shops. In the ten days that followed Dreier's arrest, the newspapers reported all facets of the strike, focusing on the treatment of the strikers. The union capitalized on the situation. As Marot wrote, "It knew the temper of the workers and pushed the story still further through shop propaganda. After three weeks of newspaper publicity and shop propaganda the reports came back to the union that the workers were aroused."[51] The role of publicity in spreading word of the strike and in organizing workers was now followed by a campaign to arouse public support for the strikers and refute newspaper accounts that threatened to undermine the strike.[52]

In her initial work on the strike, Valesh helped to organize the volunteer brigade of elite women picket-watchers to stave off unwarranted arrests. Speaking before such groups as the Civic Forum of New York and to newspaper reporters, many of whom knew her from her work, Valesh made sure the strike was covered. As WTUL leaders later remarked, the newspaper coverage of the strike highlighted her as an unofficial spokeswoman. Time and again, when journalists reported on the welfare of strikers or the possibilities that the strike would be settled, they quoted—and therefore had asked—Valesh.[53] While Valesh's proud claim always to "get good coverage" was proved again, her connections to the press and the elite women of the NCF cast suspicion on her intentions. Her membership in the WTUL was not even confirmed until February, and she had an uncertain relationship to the AFL. Her autonomy made it difficult for the WTUL to hold her accountable. Furthermore, Valesh's entrepreneurial instincts had given her the confidence to act as a mediator or cultural broker. Acting as a "go-between" was precisely the charge that Socialists like Theresa Serber Malkiel, author of *Diary of a Shirt Waist Striker*, and WTUL leaders later made against Valesh.[54]

By January 1910, Valesh's activities had raised the ire of many WTUL allies and leaders with a public statement that condemned the socialist influence in the strike. At that point, the garment union had rejected an informal offer to settle from the Shirtwaist Manufacturers Association. Negotiated by AFL president Samuel Gompers and the miners' John Mitchell, the settlement conceded several of the strikers' demands but refused union recognition. State arbitration also failed.[55] Incredulous that the offer was rejected, Valesh attacked the union in front of a Civic Forum audience. She charged that the Socialists in the union and the WTUL were using the shirtwaist strikers for their own "dangerous purposes." As Valesh claimed, it was the union men, who far outnumbered women on the strike committee but not among the strikers, who turned down the mediated settlement. They were "ignorant of what the girls want." Furthermore, she said that "those girl strikers are actually grateful to the men who are using them for their own purposes." In response, Valesh announced, she was beginning a "campaign against socialism." The *New York Tribune*, which reported the meeting, claimed that Valesh charged that socialism only made "ignorant foreigners discontented, set them against the government, [made] them want to tear it down."[56] The incident served as a catalyst to the breakdown of relations between Valesh and the WTUL. Valesh's offhand comments, as a former compatriot in Gompers's anti-Socialist campaign, were seen as a fundamental betrayal.

After the Civic Forum meeting, the New York WTUL was in a quandary about how to proceed with Valesh. Dreier had warned Valesh even then that it was impossible for her to work with the WTUL. More immediately, the WTUL had an invitation from her—and from Gompers—to attend a meeting about how the AFL might aid the WTUL in organizing the shirtwaist industry. According to Robins, Gompers "deplored" Valesh's statement but would not reveal if she was still connected to the AFL. He asked Robins to attend a meeting with Morgan, Marbury, Belmont, Ida Tarbell, and Valesh to try to find constructive means to deal with the waning strike effort. His effort seems to have been in vain.[57]

While Raymond Robins congratulated his sister-in-law Dreier on the "victory over the Valesh cabal," the WTUL still lacked an appropriate, agreed-on response to what most perceived as Valesh's treason. "What an Old Pup the Hon. Samuel Gompers really is," exclaimed Robins. Like his wife, Margaret Robins, and her sister, he saw the situation fraught with risks for the WTUL, but he also wished that such "ill-tempered and low natured people [Gompers and the Socialists] scrap among themselves." It was better to ignore Valesh than to give her publicity. By mid-February, Dreier reported that the New York WTUL wanted to formally expel Valesh. Despite Dreier's arguments that the New York WTUL "would be playing into [Valesh's] hands," Executive Board members' outrage at her actions dictated a firmer response.[58]

In her fictionalized account of the strike, *Diary of a Shirt Waist Striker*, Malkiel wrote of Valesh: "These curses ain't strong enough for her that's mixing in our affairs. I've come to realize that there ain't no worse plague than a false labor leader. . . . She ain't satisfied with arranging all these tom fool conferences—nay, she must needs give out false reports to the newspapers." Condemning the fictional double of Valesh as "a sleek temptress" and an "Eve,"[59] Malkiel's injunction fit with larger cultural prejudices against women speaking in public, especially on political matters and in front of mixed audiences. Women were not supposed to speak in public places; such an act revealed their private selves to a public audience. Even in the twentieth century, a woman speaking in public in many ways continued to be an act of transgression, a boundary breaking, a dislocation of the private into the public. Women's public speeches were often heard as hissing, gossip, entrapment, treachery, and subversion. Their voices were thought to be not human voices engaged in moral public speech and affirmation of self in the polis but slippery and cacophonous.

Even the use of the word *go-between* to describe Valesh called up images of Satan, Lilith, and those who do not possess either one state or the other but constantly transgress states of being, slithering between the two. It was a caricature of the socially mobile. As an upwardly mobile daughter of the working class, Valesh was a go-between across the class divide—between workers and employers, elite and working-class women, labor and capital, those who wrote and led and those who read and followed. "Go-between," however, is the name not only of those who exchange messages or favors between two parties, often under cover of darkness and secrecy. It is also the role of peacemaker, of mediator, of broker. Those who "go between" can go between states and identities, much as Valesh did, in her sometimes heroic and sometimes opportunistic career. In all of her life, she became what we can only describe as "transclass" and perhaps even "transgender," in the sense of enlarging her role as woman and taking on the responsibilities and perspectives traditionally given over to men.

The remarks of Malkiel, a Socialist, were not far removed from the way in which WTUL women increasingly characterized Valesh. Her "betrayal and disloyalty" were, after all, the chief charges against her as the WTUL moved to extricate itself from depending on her skills as publicist. As Valesh had learned, publicity did not always bring good news to public attention. An earlier fiasco over the conservative antisuffragism of the NCF Women's Committee had given her a taste of how publicity could backfire. In a letter at the time, Valesh cautioned the NCF to the limited use of such publicity. "I am not so enthusiastic about press work," she wrote, "for I realize the danger of making a mistake or being misrepresented and perhaps causing vexation when only helpfulness was intended, however, I'll do the best I can." "The yellow journals," she wrote, "will twist an expression of individual opinion into something official."[60] Damning statements of her own reinforced Valesh's practical knowledge that the press knew how to elicit misstatements or simply invent their own. As she protested to Helen Marot, she did not know "any way of escaping inaccurate reports in the newspapers. Everybody in public life suffers from it more or less."[61]

In her own defense, Valesh insisted that she had been misquoted and acted with wounded pride to the WTUL effort to expel her. As she wrote Dreier, "You are of course quite at liberty to decline or accept whatever character of assistance you choose in the work of organizing, and I am equally free to do my work without reference to your organization, since my services have been declined by you." After demanding proof of what she said at the Civic Forum, Valesh returned, "What I did do was to point out the harm done by the Socialistic influences which were using both your organization and other forces in the effort to spread socialistic propaganda and prevent an honorable settlement of the strike." Claiming that she was defending the WTUL, Valesh then stood on her "twenty years' service in the trade union movement" as a measure of her character. Dreier complied with Valesh's request for a transcript of the *New York Tribune* article, which only angered Valesh further. The incident escalated with countercharges and the request that Valesh appear before the WTUL Executive Board.[62]

As the controversy grew, Valesh seemed to want the crisis to end as much as WTUL leaders Robins and Dreier. In mid-April, Valesh resigned from the WTUL, but her subsequent letters continued to battle on. The New York WTUL's Executive Board wanted their hearing on the matter, in part as a pledge of faith to the working-class members who saw Valesh's behavior in a far more serious light than did their upper-class allies. The hearing reiterated charges of falsehood and disloyalty that had surfaced during the Civic Forum meeting. They declared that Valesh was "no true trade unionist." Her statements, members declared, were "calculated or devised" to "mislead and confuse." Furthermore, in the "cunningly devised" report of the strike in her syndicated newsletter, Valesh had "suppressed all mention of the help and support of the WTUL." The Executive Board, with two exceptions, voted to sustain the charges and expel Valesh from membership.[63]

By the time of the shirtwaist-makers' strike, Valesh was no longer an inexperienced publicist. Both Raymond and Margaret Robins were right that Valesh could use for her own purposes reports of the WTUL Executive Board's decision to expel her. The trouble was that the WTUL board members wanted to use the press as much, if not more, than Valesh did to promote both the WTUL and their individual efforts at social reform and uplift. There was no innocence on either side. In the end, the WTUL Executive Board succeeded in expelling its most reluctant and troublesome member.

Crossing the Bar between the Classes

A theme that runs through the conflict between Valesh and her WTUL allies is that of class and its definition. In some ways, it was not surprising that Valesh was more comfortable with Morgan and Marbury, who were secure in their class position, than she was with the WTUL, which encompassed both middle- and upper-class women on the make. The class differences between Valesh and her NCF allies were greater than with those between Valesh and middle-class women reformers, but her social place among elite women was at least well-defined. In subsequent years, she maintained friendships with Morgan, Marbury, and other clubwomen, owing partly to common interests in reform and partly because Valesh was to marry a man of their class. At the same time, their political connection begs the question, What political purposes bound together the daughters of bankers with the daughter of a workingman?

Let us begin with what had been called "social distinction" and what we call "class." The former term connotes something more complex than a position in a rigid social hierarchy and encompasses the shadings and gradations of status as well as money and power. "Social distinction" provides, in effect, a more finely tuned concept of how class difference is constructed and understood. The concept also implicitly associates class identity and class attribution with public performance and civic attachment. May King Van Rensselaer devoted a chapter of *The Social Ladder* to discussing the breakdown of old distinctions and their resurrection in elite society. Formerly rooted in property, family, and lineage, social distinction by the late nineteenth century had evolved to where artistic talent, political savvy, and, most of all, money transformed society and made possible the mingling of old and new families. Van Rensselaer thus described the families who invaded New York society in the 1870s—the nouveau riche of finance and transport—as "bouncers." They broke through the insulated world of Knickerbocker society, she wrote, through "counter-attraction." The newcomers were not allowed into the charmed circle of the New York elite until old monied families like the Astors grew afraid that their daughters or sons would be excluded from the new social world. It was Alva Vanderbilt's costume ball (nicknamed "the Bouncers Ball") that opened the doors of New York society to the fortune-laden interlopers. Vanderbilt created and generously shared among her elite friends the social resources—that is, education, networks, and social gatherings—that even old money envied.

If social distinction can describe the gradations of social status and public influence among the upper classes, it is even more important in tracing the changes in working-class communities and politics over the same period of time. The career of Eva McDonald Valesh has helped us to understand the importance of publicity in generating support for labor protests and political campaigns over the two decades between 1888 and 1910. Her livelihood and popularity as a labor speaker and journalist certainly depended on publicity as it supported labor's cause but also as it helped to generate new and greater sources of income. Publicizing the Farmers' Alliance, the eight-hour campaigns, and the just grievances of strikers in many far-flung battles also advertised her own success, reputation, and ability. Having risen, as she liked to remind audiences, from the printing press to the podium, she could help the labor movement collectively and workers individually to see and achieve a different future. Making labor's politics visible, Valesh had earned a certain status in labor movement politics—a world to which elite women now sought access.

In defining social distinction, Van Rensselaer described the importance of publicity in changing perceptions of class. She declaimed that "society once connoted first of all family; its primary meaning at present is fortune. Years ago, it also stood for breeding; now it represents, instead, self-advertisement."[64] That advertisement began as who gave the largest and most elaborate balls and ended with attention to their public "good works." While Van Rensselaer viewed this change as inevitable, she still retained the memory of distinctions that restrained social and political mingling. By the turn of the century, while Knickerbocker families still remembered who belonged to Old New York, the elite cheerfully intermarried, and the Harrimans, the Vanderbilts, and the Belmonts were now the old families. They, too, married only within the circle of wealthy families, educated their children in the best schools, belonged to the right clubs, and participated in the correct social causes. In the new social world, they required the services of publicists, advertising agents, and news reporters. And it was these skills that Valesh possessed in abundance.

But if the memory of transitional social status could haunt the accomplished upper classes, how much more so was it likely that the origins of Valesh, the daughter of a workingman, would be remembered and her difference attributed to humble origins? In her autobiography, Marbury wrote that she had "always maintained that to climb socially is legitimate, provided that in the struggle the machinery does not creak too loudly."[65] In an age that valued money above family, it still remained difficult to move between classes and among the elite groups. Coming from the wrong place could never be overcome. As for social distinction based on good works, Marbury wrote, "Social reform is rapidly developing into a fine art. It has created a new industry, hence a new channel of employment. It provides more salaried positions for mediocre minds than can be found in any other walk of life."[66] In her pursuit of a career in the realm of reform, Valesh broke the rules and made noise climbing the rungs.

"Working" Women and Workingwomen

For all the noise, there were effectively three reasons why the relationship between Valesh and the elite women of Morgan's circle worked to create alliances
despite conflicting personalities and agendas. First and ironically, Valesh's
origins mattered in another way to "the Mink Brigade" that supported the
shirtwaist-makers' strike. She was an authentic "working-class woman." Second,
she had education and knowledge of social conditions and publicity that they did
not have and could not easily obtain. Finally, elite women in the period increasingly came to view themselves, as historian Ellen Du Bois has argued, as workingwomen. In "Organization the Remedy," Marbury wrote that the right to work
was more important than suffrage and advocated self-support and independence
for all women. When Valesh spoke at length to the NCF women on the pay and
working conditions of workingwomen, her topic was one that they had chosen.
Born into the upper class and thereby having no need for wage work, NCF
women nonetheless believed that they, too, were workingwomen.[67] They came
to celebrate the autonomy that they now had in political work.

In her autobiography, *My Crystal Ball*, NCF member Marbury celebrated
independence and work as that which separated the "builders" from idle "mas-
ters" and "molluscs." She stressed the importance of "the independent bank
account" as an important "anchor to windward" for women. Her speech before the Bureau of Printing women resonated with praise for work, self-
reliance, and equality rooted in not the political but the economic sphere. And
yet, like the trade-union rhetoric they emulated, the NCF women in their public speeches and writings oscillated between the rights of women to work and
compelling social arguments that women remain domestic. So it was that
Marbury in her autobiography sought to explain why she remained single: "I
never really had a good offer. The best was but anemic. I attracted all the lame
ducks that were limping about; I was the magnetic lodestar of the weaklings."
If she had "escaped a fate worse than single blessedness," she still publicly argued that woman should marry as "the end for which God intended her."[68]
Marbury's affirmation of married life thus coexisted with her affirmation of
both work and her lifelong relationship with Elsie de Wolfe, in whom she
found "the relation of sister and companion."[69] In no way did Marbury admit
or explore the contradictions. Independence, she implied, could and must un-
derwrite women's private lives, too.

Suffice to say, Valesh was a self-supporting career woman, as were Marbury
and women political activists in the settlement houses, the WTUL, the National Consumers' League, the National American Woman Suffrage Associa-

tion, and the General Federation of Women's Clubs.[70] Their battle to participate in work was waged against continuing public opposition to women working even as citizenship—for the corporate elite, the middle class, and the trade
union—was economic engagement, whether in wage labor, salaried and commissioned work, or investment. In a context that revalued citizenship and re-
oriented it toward wage work, it is thus little wonder that women labor reformers were obsessed with obtaining certain forms of political and industrial
citizenship. The way to women's equality was through self-support, economic
as well as political.

Whatever the political fate of Eva McDonald Valesh, she was not unlike the
women of the WTUL and the Socialist party with whom she tangled in the
course of the uprising. She shared the experience of upward mobility within
the political Left with Socialist trade unionists like Malkiel, Pauline Newman,
and Rose Schneiderman and the instinct toward the protection of workingwomen expressed by the WTUL and the wealthy women of the NCF. Unlike
them, however, Valesh believed that as the "authentic voice" of workingwomen,
she could single-handedly create an alliance by going between women's paternalist politics and the working class. Despite her efforts to maintain the balance between her identities, Valesh would find herself, after a second marriage,
a workingwoman again and a private individual, desperate to maintain a life of
respectability and culture in moderate circumstances.

PROOFING THE TRUTH

Eva Valesh's Life and Labor

> I should mention in discussing my philosophy of life that I never save any money and never expect to. My tastes for expensive things in the way of artistic surroundings and pretty gowns always absorb what I earn, and then I feel dreadfully poor because there are so many beautiful things in the world that I shall never be able to get.
>
> —Eva McDonald Valesh, *Human Life*, December 1908

For more than twenty years, Eva McDonald Valesh was a committed trade unionist and labor journalist. In the wake of the WTUL debacle, however, she looked for new avenues of endeavor. Returning to Minneapolis, she spoke to a reporter of having "arrived in New York at the psychological moment" during the shirtwaist strike the year before. Since that time, she claimed, she had been "besieged by women of leisure and wealth who wanted to know what they could do to help working women." Invitations to lecture before women's club audiences followed. Turning away from "self-culture" and toward the study of "civic and industrial matters," clubwomen now sought to examine "the problems of working women," and Valesh became their labor expert.[1]

Valesh's friend Anne Morgan urged her to take up the investigation of abuses in the trades. While, as she recalled, "back in my mind I had had an idea that I would attach myself to one of those projects,"[2] personal life intervened. Within six months, sometime in 1910, she married Captain Benjamin Franklin Cross, a broker on the cotton exchange and the playboy son of a wealthy Rhode Island family. She was forty-four, and he forty-two. As she recounted, "Captain Cross was of a very alert and worldly disposition. He lived a colorful life and was very fond of gaiety and excitement."[3] While Eva enjoyed parties and receptions, her own mind and heart were bent on "constructive work." She disliked being dragged to nightclubs. Their marriage provided new opportunities for publicity but also meant that she had to keep on "good terms with his family," to keep from having to worry about money.[4] Cross had little money of his own to spend.

For nearly fifteen years, the oddly matched couple—the daughter of a workingman and the playboy even more thriftless than herself—made their life together. They established a women's magazine, funded by the Cross family, and organized the War Children's Relief Fund. They spent his mother's money, bought a farm in upstate New York, and became modern-day patrons, setting up a community center on the property. In these years Eva learned to play the role of the lady, and she earned a kind of grudging affection from her neighbors. Her lifestyle, however, was dependent on a husband with whom she shared few intellectual interests and family money to which she had no legal right.

"Idleness Didn't Agree with Me"

As Valesh discovered, the problem with becoming a lady of leisure was that she hated to be idle. Although she once told reporter Ada Patterson that she believed "a continual rush of work keeps one from absorbing the lessons of life in their proper proportion," she had trouble taking time off. She had "tantalizing visions of the things [she] might learn and enjoy," if she had leisure, but her own history provided contradictory evidence. As Patterson wrote, "A persistent and prodigious worker, Mrs. Valesh has had but three vacations in the twenty years of her career." She listened to a little music every day and read a little "in some language other than [her] own, preferably French." None of this suggests that Valesh could settle into the leisure class easily or permanently.[5]

Bored with the lack of steady occupation, Valesh sought out new work. From her days on the *Journal*, she had retained the friendships of the clubwomen with whom she had worked. It was these women to whom she addressed her next project. She had wanted, she testified in her oral history, to work in a suffrage campaign; and she became a member of Alma Belmont's Political Equality League. Cross's family, however, were conservatives who disdained the woman suffrage movement. In order to keep from alienating her in-laws, Valesh put most of her energy into creating a journal, *American Club Woman*, which reconnected her with the work of publicity. She hoped to tap into support from the General Federation of Women's Clubs, one of the largest women's organizations of the Progres-

The journalist as clubwoman: Eva McDonald Valesh in her fifties, ca. 1920s. Although she had little use for a life of leisure, Valesh posed as a clubwoman from time to time. This is probably a publicity photograph for women's club lectures. Photo courtesy of Dolores Lautman.

sive Era, which had just begun to support woman suffrage and engaged in a range of reform issues.[6]

American Club Woman published its first issue in December 1911.[7] As edited by Valesh, the journal had a decade-long history of representing the chief concerns of clubwomen's civic work in the United States. Its mission statement expressed the hope that the journal would be a "free forum for impartial consideration of broad and vital issues." In this role, the journal would "tell the story of the cleaning up of cities, placing children in proper schools, establishing juvenile courts, securing better conditions for working girls, and a score of other notable achievements." The dream that inspired the journal was to provide "a common meeting ground where the working woman and the woman of leisure may find out how they can be helpful to the other, where the club woman and the home woman may talk things over with the woman of affairs."[8] The editorials that followed often opened the door for debate, but the magazine was, much as Valesh had hoped, a neutral meeting place. Her editorial opinions, if anything, echoed sentiments familiar to her clubwomen readership.

As a business, the journal had less success than it might have had. Serving as business manager, Frank Cross cared little for the enterprise's profit margin. As he said, "We spent fifty thousand dollars of Mother Cross's money, but we stepped high, wide and handsome."[9] Within five years of its founding, some 150,000 women subscribed to the journal.[10] While the figure was respectable, the readership was not large enough for the journal to really succeed. The problem lie in the magazine's audience. Designed for wealthier women, it had a price tag to match and limited the number of advertisers. As Valesh later recalled, "We had a national circulation, but it was not as large as we would have liked to have had. It's too expensive to get circulation. We were not on the news stands. That's where we made a mistake."[11]

The major success of the *American Club Woman* was in its advocacy of issues, not its bottom line. Valesh nurtured along a fire-prevention effort, wrote on the Triangle Shirtwaist Company fire, pushed pure food efforts, investigated morality campaigns, and dealt with the niceties of club meetings and dress reform. Before World War I broke out, she echoed the wavering pacifism of the conservative women who read the journal. When war was imminent, Valesh became a profound patriot who spoke repeatedly on Americanization and the war effort. Her pride, though, was in her two great victories while editor—the campaign to stop the production of phosphorus matches and the War Children's Christmas Fund. In the first case, Valesh provided public education on the issue of poisonous matches in the early editorial columns of *Club Woman*. Scarcely a magazine number went by when she did not comment on legislation barring the matches or on the efforts to enforce new laws through consumer boycott and voluntary actions. The War Children's Christmas Fund, begun in 1914, raised money to provide clothing, toys, candy, and cash for children in war-torn Europe. While other, national war-relief campaigns had greater funding, Valesh and her husband stubbornly pursued their own mailing campaign. The financial statements in *American Club Woman* recorded the amounts donated and spent in the effort. While donations were modest, more than $50,000 in goods and cash was sent to European agencies for distribution.[12]

By the end of World War I, the publishing scene was changing drastically.[13] Older forms of women's politics were losing out to newer ones, and that meant that *American Club Woman* became a less promising audience. In this atmosphere, Valesh did not believe that the journal could long continue. Her heart attack in 1919 proved to be the final blow. She and Cross sold the magazine.[14] For a brief period afterward, the two retired to upstate New York. With the financial support of Cross's mother, Eva and Frank Cross bought a small farm in the Catskills near Willow, New York, which they named Crosspatch.[15] Eva's restlessness soon expressed itself in a project to turn a barn on the property into a community center for local residents. She organized holiday gatherings, from Christmas parties to amateur dramatics, and continued to lecture to women's clubs in the state.[16]

Continued health problems with her heart and trouble with her husband put an end to these activities as well. The second marriage proved as transient as the first. While Valesh later asserted that it was Cross's death that led to her changed circumstances, she had, in fact, divorced him quietly in 1923. In public, however, she claimed to be a widow. "Up to his neck in debts,"[17] Cross gave her nothing but Crosspatch, the title of which was in her name anyway. Needing to find work, Valesh left for New York City. She retained the cottage for weekends and holidays, but her only involvement in the Willow community in subsequent years was neighborly hospitality and occasional pieces written for the local newspaper, the *Kingston Freeman*, under the name Evelyn Cross.[18] At age fifty-six, Eva Valesh thus found herself seeking employment in the changed world of journalism.

By 1925, Valesh had transplanted herself and her career back to New York City. She could not bring herself to go back to the daily grind of reporting. As she confessed, "If you went to work as a reporter or special writer for a newspaper, you had no security. A new editor might come in, or a new policy be started, and you'd be pushed out. It might be six months before you could find anything to do." At that point, her sister Blanche suggested she try proofreading. Valesh renewed her union card and went to work. At first, she found a job on a woman's magazine, *The Pictorial Review*. As final proofreader, she had little work to do, and she was bored stiff.[19] Four years later, picking up substitute work at the *New York Times*, she managed to get a full-time position as proofreader there. Yet, as she told an interviewer, "It's so monotonous. You just correct other people's mistakes."[20] The *Times*, however, offered her security, and she worked there for twenty-seven of her last thirty years. As she summed up to the interviewer, "My world had changed with the times. I was no longer young and not in good health. I felt as an actor might when the audience goes, the lights are out, and the stage looks barren and forlorn and dark."[21] She sought to avoid the genteel poverty of middle-class women who no longer could rely on family support. Returning to newspaper work in the role of proofreader, she subsequently withdrew from public life. Her world became that of work, friends, and the son with whom she had to reacquaint herself.

During the hectic years as editor of *American Club Woman*, Valesh had seen little of her son. Both the death of his father and his own harried—if brief—career in his father's cigar business seems to have kept her son from regular visits to New York. Still, in 1914, on his honeymoon trip, Frank dutifully brought his new bride, Alice, to his mother's home in New York City. A letter written afterwards revealed warm sentiments on Eva's part and an attempt to welcome her new daughter-in-law into the fold. There was, however, little love lost between Alice and her new in-law. Eva's influence over her son, and the bitterness that arose when Cross pressured Frank to give his mother the only asset he had, Crookston Water Stocks, were bad memories for the young woman. The bankruptcy of the cigar factory soon afterward and the debts from his father's estate left young Frank Valesh without an income. He and Alice left her hometown of Graceville and moved to the Twin Cities, where he became a bricklayer and then a probation officer. They had three children, and their marriage lasted over twenty years. Frank and Alice divorced in 1937.[22]

Eva Valesh reconciled with her son when he moved to the East Coast, and she later introduced him to his second wife, Mary. A dutiful son, Frank had seen little of his working mother during childhood, but he now visited her almost every weekend. She rewarded him and his wife with attentions, letters, and stories. She lived a rich, long life as a private citizen, going to Europe again and enjoying Manhattan's cultural life and holidays at the cottage. She is still remembered today by older residents of the Willow community. She only retired when her heart condition made work difficult. In 1956, shortly after her ninetieth birthday, she died at her son's home in Westport, Connecticut. She is buried near Crosspatch, in Chichester, New York.[23]

Proofing the Truth

"Newspaper proofreading is an art in itself," James McGrath, the secretary of the typographical union, told Eva Valesh.[24] There is some irony in Valesh spending twenty-seven of the last thirty years of her life in pursuing that art. For much of her life, she had been busy "correcting mistakes" in her own life story as she reinvented herself as printer, journalist, labor organizer, Populist, and clubwoman. The reinvention was not merely a change of work or clothes,

Eva Valesh and son, Frank Valesh, in the 1950s. Despite years of alienation and distance, Frank Valesh was reconciled with his mother, and she spent much of her later years visiting with him and his wife. Here they are probably at her cottage of Crosspatch. Photo courtesy of Dolores Lautman.

though it entailed both. "The truth" was refashioned as well in word and memory. According to her granddaughter Lordie Lautman, "Eva did believe in adjusting the facts to suit her."[25] Proofreading always contains the possibility of introducing new errors into the text and changes in meaning, both accidental and intentional. In interviews throughout her career, Valesh changed the tone and colored the story of her life in reform. She erased the episodes of uncertain outcome and meaning, made coherent her life work, and read back into time a willingness to arbitrate and mediate, to be on the side of the decent people, to avoid the radical solution. By age eighty-six, when she gave an interview to the Columbia Oral History project, the story of her radical youth consisted largely her experiences as a woman who did men's work—in printing, labor unions, politics, journalism, and proofreading. By that time, Valesh was practiced at the art. She reinterpreted her experiences to fit a story line of how a workingman's daughter made good and came to know the daughters of plenty. The conservative 1950s did not dampen her pride in having broken boundaries during her long career, but the domestic overtones of the decade certainly influenced her to rewrite the script on her marriages. The twice-divorced became the twice-widowed, for in fact both ex-husbands were dead. Proofing the truth, she corrected her mistakes for her interviewer.

"Desire for the Things of the Earth"

When I began researching Eva McDonald Valesh, I gave little thought to how we construct truths about ourselves over the life span. Asked once why I had chosen this topic, I quipped, "An unnatural fear of co-optation." Co-optation, in shorthand, explained why Valesh could invalidate and deny her experience in the labor movement and traverse reform politics from Populist to red-baiting clubwoman without recognizing the shift in attitudes that required. At the time, I knew that my response was inadequate to the task of analyzing her complex personality. Knowing little of Valesh's childhood and education and only able to speculate about her personality and emotions, it seemed wrong to impose any concept as a substitute for understanding. Valesh's hidden work as publicist, editor, and AFL organizer suggested she had accepted invisibility as the price of leading an independent life. Being ostracized and ridiculed by newspapers and competitors during much of her later career cannot have made her more willing to buck the system. As much as I disdained her red-baiting and lacked sympathy for her xenophobia, I found that labels obscured more than they revealed.

Furthermore, Valesh's search for a cross- or transclass identity meshed in some respects with my own life. Choosing a learned profession, the "life of the mind" rather than "hands-on labor," supposedly meant that I no longer belonged to the working class. Being an intellectual, a cultural worker, meant no longer knowing what value or meaning to place on the things one did. Mental labor is harder to measure than more tangible physical work, but my choice, like Valesh's choice, was for social mobility. That similarity gave me some sympathy for the sometimes zigzagging path she took through her adult life. I saw little in Valesh's personality that resembled my own; her boundless self-absorption and blissful neglect of consequence, quite frankly, appalled me. Still, I could empathize with the uncertainty that characterized much of her upward climb. Riding the rails of class mobility means that one can never be certain at which stop one will get off. One can be pulled from the train and arrested as a vagrant, wind up in a town with even worse prospects, meet violence en route, or ride the car to the end of the line and to what, one hopes, is opportunity. Even if one arrives safely, one has no sense of relief that it really is one's destination. The socially mobile take the long chance, even if in American culture, with its myth of mobility and its rhetorical respect for education, there may be some paths to mobility that lower the odds.

The other compelling parallel I found in Valesh's life was the means by which she chose to move across the class divide. In the love of language, and the acquisition of language skills, she had found the path to social mobility. Reading her early writings, one can experience the true joy she must have had discovering new words for old grievances and new ideas to address the problems of the working-class movement and the society around her. As a wordsmith, she hammered out many pieces of writing that were routine reports on labor, politics, and collective action. And yet, amid the commonplace language she used, there was the occasional treasure. In her novel *A Tale of the Twin Cities*, it was a convoluted use of Darwin's missing link in a metaphor; in a letter to a friend, it is Benedict from *Much Ado about Nothing* who crops up unawares. There are words that sing out and new knowledge that surfaces. In these moments, it is possible to recognize our own joy in learning and our zest for the play of language, intelligence, and humor.

Through her life, Eva Valesh dedicated herself to mediating and negotiating the boundaries of class and gender politics through her language skills. The political culture in which she matured was unstable and uncertain. Through the social change, political crisis, and economic upheavals of the late nineteenth century, American society experienced traumatic shifts in class structure, class politics, and above all in the meanings of class at the individual, community, and societal levels. It was Valesh's flexibility in response to this changing environment that gave her a long career in the notoriously unstable world of labor reform. Unlike Samuel Gompers, who had a longer term of service, she held no permanent post or organizational affiliation. Her responses to the political context, while not predetermined, reflected both her opportunism and her perception of what was necessary. Perhaps Valesh was not so much a chameleon or opportunist as a survivor. Still, she did not seek survival on meager terms.

While Valesh resisted her mother's wish for a respectable and settled daughter, Eva sought to make a life through reform that would not reproduce the conditions of the workers in her own life. Instead, she made what she considered a decent living. She knew, as perhaps many of the puritanically mobile do not, how to have a good time and spend money on herself. If that made her thriftless, it also no doubt made her happier than most. Her lack of self-consciousness about "bygones" seems to have mattered as well.

It would be wrong, however, to look at Valesh's upward mobility as a single-minded search for material success, any more than it is possible to view late-nineteenth-century labor reformers as a crowd of greedy, backbiting social climbers who didn't know their place. They did not believe they had a determined place, and they resisted the imposition of the hardships and hazards of class upon both themselves and their followers. It is also important to remember that the reason for taking the chance of social mobility in either individual or group terms is not the desire to become a money mogul or a lord of creation. The pursuit of social mobility can feel ambivalent and risky. In the nineteenth century, the chances for even intergenerational social mobility were marginal. The respectable working-class family bought a house in the second generation, acquired a college or normal-school education in the third or fourth, and worked its way up in a kind of multigenerational family strategy. Thus the aspirations of the upwardly mobile tend to be limited in scope by pragmatic vision, and—I believe—by the desire not so much for a better set of things as for a more secure and meaningful life.

Invoking the words that have long characterized the 1912 Lawrence textile strikers, I suggest that the demand for "Bread and Roses" captures the working-class desire, whether individual or collective, to live life more fully. Throughout the autobiographies and biographies of working-class men and women, we hear that desire invoked to be a better person and have a richer life in qualitative terms. Eva Valesh had a consuming desire to know the things she had read about. While she did love "pretty things," her desire was not for the material so much as the meaning she assigned to certain objects and designs. To understand the attraction and experience of social mobility, we need to invoke the ritualistic meaning of goods—that is, their symbolic value. Furthermore, we have to recognize social mobility not as a ladder but as a transitional state, a liminal status, defined by vulnerability, risk, and sometimes power. The transclass individual experiences a different relationship to his/her class of family origin and always stands a little askew of the newly acquired one. The complex reworking of class identity within a single life thus alters where one stands politically and personally, even if not in a predetermined direction. As Carolyn Steedman has argued, class perspective requires us to explore how "desire for the things of the earth" shapes one's class position and politics. The goods that come with social mobility serve both as markers for the new position and as talismans to prevent the subject from sliding into a liminal state.

The importance of material goods in Eva Valesh's life—her brownstone, her lost china, oriental rugs, and a piece of cretonne—thus provides clues as to who she was as a publicist, a reformer, and a woman. In defining and refining her class and gender identity, these goods had both real and symbolic value to her. Language and learning, above all, were treasured possessions. Still, there were more concrete ones. In the only letter to her daughter-in-law, Alice, which still exists, Valesh wrote, "Send me a little piece of your cretonne so I can picture in my mind how it will all look." During a honeymoon visit to his mother, young Frank Valesh and his wife had an oriental rug thrust on them at Eva's insistence. While a bill for the rug followed in the mail,[26] what was important for her was the sense that her daughter-in-law had goods similar to her own, which bound them together through the ritual of consumption.

So it is, in one tale of upward mobility after another, that word and object take on extraordinary power. Just as Valesh's elocution lessons with Jack McGaughey shaped her life, so, too, did the facility with language and the possessions of respectability matter in the lives of those moving from the working class to the middle class. From Anzia Yezierska's *The Breadgivers*, we have the image of the heroine learning lessons by fixing pages of books in front of her manual labor. She exhausts herself in the search for knowledge, driven culturally by the respect for that knowledge in Jewish culture but also by the accouterments of education—a clean dwelling place, simple but solid furniture, respectable clothing, stable relationships. In *Coming of Age in Mississippi*, Anne Moody speaks to the physical accompaniments of education—the pride in one's luggage and clothing as well as new knowledge. In Cheri Register's *Packinghouse Daughter*, there is the movement toward better clothing and home ownership. And in *Landscape for a Good Woman*, Carolyn Steedman connects her mother's conservative politics to the desire for a life that reaches beyond puritanical labor and self-sacrifice to goods that give meaning and richness to her class-bound life. The good clothing and leather shoes that enable a working-class woman to migrate through the class structure and negotiate her new middle-class status are intimately bound up with the desire not so much to be a member of the elite but to protect one's self from the vagaries and hazards of class transition. Protection, not just celebration, is seen in the hat, the shirtwaist, and the cretonne.[27]

When I began to write the biography of Eva Valesh, I had no idea that I would come to speak of magic talismans and the transforming power of language. Yet I find myself seeking the words to bring closure to this biographical journey. A narrative junkie, and a true lover of parables, I looked in vain for the moral to Valesh's story. Abandoning the idealism of her working-class youth for the pragmatic adjustments of middle age brought her neither ultimate victory nor tragic defeat. The truth is, though, that the stories I loved best as a child were the "fractured fairy tales" of *The Adventures of Rocky and Bullwinkle*.

Comeuppance, not justice, reigned, and bad puns provided the necessary end to every tale. As with most biographers, I have felt as though I have been in dialogue with my subject for years. Eva McDonald Valesh, whose stories inspired workers to strike and kept neighbors entertained, told me one morning, while I puzzled over the twists and turns in her life, to tell a good story, not to provide a good moral. You, dear reader, have to draw the rest of the conclusions yourself.

NOTES

Introduction: Truth-Telling Fictions

1. Eva McDonald Valesh to Albert Dollenmayer, 19 July 1891, Belmont, N.Y., Box 2, Albert Dollenmayer and Family Papers, Minnesota Historical Society (hereafter cited in notes as MHS).

2. At age twenty-five, when she married, Eva Valesh was older than the usual bride. The median age at first marriage for women in 1890 was twenty-two. U.S. Bureau of the Census, *Historical Statistics of the United States*, Bicentennial Edition (Washington, D.C., 1975), Series A 158–59, p. 19. It was also exceptional in that Eva McDonald, a lower-middle-class Protestant Scots-Anglo-Irish woman, married a Catholic Czech immigrant and skilled tradesman. Religious and ethnic intermarriages were rare.

3. "The Alliance Picnic," n.p. [1891], Ignatius Donnelly Papers, Scrapbook, reel 158, fr. 402–406, MHS; "Donnelly's Predicament," *Pioneer Press*, 3 January 1891; *St. Paul Trades and Labor Bulletin* 2:5 (June 1893): 1. On the "feminine comet" that was Eva McDonald Valesh, see Rhoda R. Gilman, "Eva McDonald Valesh, Minnesota Populist," in *Women of Minnesota*, ed. Barbara Stuhler and Gretchen Kreuter (St. Paul, 1977), 55–76.

4. For an overview of recent trends in biography, see Paula Backscheider, *Reflections on Biography* (New York, 1999). See also Eric Homberger and John Charmley, eds., *The Troubled Face of Biography* (London, 1988); Sara Alpern, Joyce Antler, Elisabeth Israels Perry, and Ingrid Winther Scobie, eds., *The Challenge of Feminist Biography* (Urbana, 1992); Mary Rhiel and David Suchoff, eds., *The Seductions of Biography* (New York and London, 1996).

5. David Paul Nord, "Tocqueville, Garrison, and the Perfection of Journalism," *Journalism History* 13:2 (Summer 1986): 56–63; Thomas Leonard, *The Power of the Press: The Birth of American Political Reporting* (New York, 1986), 137–65, 193–231.

6. See, for example, Craig Phelan, *Divided Loyalties: The Public and Private Life of John Mitchell* (Albany, 1994), 1–17, and *Grand Master Workman: Terence Powderly and the Knights of Labor* (New York, 2000), 11–15; also note the autobiographies of Mary Anderson, *Woman at Work: The Autobiography of Mary Anderson*, as told to Mary N. Winslow (Minneapolis,

1951), 3–26; Agnes Nestor, *Woman's Labor Leader: An Autobiography of Agnes Nestor* (Rockford, Ill., 1954), 3–19; Rose Schneiderman (with Lucy Goldthwaite), *All for One* (New York, 1967). Such mobility was also experienced by working-class men who became part of ward and city machine politics.

7. Samuel Gompers, *Seventy Years of Life and Labor, An Autobiography*, vol. 1 (1925; New York, 1957), 2, 15, 56, provides insight into his class background. For the only full-scale biography of Gompers, see Bernard Mandel, *Samuel Gompers: A Biography* (Yellow Springs, Ohio, 1963).

8. Mary Jo Maynes, *Taking the Hard Road: Life Course in French and German Workers' Autobiographies in the Era of Industrialization* (Chapel Hill, N.C., 1995), 200–201; Carolyn Steedman, *Landscape for a Good Woman: A Story of Two Lives* (New Brunswick, N.J., 1987), 5. The effects of social mobility on working-class advocates and their "cross-class" or "transclass" identities only rarely have been noted. See, for example, the tensions discussed in Mary J. Bularzik, "The Bonds of Belonging: Leonora O'Reilly and Social Reform," *Labor History* 24:1 (Winter 1983): 60–83; Alice Kessler-Harris, "Rose Schneiderman and the Limits of Women's Trade Unionism," in *Labor Leaders in America*, ed. Melvyn Dubofsky and Warren Van Tine (Urbana, 1986), 160–84; and Annelise Orleck, *Common Sense and a Little Fire: Women and Working Class Politics in the United States, 1900–1965* (Chapel Hill, N.C., 1995). Phelan, in *Divided Loyalties*, also notes the growing gap between labor leader John Mitchell and the rank and file.

9. See the Essay on Sources at the end of the volume.

Chapter 1. Stealing the Trade

1. "The Plain Facts," *Tribune*, 13 May 1888. McDonald's role in the strike was through her membership in the Knights of Labor. The strikers belonged to the Ladies' Protective Association, Local Assembly 5261, Knights of Labor. See Albert Dollenmayer, "Eva McDonald Valesh," in *American Women*, ed. Frances E. Willard and Mary A. Livermore (New York, 1897), 729–30.

2. "The Plain Facts," *Tribune*, 13 May 1888.

3. *Reminiscences of Eva McDonald Valesh* (1952), p. 1, in the Columbia University Oral History Research Office Collection (hereafter cited in the notes as *Reminiscences*). In the interview, she gives 1874 as the year she was born.

4. See Marcus Lee Hansen (with John Bartlet Brebner), *The Mingling of the Canadian and American Peoples* (New Haven, Conn., 1940), 140–58.

5. On the birth date, see Eva McDonald Valesh to Albert Dollenmayer, 19 July 1891, Albert Dollenmayer and Family Papers, Box 2, MHS. For a family genealogy, see Letters, Dolores Lautman to the author, 14 February and 27 March 1993; Dolores Lautman, Family Group Record, dated July 25, 1993, Dolores V. Lautman, private papers, Seattle, Washington.

6. *Reminiscences*, 1.

7. Rhoda R. Gilman, "Eva McDonald Valesh, Minnesota Populist," in *Women of Minnesota*, ed. Barbara Stuhler and Gretchen Kreuter (St. Paul, 1977), 55–76; Lautman Family Group Record.

8. *Reminiscences*, 4–5.

9. Gilman ("Eva McDonald Valesh," 56) states that the family moved first in 1875 to Stillwater, Minnesota. The family is recorded in Minneapolis in the 1880 census. U.S.

Census Manuscript Population Schedules, Minnesota, Hennepin County, v. 6, District 2, Enumeration District 251, Sheet 46, Line 34. Blanche McDonald was born in 1880; Bernice followed in 1883.

10. Joseph Stipanovich, *City of Lakes: An Illustrated History of Minneapolis* (Minneapolis, 1983), 9.

11. Minneapolis's population grew from 46,887 in 1880 to 130,00 in 1885 and 164,738 in 1890, and St. Paul's grew from 41,473 to 133,156 in the same decade. U.S. Bureau of the Census, *Abstract of the Eleventh Census, 1890* (Washington, 1896), 36; Albert Shaw, "Cooperation in a Western City," *American Economics Association Publications*, vol. 1 (Baltimore, 1886), 199.

12. Shaw, "Cooperation in a Western City," quoted in Bradley L. Morison, *Sunlight on Your Doorstep: The Minneapolis Tribune's First Hundred Years* (Minneapolis, 1966), 12.

13. Minnesota Writers' Project, *Minneapolis: The Story of a City* (Minneapolis, 1940), 72–94.

14. *Reminiscences*, 5.

15. Gilman ("Eva McDonald Valesh," 349n3) records that John McDonald was listed as a grocer in Minneapolis city directories from 1883/84 to 1887/88. The following year, he once again listed as a carpenter.

16. *Reminiscences*, 1–2.

17. Ibid., 23.

18. Ibid., 10–11.

19. Ibid., 18.

20. Dollenmayer, "Eva McDonald Valesh," 729.

21. *Reminiscences*, 2.

22. Ibid., 23.

23. On working-class domesticity, see Susan Levine, "Labor's True Woman: Domesticity and Equal Rights in the Knights of Labor," *Journal of American History* 70 (September 1983): 323–39; Robert E. Weir, *Beyond the Veil: The Culture of the Knights of Labor* (University Park, Penn., 1998), 180–90. See also Stephanie Coontz, *The Social Origins of Private Life: A History of American Families, 1600–1900* (New York, 1988), 251–329; Steve Mintz and Susan Kellogg, *Domestic Revolutions: A Social History of American Family Life* (New York, 1988), 83–106.

24. *Reminiscences*, 7.

25. "As to a Well-Bred Girl," *Minneapolis Journal*, 2 November 1889.

26. Coontz, *Social Origins of Private Life*, 261.

27. Dollenmayer, "Eva McDonald Valesh," 729.

28. *Reminiscences*, 2.

29. Dollenmayer, "Eva McDonald Valesh," 729.

30. *Reminiscences*, 3.

31. Ada Patterson, "Eva McDonald Valesh, Joan of Arc of the Women of the Laboring Classes," *Human Work* (December 1908): 21.

32. "Girls Make Money," *Globe*, 13 May 1888.

33. *Reminiscences*, 8a.

34. Ibid., 8a–9.

35. Ibid., 9.

36. "Girls Make Money," *Globe*, 13 May 1888.

37. Edith Abbott, *Women in Industry: A Study in American Economic History* (1909; New York, 1918), 246–61, quote on p. 254; Elizabeth Butler, *Women and the Trades, Pittsburgh,*

1907–1908, introduction by Maurine Weiner Greenwald (Pittsburgh, 1984), 275–81; Ava Baron, "Questions of Gender: Deskilling and Demasculinization in the U.S. Printing Industry, 1830–1915," *Gender and History* 1 (Summer 1989): 178–99.

38. See Hellen Asher, "The Labor Movement in Minnesota," unpublished paper, MHS, 1925, 6; W. E. McEwen, "The Minnesota Labor Movement," *Minnesota State Federation of Labor Yearbook* (St. Paul, 1915), 37; "The Boycotters," *Saturday Evening Spectator*, 14 January 1888; "Girls Make Money," *Globe*, 13 May 1888.

39. *Reminiscences*, 10.

40. Patterson, "Eva McDonald Valesh," 21.

41. For sources on the history of the Knights in Minnesota and in Minneapolis, see these works by George B. Engberg: "The Rise of Organized Labor in Minnesota," M.A. thesis (University of Minnesota, 1939); "The Knights of Labor in Minnesota," *Minnesota History* 22 (1941): 367–91; and "The Rise of Organized Labor in Minnesota," *Minnesota History* 21 (1940): 372–94. The labor movement began to write its history in labor newspapers and columns and in yearbooks; see, for example, "From Shop and Mill," *Globe*, 19 April 1885; "First Temple to Labor," *Globe*, 30 May 1887; "Labor and Laboring Men," *Globe*, 14 August 1887.

42. The North Star Labor Club, Knights Local Assembly 805, went by different names, including the Dirigo Assembly (1883; see Weir, *Beyond the Veil*, 56). Its leadership included railroad clerk Jack McGaughey, shoemaker Timothy Brosnan, surveyor John Lamb, printer George William Morey, Dr. Michael Finnegan, and printer Thomas Clark; "Labor," *Tribune*, 28 July 1895.

43. Nord, "Tocqueville, Garrison, and the Perfection of Journalism," 59.

44. Frank Valesh to W. E. McEwen, quoted in Minnesota State Federation of Labor, *Yearbook*, 15.

45. Frank Valesh to W. E. McEwen, Duluth, 18 February 1914, Lautman papers. On the importance of the working-class press, see Weir, *Beyond the Veil*, 152ff; Philip Ethington, *The Public City: The Political Construction of Urban Life in San Francisco, 1850–1900* (Cambridge, 1994), 208, 231–41, 308–319; Jon Bekken, "The Working Class Press at the Turn of the Century," in *Ruthless Criticism: New Perspectives in US Communications History*, ed. William S. Solomon and Robert W. McChesney (Minneapolis, 1993), 151–75. On public opinion and labor reform, see Alexander Yard, "Coercive Government within a Minimal State: The Idea of Public Opinion in Gilded Age Labor Reform Culture," *Labor History* 34 (Fall 1993): 443–56.

46. "Women's Column," *Labor Echo*, 6 August 1887; "Women's Column," *Labor Echo*, 24 March 1888; Mollie Lee and Margaret Christie, Report on the Committee on Woman's Work, *Proceedings of the Twelfth Regular Meeting of the Knights of Labor, District Assembly* 79 (1887), 71–72, John P. McGaughey Papers, MHS; Katie F. Cronin and Annie Esler, "Report of the Committee on Women's Work," *Proceedings of 21st Annual Meeting of District Assembly* 79 (1889), 33–4, reel 65, series A, part 4B, and Katie F. Cronin and Annie Esler, "Report on Women's Work," *Proceedings of the 25th Annual Meeting of District Assembly* 79, 34–35, reel 65, series A, part 4B, both in the Terence Vincent Powderly Papers, Catholic University, Washington, D.C., microfilm edition.

47. Patterson, "Eva McDonald Valesh"; "The Kirmess," *Journal*, 9 April 1887; meeting notice, *Labor Echo* 3:4 (16 March 1888): 5. Eva and her father, John McDonald, were both listed as stockholders of the Knights of Labor Building Association. See *The Labor*

Temple, Now in the Course of Erection by the Knights of Labor Building Association, Minneapolis, Minnesota (Minneapolis, 1887), in *Pamphlets in American History*, microfiche collection, Labor, L3294, 42.

48. The story of her first *St. Paul Globe* article is told in several places and serves as a touchstone for her own narrative of upward mobility. See *Reminiscences*, 10–11, 19–22.

49. *Reminiscences*, 21.

50. "Workers in Wool," *Globe*, 20 May 1888.

51. *Reminiscences*, 21.

52. Patterson, "Eva McDonald Valesh"; "'Mong Girls Who Toil," *Globe*, 25 March 1888.

53. "Workers in Wool," *Globe*, 20 May 1888.

54. "Working in the Wet," *Globe*, 15 April 1888; "Girls Make Cigars," *Globe*, 27 May 1888.

55. See "'Mong Girls Who Toil," *Globe*, 25 March 1888; "Eva Gay's Travels," *Globe*, 6 May 1888; "Workers in Wool," *Globe*, 20 May 1888; "Girls in Politics," *Globe*, 19 August 1888; "How Girls Clerk," *Globe*, 17 June 1888; "That You, Central?" *Globe*, 12 August 1888.

56. "'Mong Girls Who Toil," *Globe*, 25 March 1888; "Behind the Scenes," *Globe*, 22 July 1888; "On the Bright Side," *Globe*, 24 June 1888; "Their Sunday Out," *Globe*, 14 October 1888.

57. "Girls Make Money," *Globe*, 13 May 1888; "The Girls Rejoice," *Globe*, 1 July 1888; "Girls in Politics," *Globe*, 19 August 1888.

58. *Tribune Handbook of Minneapolis* (Minneapolis, 1884), 79; *Minneapolis Business Souvenir* (Minneapolis, 1885), 10–11.

59. "'Mong Girls Who Toil," *Globe*, 25 March 1888.

60. "'Mong Girls Who Toil," *Globe*, 25 March 1888; "A Committee of Jobbers," *Globe*, 12 May 1888; *Minneapolis Business Souvenir*, 11.

61. "'Mong Women Who Toil," *Globe*, 25 March 1888.

62. "Wage Working Women," in Minnesota Bureau of Labor Statistics, *Biennial Report*, 1st, 1887–88 (St. Paul, 1888), 148, 190–94; "'Mong Girls Who Toil,'" *Globe*, 25 March 1888; "Out on Strike," "The Strikers," and "Against Convict Labor," *Tribune*, 19–21 April 1888.

63. "Out on Strike," *Tribune*, 19 April 1888.

64. Ibid.

65. "We Won't Be Back," *Globe*, 20 April 1888.

66. At least a portion of the women working at Shotwell were members of the Knights of Labor, but it is unclear how many or what the timing was. See "Out on Strike," *Tribune*, 19 April 1888; "Two Sides," *Globe*, 18 April 1888; "Strike Still On," *Pioneer Press*, 20 April 1888; Dollenmayer, "Eva McDonald Valesh," 729.

67. The St. Paul Ladies' Protective Association, established in 1885, was suspended in 1892; the Minneapolis assembly existed from 1886 to 1894. See John B. Andrews and W. D. P. Bliss, *History of Women in Trade Unions* (1911; New York, 1974), 117, 119, 127, 129–31.

68. "Two Sides," *Globe*, 18 April 1888; "A Strike at Home," *Pioneer Press*, 19 April 1888.

69. "Our Female Strikers," *Globe*, 19 April 1888.

70. "'Mong Girls Who Toil," *Globe*, 25 March 1888.

71. "Art Gallery Visitors," *Globe*, 10 September 1888, and "Schoolma'am Talk," *Globe*, 23 September 1888. See Mariana Valverde, "The Love of Finery: Fashion and the Fallen

Woman in Nineteenth Century Social Discourse," *Victorian Studies* 32 (Winter 1989): 169–88.

72. "Two Sides," *Globe*, 18 April 1888; "A Strike at Home," *Pioneer Press*, 19 April 1888.

73. "Strike Still On," *Pioneer Press*, 20 April 1888.

74. "Our Female Strikers," *Globe*, 19 April 1888; "Out on Strike," *Tribune*, 19 April 1888; "Strike Still On," *Pioneer Press*, 19 April 1888.

75. For late-nineteenth-century uses of white-collar jobs as security for sons, see Ileen DeVault, " 'Give the Boys a Trade': Gender and Job Choice in the 1890s," in *Work Engendered: Toward a New History of Labor*, ed. Ava Baron (Ithaca, N.Y., 1991), 191–215.

76. "What an Amateur Reporter Saw at the Knights of Labor Picnic," *Globe*, undated clipping, Scrapbook, McGaughey Papers, MHS.

77. "Giddy Male Mashers," *Globe*, 1 January 1889.

78. Ibid. Dislike of "dudes" was widely shared in labor circles. See "What an Amateur Reporter Saw at the Knights of Labor Picnic," addressed to editor of the *Globe*, undated clipping, Scrapbook, McGaughey Papers, MHS.

79. Ibid.

80. "Our Female Strikers," *Globe*, 19 April 1888; "Out on Strike," *Tribune*, 19 April 1888; "A Strike at Home," *Pioneer Press*, 19 April 1888.

81. Eva McDonald, "The Factory's White Slave," *Journal of United Labor* 9 (18 April 1889). See also "Girls Who Work," *Globe*, 19 July 1885, on the "guileless girls" who try to conceal they are wage-earners through dress.

82. For insights into the importance of clothing, see McDonald's Eva Gay articles in the *Globe* and "The Woman's Organization," *Journal of United Labor*, 17 July 1888, and "The Factory's White Slave," *Journal of United Labor*, 18 April 1889. On the importance of dress as honor, see Valverde, "The Love of Finery"; Max Weber, "Class, Status, Party," in *From Max Weber: Essays in Sociology*, trans. and ed., H. H. Gerth and C. Wright Mills (New York, 1946), 180–95. See also Nan Enstad, *Ladies of Labor, Girls of Adventure: Working Women, Popular Culture, and Labor Politics at the Turn of the Twentieth Century* (New York, 1999), which has a slightly different take, emphasizing working women's desire to appropriate middle-class "ladyhood."

83. "Striking Maidens," *Globe*, 29 April 1888.

84. "Workingmen Speak Out," *Journal*, 21 April 1888; "; 'Mong Girls Who Toil," *Globe*, 25 March 1888; "Out on Strike" and "The Strikers," *Tribune*, 19 and 20 April 1888; "The Girls Heard From," *Globe*, 13 May 1888.

85. "Status of the Strike," *Pioneer Press*, 22 April 1888.

86. "Striking Maidens," *Globe*, 29 April 1888.

87. "Council and Assembly," *Journal*, 2 June 1888; "Aid for Strikers," *Journal*, 28 April 1888; "The Working Girls' Strike," *Labor Echo*, 28 April 1888; "Not Going Back" and "Sympathize with the Girls," *Tribune*, 29 April and 7 May 1888.

88. "Strike Still On," *Pioneer Press*, 20 April 1888; "Against Convict Labor," *Tribune*, 21 April 1888; "Meeting of the Strikers," *Globe*, 22 April 1888.

89. "The Working Girls' Strike," *Labor Echo*, 28 April 1888; "Another Appeal," *Globe*, 28 April 1888.

90. "A Scathing Rebuke," *Globe*, 14 May 1888.

91. "Entitled to Credit," *Globe*, 22 April 1888.

92. "The Girls Indorsed," *Globe*, 11 May 1888.

93. Ibid. and "For Working Girls," *Tribune*, 11 May 1888.

94. "Status of the Strike," *Pioneer Press*, 22 April 1888.

95. "The Girls Indorsed," *Globe*, 11 May 1888; "For Working Girls," *Tribune*, 11 May 1888.

96. "Status of the Strike," *Pioneer Press*, 22 April 1888.

97. "Striking Maidens," *Globe*, 29 April 1888; "The Striking Girls" and "Not Going Back," *Tribune*, 26 and 29 April 1888; "In a Very Tight Place," *Journal*, 13 June 1888; "Strikers Pushing Their Boycott," *Journal*, 9 June 1888.

98. The series ran from 25 March to 31 March 1889, although there was a final installment in August 1889.

99. The Eva Gay series was published in 1888 in the *Globe*. Similar series were published in Pittsburgh, New York, Chicago, Indianapolis, and Waukesha, Wisconsin. The Chicago series in particular caused a furor similar to McDonald's work. See Brooke Kroeger, *Nellie Bly: Daredevil, Reporter, Feminist* (New York, 1994), 45–48; Nell Nelson (pseud.), *The White Slave Girls of Chicago. Nell Nelson's Startling Disclosures of the Cruelties and Inequities Practiced in the Workshops and Factories of a Great City* (Chicago, 1888), *The History of Women*, microform edition, reel 471, #3519; Genevieve G. McBride, *On Wisconsin Women: Working for Their Rights from Feminism to Suffrage* (Madison, Wis. 1993), 144ff. On the impact of the Chicago series, see Meredith Tax, *The Rising of the Women* (New York, 1980), 65–90.

100. Andrews and Bliss, *History of Women in Trade Unions*, 118.

101. Katie F. Cronin and Annie Esler, "Report of the Committee on Women's Work," *Proceedings of District Assembly 79*, Knights of Labor, 21st meeting, 1889, 33–4, in Powderly Papers, microfilm edition, Reel 65, Series A, Part 4B.

102. *Star*, 18 October 1889, in index file of the Minneapolis Historical Collection, Minneapolis Public Library; "For People Who Work," *Journal* 2 November 1889.

Chapter 2. "An Object of Solicitude at Election Time"

1. "Women on the School Board," *Journal*, 22 November 1886; "The Women Want a Vote," *Journal*, 25 March 1887; "Women on the School Board," *Journal*, 26 March 1887.

2. J. A. Chandler, Chicago, Milwaukee, and St. Paul, to C. A. Prior, Esq, 13 September 1880, John McGaughey Papers, MHS.

3. Davison's Minneapolis City Directory, 1883; untitled clipping, n.d. (probably from 1886), n.p., Scrapbook, McGaughey Papers, MHS. The clipping gives McGaughey's age as thirty-four and as being born approximately in 1852. This probably underestimates his age, as he had served in the Civil War.

4. Untitled newspaper clipping, n.d., n.p., scrapbook; John Lamb, Commissioner of Labor Statistics, to J. P. McGaughey, Esq., 28 March 1888, both in McGaughey Papers, MHS.

5. "The Knights of Labor in Hastings" (reprint Hastings *Banner*), n.d. (probably 1886), scrapbook, McGaughey Papers, MHS.

6. *Reminiscences of Eva McDonald Valesh* (1952), p. 11–12, in the Columbia University Oral History Research Office Collection (hereafter cited in the notes as *Reminiscences*).

7. Ibid., 12.

8. Ibid.

9. Ibid.

10. Ibid., 12–13.

11. Ada Patterson, "Eva McDonald Valesh, Joan of Arc of the Women of the Laboring Classes," *Human Work* (December 1908): 21.

12. *Reminiscences*, 13.

13. "The Women's Organization," *Journal of United Labor*, 17 July 1888; *Industrial Age* (Duluth), June 1888, quoted in Karen Branan, "Non-Union Maids," *Twin Cities Reader*, 2 July 1981; "Lectures to Workingmen," *Duluth Daily Times* , 8 June 1888.

14. *Mankato Review*, 25 September 1888, copy courtesy of Jeff Kolnick.

15. Patterson, "Eva McDonald Valesh," 21.

16. *Reminiscences*, 14.

17. "Labor," *Tribune*, 28 July 1895. Sources on the Athenaeum are scattered throughout local newspapers and city directories. On Brosnan, see "Labor," *Tribune*, 28 July 1895; "Timothy Brosnan," *Progressive Men of the State of Montana* (Chicago, ca. 1902), 568. On John Lamb, see "Figures for Toilers," *Journal*, 12 April 1887; "John Lamb," in Clarence Bagley, *History of Seattle*, vol. 3 (Seattle, 1916), 131–32; obituary, *Seattle Post-Intelligencer*, 29 June 1940, courtesy of the University of Washington Library Special Collections and Washington State Historical Society. On John Swift, see "Toilers and Spinners," *Tribune*, 7 May 1893; "In the Realm of Labor," *Tribune*, 28 May 1893; "In the Realm of Labor," *Tribune*, 18 June 1893.

18. *Reminiscences*, 16.

19. Ibid., 15. In her list, she identifies William (actually George William) Morey as a "professor" when he was a printer. There may be some confusion here with William Folwell, a university professor who was engaged in workingmen's reform politics between 1886 and 1889. Both Morey and Folwell frequently spoke at labor forums.

20. "From Labor's Loom," *Journal*, 27 March 1886.

21. "Women Will Organize," *Journal*, 15 September 1888.

22. "Figures for Toilers," *Journal*, 12 April 1887. His reports were widely covered in labor columns; see, for example, "For People Who Work," *Journal*, 14 September 1888.

23. There is little information on Thomas Clark. See his *The Songs of Monssini; or, The Cry of the Laborer Defrauded*, 2d ed. (Minneapolis, 1889), a Knights of Labor songbook. On the Building Association, see *The Labor Temple and K of L Building Association, Minneapolis, Minn.* (Minneapolis, 1887). On the identification of Clark as Monssini, see Robert E. Weir, *Beyond the Veil: The Culture of the Knights of Labor* (University Park, Penn., 1998), 109.

24. See "Timothy Brosnan," *Progressive Men of the State of Montana*, 568; "Labor," *Tribune*, 28 July 1895. In 1889, Brosnan moved to Great Falls, Montana, where he started a retail men's clothing store and served as state legislator from 1894 to his death in 1897.

25. "Labor," *Tribune*, 28 July 1895.

26. The argument that the Knights were utopian dreamers was first launched by labor historian John Commons and his students but was given its fullest expression in Gerald Grob, *Workers and Utopia: A Study of Ideological Conflict in the American Labor Movement, 1865–1900* (New York, 1969). For a compelling argument about the utopian designs and productive aversions of working-class intellectuals in Paris, see Jacques Rancière, *The Nights of Labor: The Workers' Dream in Nineteenth Century France*, trans. John Drury, introduction by Donald Reid (Philadelphia, 1989).

27. See Gregory Kealey and Bryan D. Palmer, *"Dreaming of What Might Be": The Knights of Labor in Ontario, 1880–1900* (Cambridge, 1982); Leon Fink, *Workingmen's Democracy: The Knights of Labor and American Politics* (Urbana, Ill., 1983); Susan Levine, "Labor's True Woman: Domesticity and Equal Rights in the Knights of Labor," *Journal of American History* 70 (September 1983): 323–39, and *Labor's True Woman: Carpet Weavers and Labor Reform in the Gilded Age* (Philadelphia, 1984); Peter Rachleff, *Black Labor in the South: Richmond, Virginia, 1865–1890* (Philadelphia, 1984); Richard J. Oestreicher, *Solidarity and Fragmentation: Working People and Class Consciousness in Detroit, 1875–1900* (Urbana, Ill., 1986).

28. See Fink, *Workingmen's Democracy*, 26–30, on labor tickets; on the uses of politics in general, see 18–37. Compare to the argument in David Scobey, "Boycotting the Politics Factory: Labor Radicalism and the New York City Mayoral Election of 1884," *Radical History Review* 28–30 (1984): 280–325, that by the mid-1880s labor and mainstream politics "had grown very far apart." I would argue that, in fact, labor was still invested in the two major parties.

29. "Labor and Politics," *Journal*, 30 June 1888.

30. See Michael McGerr, *The Decline of Popular Politics* (New York, 1986); Paula Baker, *The Moral Frameworks of Public Life: Gender, Politics, and the State in Rural New York, 1870–1930* (New York, 1991), 24–55.

31. On Doc Ames, see Harold Zink, *City Bosses in the United States: A Study of Twenty Municipal Bosses* (Durham, N.C., 1930), 334–49, quote from p. 341; Lincoln Steffens, *The Shame of the Cities* (1904; New York, 1948), 63–100.

32. "From Shop and Mill," *Globe*, 5 April 1885; "Saturday in the City," *Globe*, 29 January 1888; "The Labor Candidate," *Globe*, 1 February 1888; "Labor and Politics," *Globe*, 13 February 1888; Eva McDonald to Sarah Christie Stevens, 5 and 12 January 1891, James C. Christie and Family Papers, Box 14, MHS.

33. "Figures for Toilers," *Journal*, 12 April 1887.

34. John Lamb, "Other People's Notions; Principles at Stake," *Journal*, 14 April 1886.

35. "A Word from Powderly," *Journal*, 19 March 1887.

36. See Richard Hofstadter, *Social Darwinism in American Thought*, rev. ed. (Boston, 1955); Sidney Fine, *Laissez Faire and the General-Welfare State: A Study of Conflict in American Thought, 1865–1901* (Ann Arbor, 1956).

37. "Ames Was Absent," *Tribune*, 11 October 1888.

38. "Their Night Out," *Tribune*, 2 November 1888; "The Lessons of Parades" and "The Biggest Yet," *Tribune*, 4 November 1888.

39. "It May Reach 50,000," *Globe*, 31 October 1888.

40. "Politicians in Skirts," *Journal*, 24 July 1888; "Women in Politics," *Tribune*, 28 October 1888.

41. See election coverage in the *Journal, Tribune*, and *Globe*. For specific examples, see "American Manhood," *Globe*, 26 April 1888; "One Kind of Harmony," *Journal*, 12 May 1888; "Akin to Anarchy" and "Feathers on It," *Globe*, 23 June 1888; "Cut the Taxes," *Globe*, 10 September 1888.

42. *Reminiscences*, 24.

43. "Women in Politics," *Globe*, 28 October 1888.

44. See "Local News," *Labor Echo*, 29 September 1888. Her views on education appeared in "Women in Politics," *Globe*, 28 October 1888. The next year, she continued

to lecture on education, see "Industrial Fields," *Globe*, 3 March 1889. Her column "The New Political Economy" in the *Great West* emphasized education.

45. For the quote, see McDonald to Sarah Christie Stevens, 5 January 1891, Box 14, Christie Family Papers, 1891, MHS. On her evaluation of teachers, see "Their Work Well Done," *Tribune*, 30 October 1888.

46. The debate began with "Votes for Women" and "Miss McDonald's Case," *Star*, 24 and 25 October 1888; Mrs. John McLaughlin, "And Still Another," and C. J. W., "One on the Other Side," *Star*, 25 October 1888; "She Must Submit" and "A Woman Voter Replies," *Star*, 26 October 1888; "Will Vote for the Girls," *Tribune*, 30 October 1888. The microfilming process left portions of the text of these letters unreadable.

47. "Votes for Women," *Star*, 24 October 1888; "A Careless Teacher," *Tribune*, 30 October 1888.

48. "It May Reach 50,000," *Globe*, 31 October 1888.

49. "Democratic Doings," *Globe*, 31 October 1888; "A Spontaneous Turnout," *Globe*, 1 November 1888; "Ten Thousand Men," *Globe*, 2 November 1888.

50. "Ten Thousand Men," *Globe*, 2 November 1888.

51. "Hennepin for Ben," *Globe*, 7 November 1888. For accounts of election practices, see Frank H. Heck, *The Civil War Veteran in Minnesota Life and Politics* (Oxford, Ohio, 1941), 112–15.

52. Robert Brekken, "From the Prairie to the City: Minnesota Populism, 1881–1896," M.A. thesis (University of Minnesota, 1980), 21.

53. Minnesota tended to vote Republican in most elections between 1865 and 1898. St. Paul voted Democratic more often than not; Minneapolis, in local politics, had a more varied history.

54. For the women's reaction, see "Women in Politics," *Tribune*, 28 October 1888; "Flour City Dust," *Globe*, 4 November 1888; "Hennepin for Ben," *Globe*, 7 November 1888; "Politics Running Wild," *Journal*, 11 November 1888. On woman suffrage, see Julia B. Nelson, "Minnesota," in *The History of Woman Suffrage*, vol. 4, ed. Susan B. Anthony and Ida Husted Harper (Rochester, Minn., 1900), 772–82; Marjorie Bingham, "Keeping at It: Minnesota Women," in *Minnesota in a Century of Change: The State and Its People since 1900*, ed. Clifford E. Clark, Jr. (St. Paul, 1989), 441ff.

55. See "Hennepin for Ben," *Globe*, 7 November 1888; "Politics Running Wild," *Journal*, 11 November 1888.

56. "The Eight Hour System," *Globe*, 27 January 1886; "Eight Hours—the Movement to Reduce the Hours of Labor," *Globe*, 28 January 1886, transcribed in the Minnesota Federal Writers' Project, *Annals of Minnesota*, Subject File, 1849–1942, reel 91, fr. 1583, 1189, MHS; "Eight Hours," *Northwestern Labor Union*, 20 April 1889.

57. "Some Eight Hours Talk," *Globe*, 23 February 1889.

58. Ibid.

59. "Eight Hour System," *Globe*, 13 May 1887.

60. W. E. McEwen, "History of the Labor Movement in Minnesota," *Official Yearbook of the Minnesota State Federation of Labor* (St. Paul, 1916), 15–16. "Industrial Topics," *Globe*, 24 March 1889, notes the meeting to be held on 7 April 1889.

61. *Reminiscences*, 17.

62. Patterson, "Eva McDonald Valesh."

63. *Reminiscences*, 17–18.

64. See "Eight Hours," *Northwestern Labor Union*, 10 August 1889, and "People Who Work," *Journal*, 2 November 1889, on McDonald's appointment. See also Knights of

Labor, *Proceedings of the 23rd Regular Meeting, District Assembly 79*, 20 January 1889, Minneapolis, Minnesota, Powderly Papers, microfilm edition, reel 65, Series A, Part 4B, afternoon session, report, 16 July 1888, p. 22.

65. Fink, *Workingmen's Democracy*, 18–37.

66. "The Wants of Workers," *Journal*, 4 August 1888.

Chapter 3. Telling Tales

1. Eva Gay, *A Tale of the Twin Cities: Lights and Shadows of the Street Car Strike in Minneapolis and St. Paul, April 1889* (St. Paul, 1889), 44 (hereafter cited in notes as *Tale*).

2. In *A Guide to Local Assemblies of the Knights of Labor* (Westport, Conn., 1982), 230, Jonathan Garlock lists only the local assembly number for the Minneapolis Street Railway Employees Protective Association, organized in 1886 and disbanded in 1889; none is listed for St. Paul. See the editorial "Not a Local Question," *Globe*, 13 April 1889.

3. *Globe*, 12, 14, 18–19 April 1889. See Goodrich Lowry, *Streetcar Man: Thomas Lowry and the Twin City Rapid Transit Company* (Minneapolis, 1979), 85–95.

4. *Tribune*, 28 February 1886, 21–22 June 1886, and 24 August 1886, transcribed in the Minnesota Federal Writers' Project, *Annals of Minnesota*, subject file "Labor–General," microfilm reel 91, fr. 1091, 1309, 1174–75, MHS.

5. *Tale*, 7–8; "They All Walk," *Globe*, 12 April 1889; "The Men Go Out," *Tribune*, 12 April 1889.

6. Lowry, *Streetcar Man*, 85–107. For other strikes focused on workers' control and technological innovation, see Robert E. Ziegler, "The Limits of Power: The Amalgamated Association of Street Railway Employees in Houston, Texas, 1897–1905," *Labor History* 18 (Winter 1977): 71–90, and Sarah M. Henry, "The Strikers and Their Sympathizers: The Brooklyn Trolley Strike of 1895," *Labor History* 32 (Winter 1991): 329–53.

7. See Goodrich's remarks in "They All Walk," *Globe*, 12 April 1889; "Bells Jingle Not," *Globe*, 14 April 1889. For similar cases, see Ziegler, "The Limits of Power"; Henry, "The Strikers and Their Sympathizers." In the Brooklyn strike, the issue was workforce composition; the ratio of straight-run men versus trippers and extras. The Brooklyn strike was, however, on an electric trolley system owned not by one but by several small companies; the resolution of the strike was somewhat more ambiguous.

8. "Twin City Industrial Gossip," *Globe*, 14 April 1889; "The True Inwardness," *Pioneer Press*, 20 April 1889; "Not a Local Question," *Globe*, 14 April 1889; "Lowry against Organized Labor," *Tribune*, 26 April 1889.

9. "They All Walk," *Globe*, 12 April 1889.

10. Ibid.; "The Men Go Out," *Tribune*, 12 April 1889. On grievances, see also "Toiler's Field," *Globe*, 7 April 1889; "In the Field of the Toiler," *Globe*, 12 May 1889.

11. "They All Walk," *Globe* 12 April 1889; for the earlier meeting, see "Twin Cities Industrial Gossip," *Globe*, 7 April 1889.

12. "Hung in Suspense," *Globe*, 16 April 1889; "Walk Still On," *Tribune*, 16 April 1889; "Cars on the Move," *Tribune*, 18 April 1889; "Women Boycott It," *Journal*, 19 April 1889; "Roast the Mayor," *Globe*, 20 April 1889; "Names the Limit," *Tribune*, 20 April 1889; "Must All Run Monday" *Pioneer Press*, 20 April 1889. For more on the petition drive, see the *Globe*, 13, 16, and 23 April 1889; *Journal*, 14 April 1889; "For the Good of the City," *Northwestern Labor Union*, 20 April 1889.

13. "Hung in Suspense," *Globe*, 16 April 1889; "No Sign of Trouble," *Globe*, 20 April 1889.

14. "Minneapolis Street Railway Co." and "Figures Talk and They Call Mr. Lowry a Lawyer," *Northwestern Labor Union*, 20 April 1889. On the earlier discussion, see "Now They Protest," *Globe*, 17 March 1889.

15. "The Strikers Confer," *Pioneer Press*, 12 April 1889; "A Day of Quiet," *Tribune*, 14 April 1889; "Minneapolis Muss," *Pioneer Press*, 14 April 1889.

16. "A Day of Quiet," *Tribune*, 14 April 1889; "Bells Jingle Not," *Globe*, 14 April 1889; *Tale*, 29. See also the discussion in "Minneapolis Street Railway Co," *Northwestern Labor Union*, 20 April 1889.

17. *Reminiscences of Eva McDonald Valesh* (1952), p. 43, in the Columbia University Oral History Research Office Collection (hereafter cited in the notes as *Reminiscences*).

18. On Eight-Hour League support, see the *Globe*, 12 and 14 April 1889. For the general campaign to reduce the workday nationwide, see David R. Roediger and Philip S. Foner, *Our Own Time: A History of American Labor and the Working Day* (Westport, Conn., 1989). For McDonald's participation, see, among other sources, the *Tribune*, 13–14, 17, 20, and 26 April 1889; *Globe* 12–14, 17, 20, and 26 April 1889; *Journal*, 24 April 1889. Quotes from "A Day of Quiet," *Tribune*, 14 April 1889, and "The End at Last," *Tribune*, 23 April 1889.

19. "A Hay Market Hurrah," *Pioneer Press*, 23 April 1889.

20. "The Strikers Confer," *Pioneer Press*, 12 April 1889; "A Hay Market Hurrah," *Pioneer Press*, 23 April 1889.

21. "Hung in Suspense," *Globe*, 16 April 1889 and subsequent issues; *Northwestern Labor Union*, 20 April 1889; *Tale*, 34–37, 44–46, 66–68.

22. See coverage of crowd actions in the *Globe*, 13–15, 22–23, and 25 April 1889; *Journal*, 12, 14, 17, and 22 April 1889; *Tribune*, 12–14 and 22 April 1889; *Pioneer Press*, 12–14, 17, and 22 April 1889.

23. "The People Sympathize," *Tribune*, 16 April 1889; "Roast the Mayor," *Globe*, 20 April 1889.

24. "Women Boycott It," *Journal*, 19 April 1889; *Globe*, 19–20 and 22 April 1889.

25. "North Minneapolis Stir," *Globe*, 20 April 1889; "Women Boycott It," *Journal*, 19 April 1889; "Was Almost a Mob," *Tribune*, 13 April 1889. See also the *Globe*, 18, 20, and 22 April 1889.

26. See, for example, "Women Will Organize," *Globe*, 15 September 1888. See also Viviana Zelizer, *Pricing the Priceless Child: The Changing Social Value of Children* (New York, 1985); Randolph E. Bergstrom, *Courting Danger: Injury and Law in New York City, 1870–1910* (Ithaca, N.Y., 1992).

27. For example, see "Girls after Farms," *Globe*, 15 April 1889; "The Woman Experiment," *Globe*, 19 April 1889; "El Dorado's Border," *Globe*, 22 April 1889; "Scuffling for Soil," *Globe*, 23 April 1889; "Sioux Take in the Sights," *Globe*, 26 April 1889.

28. "They All Walk," *Globe*, 12 April 1889.

29. "And Now Pistols," *Journal*, 17 April 1889; "The Kansas City Importations," *Journal*, 18 April 1889; "Kansas City Men" and "Here They Come," *Globe*, 19 and 20 April 1889; "50 Determined Men," "Professional Scab," and "New Men at the Junction," *Tribune*, 17, 19, and 20 April 1889.

30. "The Easter Riot," *Globe*, 22 April 1889. See the discussion on the outlaw figure in dime western and strike novels in Michael Denning, *Mechanics Accents: Dime Novels and Working Class Culture in America* (London, 1987), 157–66.

31. *Tale*, 43–44; "Cowboys in Town," *Tribune*, 20 April 1889; "The Strike Over," *Tribune*, 21 April 1889.

32. "Women Boycott It" and "The Motors Doped," *Journal*, 19 and 20 April 1889; "No Sign of Trouble," *Globe*, 20 April 1889. There was coverage of the Gray County seat war in the St. Paul *Globe* earlier in the year; see, for example, "Women under Arms," *Globe*, 14 January 1889.

33. "The Motors Doped," *Journal*, 20 April 1889; "An Easter Riot," *Globe*, 22 April 1889; "Worse and Worse," *Tribune*, 22 April 1889; "Quiet Now Reigns," *Journal*, 22 April 1889. On the racialization of class conflict, see Richard Slotkin, *The Fatal Environment: The Myth of the Frontier in the Age of Industrialization, 1800–1890* (New York, 1985), 477–98.

34. "An Easter Riot," *Globe*, 22 April 1889; "The Men Weaken," *Journal*, 23 April 1889.

35. "An Easter Riot," *Globe*, 22 April 1889.

36. "An Easter Riot" and "The End Seems Near," *Globe*, 22 and 23 April 1889; "The Men Weaken," *Journal*, 23 April 1889.

37. "An Easter Riot," *Globe*, 22 April 1889; "Worse and Worse," *Tribune*, 22 April 1889; "A Riot on Sunday," *Pioneer Press*, 22 April 1889; "Quiet Now Reigns," *Journal*, 22 April 1889.

38. The ordinances were the product of the 1877 railroad strike.

39. On the ordinances, see the *Globe*, 18, 22, and 28 April 1889; *Journal*, 23 April 1889. On the special police, see the *Globe*, 16 April 1889; *Journal*, 15 April 1889.

40. Calvin Schmid, *Social Saga of the Twin Cities: An Ecological and Statistical Study of Social Trends in Minneapolis and St. Paul* (Minneapolis, 1938), esp. 56–88; Lowry (*Streetcar Man*, 17–52) describes the building of Lowry's real-estate empire. On city expansion and streetcar development, see Sam Bass Warner, *Streetcar Suburbs: The Process of Growth in Boston, 1870–1900*, 2d ed. (Cambridge, 1978).

41. See Warner, *Streetcar Suburbs*; William Cronon, *Nature's Metropolis: Chicago and the Great West* (New York, 1992).

42. The population of Minneapolis in 1890 was 164,738, according to the Census Bureau, *17th Census of the United States, 1950, Population*, vol. 1, *Number of Inhabitants* (Washington, D.C., 1953), Table 4, 23–11.

43. On the Senate, see *Tale*, 66. The characterization of the petition as "misdirected energy" comes from McDonald's description of the fire that destroyed it (*Tale*, 44–45).

44. See Sidney L. Harring, *Policing a Class Society: The Experience of American Cities, 1865–1915* (New Brunswick, N.J., 1983), 101–48. For the legal implications, see Victoria Hattam, *Labor Visions and State Power: The Origins of Business Unionism in the United States, 1806–1896* (Princeton, N.J., 1993); Christopher L. Tomlins, *The State and the Unions: Labor Relations, Law, and the Organized Labor Movement in America, 1880–1960* (New York, 1985).

45. The coverage of the strike in the *Globe*, *Journal*, and *Tribune* periodically names those accused and sentenced for strike-related crimes. The greatest number were clustered in the period from April 17 to April 21, the last was the day of the Easter riot in

which more than twenty laborers were arrested in the Riverside area and a few scattered arrests were made around the city.

46. "The Men Weaken," *Journal*, 23 April 1889; "Strike Stricken Out," *Globe*, 26 April 1889.

47. See Helen Asher, "The Labor Movement in Minnesota, 1850–1900," unpublished paper, 1925, in the possession of MHS, 6.

48. "Workmen's Meeting," *Globe*, 24 August 1880, transcribed in the Minnesota Federal Writers' Project, *Annals of Minnesota*, Subject Files, 1849–1942, microfilm reel 91, fr. 1506, MHS.

49. Minnesota State Federation of Labor, *Yearbook* (St. Paul, 1916), 17.

50. "Hung in Suspense," *Globe*, 16 April 1889; "The End Seems Near," *Globe*, 23 April 1889; "The Men Weaken," *Journal*, 23 April 1889. See also the satirical account in *Tale*. The pun here on "printer's devil" is worth noting.

51. "The Toilers' Field," *Globe*, 28 April 1889. See the editorial response to E. M. Corser's letter that follows the article, "Professional Scab," *Journal*, 19 April 1889.

52. On the rocky history of the People's Herdics, see "All the Lines Running," *Journal*, 27 April 1889; "The Herdics," *The Progress* (East Minneapolis), 29 June 1889; "The Labor Legislature," *Journal*, 21 September 1889; "For People Who Work," *Journal*, 28 September 1889; "Defunct Herdics," *Globe*, 2 November 1889.

53. There is a longstanding argument about the nature of working-class fragmentation in the Gilded Age, especially along ethnic lines. Herbert Gutman, *Work, Culture, and Society in Industrializing America* (New York, 1976), was the first of many formulations in the new labor history. See also Richard Oestreicher, *Solidarity and Fragmentation: Working People and Class Consciousness in Detroit, 1875–1900* (Urbana, Ill., 1986); Kim Voss, *The Making of American Exceptionalism: The Knights of Labor and Class Formation in the Nineteenth Century* (Ithaca, N.Y., 1993).

54. See Sidney Fine, *Laissez Faire and the General Welfare State* (Ann Arbor, 1964); Daniel Rodgers, *The Work Ethic in America, 1850–1920* (Chicago, 1978); Edward Kirkland, *Dream and Thought in the American Business Community* (Ithaca, N.Y., 1956).

55. On class reconfigurations in the Progressive era, see James Weinstein, *The Corporate Ideal in the Liberal State, 1900–1918* (Boston, 1968).

56. Editorial, *Northwestern Labor Union*, 10 August 1889.

57. "Now They Protest," *Globe*, 17 March 1889.

58. See Harring, *Policing a Class Society*, 52–53.

59. *Tale*, 26.

Chapter 4. "They Walk on My Collar in Their Party Organs"

1. Stevens's comment in handwriting on the bottom of letter, Eva McDonald to Sarah Christie Stevens, 5 January 1891, Box 14, James C. Christie and Family Papers, 1891, MHS.

2. Annie Diggs, "Women in the Alliance Movement," *Arena* 6 (1892): 172–73.

3. See the accounts in Eleanor Flexner, *Century of Struggle: The Women's Rights Movement in the United States* (1959; New York, 1974); Gerda Lerner, *The Grimké Sisters of South Carolina: Rebels against Slavery* (Boston, 1967); Mary P. Ryan, *Women in Public: Between Banners and Ballots* (Baltimore, 1990); Nancy Isenberg, *Sex and Citizenship in Antebellum America* (Chapel Hill, N.C., 1998).

4. Paula Baker, "The Domestication of American Politics," *American Historical Review* 89 (June 1984): 620–47, and *The Moral Frameworks of Public Life: Gender, Politics,*

and the State in Rural New York, 1870–1930 (New York, 1991). See also Suzanne Lebsock, "Women and American Politics, 1880–1920," in *Women, Politics, and Change in Twentieth Century America,* ed. Louise Tilly and Patricia Gurin (New York, 1990), 35–62; Rebecca Edwards, *Angels in the Machinery: Gender in Party Politics from the Civil War to the Progressive Era* (New York, 1997).

5. On nonpartisanship, see Baker, *The Moral Frameworks of Public Life,* 44–50; Michael Goldberg, "'An Army of Women': Gender Relations and Politics in Kansas Populism, the Woman Movement, and the Republican Party, 1879–1896," Ph.D. diss. (Yale University, 1992), esp. 105–25, 251–67.

6. "Labels for Labor," *Globe,* 19 May 1889.

7. Robert Brekken, "From the Prairie to the City: Minnesota Populism, 1881–1896," M.A. thesis (University of Minnesota, 1979); Donald Warner, "Prelude to Populism," *Minnesota History* 32 (September 1951): 132–34; Martin Ridge, *Ignatius Donnelly: Portrait of a Politician* (Chicago, 1962), 247–52.

8. *Great West,* 13 February 1891.

9. See Mari Jo Buhle's comments, "Politics and Culture in Women's History," *Feminist Studies* 6 (1982): 26–63.

10. Eva McDonald Valesh to Albert Dollenmayer, 20 August 1891, Corning, N.Y., Albert Dollenmayer and Family Papers, Box 2, MHS.

11. "Live Meetings," *Great West,* 28 February 1890.

12. "The Alliance Picnic" (n.p., *Herald,* n.d.), clipping, Scrapbook, reel 158, fr. 402–406; "Alliance No. 451, Alliance Meeting at Witoka," *Winona Republican,* 29 June 1890, clipping, Scrapbook, reel 158, fr. 421–2; "The Alliance Rally," n.d., n.p., clipping, Scrapbook, reel 158, fr. 234–35; "Agitation," *Rock Co News,* 12(?) June 1890, clipping, Scrapbook, reel 158, fr. 242, Ignatius Donnelly Papers, microfilm edition, MHS; *Great West,* 17 October 1890.

13. On Eva McDonald Valesh, see Diggs, "Women and the Alliance Movement."

14. The series was initiated in February. See "The New Political Economy," *Great West,* 9 February 1890, for an overview of McDonald's political views.

15. "The New Political Economy," *Great West,* 21 February and 16 May 1890; Eva McDonald Valesh, Minnesota state lecturer, address, *Proceedings of the National Farmers' Alliance, 11th Annual Meeting at Omaha* (Des Moines, 1891), evening session, 28 January 1891, microfilm, State Historical Society of Wisconsin.

16. Donnelly diary, 18 June 1890, Donnelly Papers, reel 147, fr. 464, MHS.

17. Warner, "Prelude to Populism," 135.

18. Lawrence Goodwyn's *Democratic Promise: The Populist Movement in America* (New York, 1976) remains the best account of the creation of a movement culture through new economic institutions, political means, and public debate, although it undervalues the democratic culture of labor reform. For a general survey of Populist history, see Robert McMath, *American Populism* (New York, 1993).

19. Donnelly diary, 26 June 1890, Donnelly Papers, reel 147, fr. 473–74, MHS.

20. Frank Heck, *The Civil War Veterans in Minnesota Life and Politics* (Oxford, Ohio, 1941), 99.

21. *Reminiscences of Eva McDonald Valesh* (1952), pp. 36–39, in the Columbia University Oral History Research Office Collection (hereafter cited in the notes as *Reminiscences*).

22. "The Alliance Picnic" (n.p., *Herald,* n.d.) clipping, Scrapbook, Donnelly Papers, reel 158, fr. 402–406, MHS.

23. Eva McDonald to Sarah Christie Stevens, 8 May 1891, Christie Family Papers, Box 14, MHS.

24. Jean Christie, "Sarah Christie Stevens, Schoolwoman," *Minnesota History* 48 (Summer 1983): 245–54, esp. 249–50; *Mapleton Enterprise*, 17 October 1890; *Progressive Age*, 24 October 1890. Also see *Mankato Journal*, 25 October 1890; "Correspondence," *Mankato Journal*, 25 October 1890; "Two Speeches," *Mankato Free Press*, 31 October 1890, clippings, Box 13, Christie Papers, MHS. Information on the Blue Earth School superintendent election was provided by Jeffrey Kolnick.

25. Eva McDonald to Sarah Stevens, 15 November 1890, Box 13, 1890, and McDonald to Stevens, 5 January 1891, Box 14, 1891, both in Christie Papers, MHS.

26. See Brekken, "From the Prairie to the City."

27. See John D. Hicks, "The Origin and Early History of the Farmers' Alliance in Minnesota," *Mississippi Valley Historical Review* 9 (1922): 203–15, and "The People's Party in Minnesota," *Minnesota History* 5 (1924): 531–60; Warner, "Prelude to Populism"; Carl H. Chrislock, "The Politics of Protest in Minnesota, 1890–1901," Ph.D. diss. (University of Minnesota, 1954); Martin Ridge, *Ignatius Donnelly*, 270–78.

28. Kate Donnelly to Ignatius Donnelly, 8 January 1891, quoted in Ridge, *Ignatius Donnelly*, 284; Donnelly diary, 19 May 1891, Donnelly Papers, reel 147, fr. 840, 843, MHS.

29. One might cite, for example, James E. Wright, *The Politics of Populism: Dissent in Colorado* (New Haven, Conn., 1974). See also David Montgomery, "On Goodwyn's Populists," *Marxist Perspectives* 1 (1978): 166–73; Leon Fink, *Workingmen's Democracy: The Knights of Labor and American Politics* (Urbana, Ill., 1983).

30. "The New Political Economy," *Great West*, 16 May 1890, and "The Strengths and Weaknesses of the People's Movement," *Arena* 5 (May 1892): 726–31, are McDonald Valesh's best analyses of the problems of coalition between farm and labor movements.

31. Ibid.

32. Both contemporary and retrospective sources (published in the Minnesota State Federation of Labor *Yearbook* [St. Paul, 1916], 15) described the Knights of Labor as "wrecked on the rocks of partisan politics."

33. "The Strengths and Weaknesses of the People's Movement."

34. Donnelly wrote to McDonald just before the convention: "I am a candidate for president of the Alliance at our meeting of December 30th. If I am elected I propose to push the work. Are yr engagements such that after Jany 1st you could take the field?" Ignatius Donnelly to Eva McDonald, 27 November 1890, Donnelly letterbook, Donnelly Papers, MHS, quoted in Gilman, 66. On McDonald's election, see "Proceedings of Alliance Meeting," *Great West*, 9 January 1891; "The State Convention," *Farm, Stock, and Home*, 15 January 1891, 79; Eva McDonald to Sarah Stevens, 5 January 1891, Box 14, Christie Papers, 1891, MHS.

35. The Minnesota State Farmers' Alliance Constitution and Bylaws does not specifically bar women as members. It does state that "any persons who are employed by, or working for the Alliance, during the greater part of the time, as lecturers, organizers, agents, or Alliance editors, shall be eligible to membership in any subordinate alliance, as fully as if they were practical farmers." The only other bars to membership were to railroad employees and stockholders, drunkards, and persons of immoral character. Article IV, section 5, also makes the wives and daughters or female relatives of persons eligible for membership in the Alliance with the same rights as other members. See the Minnesota State Farmers' Alliance, *Constitution and Bylaws* (1891), MHS.

36. *Great West,* 24 April 1891.

37. *Great West,* 23 January 1891.

38. "Proceedings of Alliance Meeting," *Great West,* 9 January 1891.

39. Executive Committee Report, *Great West,* 6 February 1891.

40. Early accounts include Bettie Gay, "The Influence of Women in the Alliance," in *Farmers' Alliance History and Agricultural Digest,* ed. Nelson Dunning (Washington, D.C., 1891), 308–12; Diggs, "Women in the Alliance Movement." See also Julie Roy Jeffrey, "Women in the Southern Farmers' Alliance," *Feminist Studies* 3 (Fall 1975): 72–91; Mari Jo Buhle, *Women and American Socialism* (Urbana, Ill., 1981), 82–89; Mary Jo Wagner, "Farm, Families, and Reform: Women in the Farmers' Alliance and Populist Party," Ph.D. diss. (University of Oregon, 1986); Goldberg, "An Army of Women."

41. "The New Political Economy," *Great West,* 21 March 1890.

42. Ibid.

43. Ibid.

44. Ibid. Eva McDonald Valesh, "More Leisure for Women," *Farmers' Wife* (September 1891); Eva McDonald Valesh, Minnesota state lecturer, address, *Proceedings of the National Farmers' Alliance, 11th Annual Meeting at Omaha* (Des Moines, 1891), evening session, 28 January 1891, microfilm, State Historical Society of Wisconsin.

45. Another point of contention was McDonald's appointment to a clerkship in the state House of Representatives. See Eva McDonald to Sarah Christie Stevens, 5 and 12 January 1891, Christie Papers, Box 14, MHS; "Only a Woman, but She May Have Stood between a Sage and His Ambition," *Globe,* 1 February 1891.

46. "The Alliance Rally," n.p., n.d., clipping, Scrapbook, reel 158, fr. 234–5, MHS; "Alliance No. 451, Alliance Meeting at Witoka," *Winona Republican,* 29 June 1890, clipping, Scrapbook, reel 158, fr. 421–22, Donnelly Papers, MHS.

47. See the change in political language as discussed in Kenneth Cmiel, *Democratic Eloquence: The Fight over Popular Speech in 19th Century America* (Berkeley, 1990), 236–57. Journalistic norms affected political speech-making as well as shifting tastes and composition of political constituencies. See Thomas Leonard, *The Power of the Press: The Birth of American Political Reporting* (New York, 1986), 166–231.

48. "Donnelly's Predicament," *Pioneer Press,* 3 January 1891.

49. Ibid.

50. For the Populist critique of the commercial press, see Goodwyn, *Democratic Promise,* 354–86.

51. "A Discord in the Reform Chorus," *Globe,* 17 February 1889; "Donnelly's Predicament," *Pioneer Press,* 3 January 1891; J. L., Sparta, "Beware of the Ambitious," *Farm, Stock, and Home,* 15 March 1891, 152.

52. David Paul Nord, "Tocqueville, Garrison, and the Perfection of Journalism," *Journalism History* 13 (Summer 1986): 56–63, addresses journalism as an aspect of voluntary association.

53. Ridge, *Ignatius Donnelly,* 268–69.

54. Donnelly, who accused numerous politicians of corruption, built his career on a steady oscillation between and among parties and causes. See Ridge, *Ignatius Donnelly.*

55. Eva McDonald Valesh to Albert Dollenmayer, Red Wing, Minn., 24 November 1891, Dollenmayer Papers, Box 2, MHS.

56. "Address," *Great West,* 8 January 1892.

57. Ibid.

58. Ibid.

59. *Great West*, 13 February 1891; *Globe*, 1 February 1891; *Pioneer Press*, 23 April 1891.

60. *Reminiscences*, 25.

61. Dolores Valesh Lautman to Elizabeth Faue, 27 January 1993, letter in author's possession.

62. *Reminiscences*, 25.

63. Ada Patterson, "Eva McDonald Valesh, Joan of Arc of the Women of the Laboring Classes," *Human Life* (December 1908); application for marriage license, Frank S. Valesh and Eva McDonald, 2 June 1891, marriage records, Hennepin County, 24 July 1891, Book 51, 103 (microfilm 22–435), Eva McDonald Valesh Papers, MHS. Witnesses were Frederick Valesh, Frank's brother, and Anna A. Lane, probably Eva's aunt. They were married by a Catholic priest, R. M. Blomer.

64. The principal evidence for her tour are the letters to Dollenmayer. For newspaper coverage of Populist work in New York, see "Peffer and Simpson," *New York Tribune*, 24 August 1891; "Peffer and Simpson at Mt. Gretna," *New York Tribune*, 22 August 1891. Neither article mentions McDonald Valesh as a speaker; a hurried survey of the fragmentary surviving local newspapers in New York yielded no other reports. McDonald's presence at the Illinois farmers' encampment is stated in "Facts about Farmers," *Chicago Tribune*, 15 August 1891; "Grange Speakers Heard," *Illinois State Journal*, 13 August 1891; "The Farmers Were Absent," *Illinois State Journal*, 14 August 1891; "The Encampment Is Ended," *Illinois State Journal*, 15 August 1891.

65. See Eva McDonald's address, *Proceedings of the National Farmers' Alliance, 11th Annual Meeting* (Des Moines, 1891), 28 January 1891, evening session, microfilm, State Historical Society of Wisconsin; on the Indianapolis meeting, Eva McDonald Valesh to Albert Dollenmayer, 24 November 1891, Dollenmayer Papers, Box 2, MHS.

66. Eva McDonald Valesh to Albert Dollenmayer, 20 August 1891, Corning, N.Y., Dollenmayer Papers, Box 2, MHS.

67. Eva McDonald Valesh to Albert Dollenmayer, 19 July 1891, Belmont, N.Y., Dollenmayer Papers, Box 2, MHS.

68. Eva McDonald Valesh to Albert Dollenmayer, 20 August 1891, Corning, N.Y., Dollenmayer Papers, Box 2, MHS; see also *Reminiscences*, 34–43.

69. Eva McDonald Valesh to Albert Dollenmayer, 19 July 1891, Belmont, N.Y., Dollenmayer Papers, Box 2, MHS.

70. Eva McDonald Valesh to Albert Dollenmayer, 1 August 1891, Belmont, N.Y., and Valesh to Dollenmayer, 20 August 1891, Corning, N.Y., both in Dollenmayer Papers, Box 2, MHS.

71. See her "The People's Movement," *National Economist*, 9 April 1892, 51; "Changes in Our Governmental System," *National Economist*, 3 September 1892, 395; Valesh, "Strengths and Weaknesses of the People's Movement," *Arena* 5 (May 1892): 726–31.

72. January meeting of the Minnesota Farmers' Alliance, address by Donnelly, in *Great West*, 8 January 1892.

73. A similar process of marginalization in reform movements that turned to politics can be observed in the precursors to the People's party, including the abolitionist movement, the Grange, and the Socialist party. When such social movements shift their tactics from petitioning to electoral politics, women have generally lost their institutional role in the movement. See Alice Rossi, "The Social Roots of the Women's Movement in America," *The Feminist Papers* (New York, 1976), 241–81; Gerda Lerner, "The

Political Activities of the Antislavery Women," in *The Majority Finds Its Past* (New York, 1979), 112–28.

Chapter 5. From Strikes to Strings

1. Eva McDonald Valesh to Albert Dollenmayer, 19 July 1891, Albert Dollenmayer and Family Papers, Box 2, MHS.

2. Brooke Kroeger, *Nellie Bly: Daredevil, Reporter, Feminist* (New York, 1994).

3. Julian Ralph, a nationally known journalist, noted in his autobiography that "if a reporter gets what he is told to, he is a good reporter; if not, he is no good." Julian Ralph, *The Making of a Journalist* (New York, 1903), 32.

4. Eva McDonald Valesh to Albert Dollenmayer, 20 August 1891; Valesh to Dollenmayer, 8 September 1891; Valesh to Dollenmayer, 24 November 1891, Box 2; Dollenmayer to Valesh, 25 July 1891; Dollenmayer to Valesh, 31 August 1891, both in Letterbook, 1891–92, vol. 5, Box 6, Dollenmayer Papers, MHS.

5. Edward Llewellyn Shuman, *Steps into Journalism: Helps and Hints for Young Writers* (Evanston, Ill., 1894), 126.

6. Michael Schudson, *Discovering the News: A Social History of American Newspapers* (New York, 1978), 61–120; Frank Mott, *American Journalism: A History of Newspapers in the United States*, rev. ed. (New York, 1950), 430–58; Edwin Emery, *The Press and America: An Interpretive History of Journalism*, 2d ed. (Englewood Cliffs, N.J., 1962), 369–446; Kroeger, *Nellie Bly*, 79–182.

7. *Reminiscences of Eva McDonald Valesh* (1952), pp. 26–27, in the Columbia University Oral History Research Office Collection (hereafter cited in the notes as *Reminiscences*).

8. Goodrich Lowry, *Streetcar Man: Tom Lowry and the Twin City Rapid Transit Company* (Minneapolis, 1979), 98.

9. Bradley L. Morison, *Sunlight on Your Doorstep: The Minneapolis Tribune's First Hundred Years* (Minneapolis, 1966), 23; George S. Hage, "Evolution and Revolution in the Media: Print and Broadcast Journalism," in *Minnesota in a Century of Change: The State and Its People since 1900*, ed. Clifford E. Clark, Jr. (St. Paul, 1989), 298.

10. Valesh, *Reminiscences*, 29.

11. Morison, *Sunlight on Your Doorstep*, 23.

12. Ibid., 15–16.

13. Albert Dollenmayer to Eva Valesh, 9 December 1891, Letterbook, 1891–1892, vol. 5, Box 6, Dollenmayer Papers, MHS.

14. Valesh, *Reminiscences*, 26.

15. Morison, *Sunlight on Your Doorstep*, 23.

16. Valesh, *Reminiscences*, 29–30.

17. Ibid., 73.

18. On Murphy and the support payments, see W. J. Murphy to Frank Valesh, 11 July 1907, Dolores Lautman Papers.

19. On news as commodity, see William S. Solomon, "Division of Labor: Editorial Practices and Changes of Status and Power in a Nineteenth Century Newsroom," in *Newsworkers: Towards a History of the Rank and File*, ed. Hanno Hardt and Bonnie Bremen (Minneapolis, 1995), 112; Gerald J. Baldasty, *The Commercialism of News in the Nineteenth Century* (Madison, 1992).

20. Christopher P. Wilson, *The Labor of Words: Literary Professionalism in the Progressive Era* (Athens, Ga., 1985), 19.

21. On the reporter as "social invention" of the 1880s and 1890s and rising status and income, see Wilson, *Labor of Words*, 17–39; Schudson, *Discovering the News*, 61–120.

22. Wilson, *Labor of Words*, 17–39; Solomon, "Division of Labor"; Julius Chambers, "The Reporter's First Murder Case," in *The Making of a Newspaper*, ed. Melville Philips (New York, 1893), 305ff; Robert Darnton, "Writing News and Telling Stories," *Daedalus* 104 (1975): 175–94. On their business arrangement, see Albert Dollenmayer to Eva Valesh, 31 August 1891, Letterbook, 1891–1892, vol. 5, Box 6, Dollenmayer Papers, MHS.

23. Ralph, *The Making of a Journalist*, 26.

24. See Ted Curtis Smythe, "The Reporter, 1880–1900: Working Conditions and Their Influence on the News," *Journalism History* 1 (1980): 1–11; Solomon, "The Site of Newsroom Labor"; Kroeger, *Nellie Bly*, 192–95.

25. Willis J. Abbot, *Watching the World Go By* (Boston, 1933), 142; Shuman, *Steps into Journalism*, 18, 46–7, 49, 67, 153.

26. Wilson, *Labor of Words*, 17; see also Schudson, *Discovering the News*, 65, 88ff.

27. Shuman, *Steps into Journalism*, 148.

28. *New Orleans Picayune*, in *The Journalist*, 13 May 1893, quoted in Kroeger, *Nellie Bly*, 223.

29. Eva Valesh to Albert Dollenmayer, 24 November 1891, Box 2, Dollenmayer Papers, MHS.

30. Eva Valesh to Albert Dollenmayer, 23 March 1892, Box 2; Dollenmayer to Valesh, 29 March 1892, Letterbook, 1891–92, vol. 5, Box 6, Dollenmayer Papers, MHS. The articles were unsigned. A search revealed two likely suspects–"They Squirm," *Tribune*, 13 February 1892; "Modest Donnelly," *Tribune*, 27 February 1892.

31. Eva Valesh to Albert Dollenmayer, 2 April 1892, Box 2, Dollenmayer Papers, MHS.

32. Frank Valesh to Albert Dollenmayer, 10 May 1892; Eva Valesh to Dollenmayer, 20 December 1892, Box 2, Dollenmayer Papers, MHS.

33. Dollenmayer started as a reporter on the *Minneapolis Tribune* in 1891. He married Claribel [Longstreet?] on 27 June 1891, just a few weeks after Eva and Frank Valesh were married. Biographical Sketch, inventory, Albert Dollenmayer and Family Papers, MHS.

34. Eva Valesh to Albert Dollenmayer, 3 December 1893, Box 3, Dollenmayer Papers, MHS. Charles Hamblin was managing editor of the *Tribune*.

35. Eva Valesh to Albert Dollenmayer, 19 July 1891, Box 2, Dollenmayer Papers, MHS. The reference to Benedict is to the marriage-scoffing bachelor of Shakespeare's *Much Ado about Nothing*.

36. Albert Dollenmayer to Eva Valesh, 25 July 1891, Letterbook, 1891–92, vol. 5, Box 6, Dollenmayer Papers, MHS.

37. Eva Valesh to Albert Dollenmayer, 19 July 1891, Box 2, Dollenmayer Papers.

38. Frank Valesh to Albert Dollenmayer, 10 May 1892, Box 2, Dollenmayer Papers, MHS.

39. Eva Valesh to Albert Dollenmayer, 3 December 1893, Box 3, Dollenmayer Papers, MHS; see also 10 September 1893, Box 3, on the children.

40. Eva Valesh to Albert Dollenmayer, 19 July 1891, Box 2, Dollenmayer Papers, MHS.

41. Eva McDonald Valesh to Sarah Christie Stevens, 18 November 1893, Box 16, James C. Christie and Family papers, MHS.

42. Eva Valesh to Albert Dollenmayer, 3 December 1893, Box 3, Dollenmayer Papers, MHS. On Frank's absences, see letters of 19 July 1893 (Box 2), 23 March 1892 (Box 2), 10 September 1893 (Box 3).

43. Eva Valesh to Albert Dollenmayer, 3 December 1893, Box 3, Dollenmayer Papers, MHS.

44. Eva Valesh to Albert Dollenmayer, 3 December 1893, Box 3, Dollenmayer Papers, MHS.

45. Eva Valesh to Sarah Stevens, 18 November 1893, Box 16, Christie Family papers, MHS; Eva Valesh to Albert Dollenmayer, 3 December 1893, Box 3, Dollenmayer Papers, MHS.

46. Eva McDonald Valesh's column ran continuously from 5 March 1893 to 8 December 1895. After a tour of Europe, she resumed working for the *Tribune* sometime in April 1897.

47. See, for example, her stories on its early organization: "The Sweat of Their Brow," *Tribune*, 19 March 1893; "In the Industrial World," *Tribune*, 26 March 1893; "The Value of the Label," *Tribune*, 9 April 1893; "From Factory to Shop," *Tribune*, 16 April 1893; "Skilled and Unskilled," *Tribune*, 23 April 1893.

48. For a Gompers's editorial, see "Labor," *Tribune*, 3 September 1893; a summary of Frank's article in the *American Federationist* appears in "Labor," *Tribune*, 28 April 1895.

49. *The St. Paul Trades and Labor Bulletin* was published between 1891 and 1894.

50. *St. Paul Trades and Labor Bulletin* 2 (April 1893): 6. Valesh covered it in her *Tribune* column as well. See, for example, "Aspirations of Labor," *Tribune*, 2 April 1893.

51. See, for example, "The Labor Market," *Journal*, 29 July and 5 August 1893; "Unemployed," *Tribune*, 17 September 1893; "Employment Club," *Tribune*, 8 December 1893; "Aid Their Brethren," *Tribune*, 4 February 1894; "Labor," *Tribune* 10, 17, and 24 June and 26 August 1894.

52. "The First Step Taken," *Tribune*, 20 August 1893; "To Tackle a Problem," *Tribune*, 27 August 1893; "Work, Not Charity," *Tribune*, 31 December 1894; "From Labor's Field," *Tribune*, 12 January 1894; "Labor," *Tribune*, 8 September 1895.

53. Eva Valesh to Albert Dollenmayer, 20 December 1892, Box 2, Dollenmayer Papers, MHS.

54. Eva McDonald Valesh, "The Tenement House Problem in New York," *Arena* 7 (1893): 580–86.

55. Ibid., 581–82.

56. Ibid., 582.

57. Ibid., 582–84.

58. Ibid. On attitudes toward immigrants and disease, see Alan M. Kraut, *Silent Travelers: Germs, Genes, and the "Immigrant Menace"* (New York, 1994).

59. On labor's view of immigration, see Gwendolyn Mink, *Old Labor and New Immigrants in American Political Development: Unions, Party, and State, 1875–1920* (Ithaca, N.Y., 1986); A. J. Lane, *Solidarity or Survival? American Labor and European Immigrants, 1830–1924* (Westport, Conn., 1987); Catherine Collomp, "Unions, Civics, and National Identity: Organized Labor's Reaction to Immigration, 1881–1897," *Labor History* 29 (1988): 450–74.

60. Valesh, "The Tenement House Problem," 580–81.

61. Ibid., 580–81; Eva Gay, "Workers in Wool," *Globe,* 20 May 1888; Eva McDonald Valesh, "Child Labor," *American Federationist* 14:3 (March 1907): 157.

62. Valesh, "The Tenement House Problem," 585.

63. William E. McEwen, "History of the Labor Movement in Minnesota," in Minnesota State Federation of Labor, *Official Yearbook* (St. Paul, 1916), 13–14, 18–19; George Barker Engberg, "The Rise of Organized Labor in Minnesota, 1850–1890," M.A. thesis (University of Minnesota, 1939), 117–18.

64. American Federation of Labor, *Proceedings of the 11th Convention,* Birmingham, Alabama, 14–19 December 1891, 26–27; Eva McDonald Valesh, "Woman and Labor," *American Federationist* 2 (February 1896): 221–23; "St. Paul Labor Circles," *Northwestern Labor Union,* 12 December 1891, 2.

65. Valesh, "Woman and Labor," 221–23; James J. Kenneally, *Women in American Trade Unions* (St. Albans, Vt., 1978), 20; Philip Foner, *Women and the American Labor Movement,* vol. 1 (New York, 1979), 220–22.

66. On developments nationally, see Norman Ware, *The Labor Movement in the United States, 1860–1895: A Study in Democracy* (1929; New York, 1959), 155–298; Philip Foner, *The History of the Labor Movement in the United States,* vol. 2, *From the Founding of the American Federation of Labor to the Emergence of American Imperialism* (New York, 1955), 78–80, 132–44, 157–88.

67. See her comments in Eva McDonald, "New Political Economy," *Great West,* 28 March 1890, 25 April 1890; Eva McDonald Valesh, "The Strengths and Weaknesses of the People's Movement," *Arena* 5:30 (May 1892): 726–31; "All Care Laid Aside," *Tribune,* 4 September 1894.

68. Samuel Gompers to Eva Valesh, 4 August 1893, reel 7, vol. 9, pp. 346–47, *The Letterpress Copybooks of Samuel Gompers,* microfilm edition, Library of Congress (hereafter cited in notes as LC).

69. Ibid.; Bernard Mandel, *Samuel Gompers: A Biography* (Yellow Springs, Ohio, 1963), 99–100.

70. Samuel Gompers to Eva McDonald Valesh, 9 February 1892, reel 7, vol. 7, p. 36, Gompers Letterbooks, LC.

71. On the AFL's national political stance, see Julie Greene, *Pure and Simple Politics: The American Federation of Labor and Political Activism, 1881–1917* (Cambridge, 1998), esp. 4–12; Mollie Ray Carroll, *Labor and Politics: The Attitude of the American Federation of Labor toward Politics and Legislation* (New York, 1923); Marc Karson, *American Labor Unions and Politics, 1900–1918* (Carbondale, Ill., 1958). An important departure is Elisabeth S. Clemens, *The People's Lobby: Organizational Innovation and the Rise of Interest Group Politics in the United States, 1890–1925* (Chicago, 1997), 100–44.

72. "An Explanation," *St. Paul Trades and Labor Bulletin* 2 (June 1893): 1.

73. *St. Paul Trades and Labor Bulletin* (April 1893).

74. "Eva's Style," *Journal,* 5 August 1893.

75. *St. Paul Trades and Labor Bulletin* 2:8 (September 1893).

76. The *Indianapolis Labor Signal* (quoted in Valesh's column, "For the Federation," *Tribune,* 3 December 1893) noted that "Mrs. Eva McDonald Valesh . . . who made such a favorable impression upon the trades union people of this city two years ago . . . was one of the leaders in the revolt against the old organization, which has ceased to be a representative body."

77. "In the Realm of Labor," *Tribune*, 11 and 18 June 1893; "Stop Out Ring Rule," *Tribune*, 23 July 1893; "Call for Council," *Tribune*, 30 July 1893; "All Falling into Line," *Tribune*, 13 September 1893; "For the Federation," *Tribune*, 3 December 1893.

78. "Stamp Out Ring Rule," *Tribune*, 23 July 1893.

79. Ibid.

80. "Eva's Style," *Journal*, 5 August 1893.

81. "All Falling into Line," *Tribune*, 13 August 1893.

82. "Eva's Style," *Journal*, 5 August 1893. See also a late rejoinder in "Labor," *Tribune*, 25 November 1894.

83. "The Value of Labels," *Tribune*, 19 November 1893.

84. "Federation Platform," *Tribune*, 25 February 1894. See also "Palace of the People," *Tribune*, 11 March 1894, about the troubles of the Labor Temple. For criticisms of both sides, especially the Knights' tradition of secrecy, see "Palace of the People," *Tribune*, 11 March 1894; "The Building Trades," *Tribune*, 18 March 1894; "Cigar Makers Active," *Tribune*, 25 March 1894; "The Union of Forces," *Tribune* 1 April 1894; "Labor," 29 April 1895.

85. Valesh dutifully reported the remarks in her column and made later comments. See "Labor," *Tribune*, 20 January 1895, and "Labor," *Journal*, 17 May 1894.

86. "Calm after Riot," *Chicago Tribune*, 28 August 1893; "Attack on a Store," *Chicago Tribune*, 29 August 1893. The riot took place on Saturday, 26 August 1893.

87. On Valesh's appearance at the Labor Congress, see "Labor's Real Voice," *Chicago Tribune*, 31 August 1893; "Labor," *Minneapolis Tribune*, 3 September 1893; Reid Badger, *The Great American World Fair: The World's Columbian Exposition and American Culture* (Chicago, 1979), 100–101.

88. See Eva McDonald Valesh, "Conditions of Labor in Europe," *American Federationist* 3 (April 1896): 23–26; (May 1896): 41–43; (June 1896): 64–66; (July 1896): 83–85; (August 1896): 111–13; and (October 1896): 155–56. See also her articles "Settled by Arbitration," *American Federationist* 1 (July 1894): 97; "Women and Labor," *American Federationist* 2 (February 1896): 221–23; "The Ethics of the Labor Movement," *Trades and Labor Directory of Minneapolis and St. Paul* (Minneapolis, 1892), 85, 88–89; "Education in the Labor Movement," *Railway Times*, 2 September 1895. On syndication, see "Sons of Toil," *Tribune*, 1 April 1894.

Chapter 6. "A Slim Chance of Making Good"

1. *Reminiscences of Eva McDonald Valesh* (1952), p. 30, in the Columbia Oral History Research Office Collection (hereafter cited in the notes as *Reminiscences*).

2. Samuel Gompers to Eva McDonald Valesh, 31 July 1896, Gompers Letterbooks, LC, microfilm edition, reel 9, vol. 15, p. 638.

3. Eva McDonald Valesh to Albert Dollenmayer, New York, 20 December 1895, Albert Dollenmayer and Family Papers, Box 4, MHS.

4. *Reminiscences*, 34.

5. "Excerpts from Accounts of the 1895 Convention of the AFL in New York City," *Samuel Gompers Papers*, vol. 4, *A National Labor Movement Takes Shape, 1895–1898*, ed. Stuart B. Kaufman, Peter J. Albert, and Grace Palladino (Urbana, Ill., 1991), 81; "Eu-

ropean Letters," *American Federationist* 3 (March 1896), 15; Eva McDonald Valesh to Albert Dollenmayer, New York, 20 December 1895, Dollenmayer Papers, Box 4, MHS.

6. *Reminiscences*, 31.

7. Ibid., 34.

8. Eva McDonald Valesh, "Conditions of Labor in Europe. I—Cannes, France," *American Federationist* 3 (April 1896): 23–26.

9. Ibid.

10. Ibid, 26.

11. Ibid, 24, 26.

12. Ibid, 25.

13. Eva McDonald Valesh, "Conditions of Labor in Europe. II—Marseilles, France," *American Federationist* 3 (May 1896): 41; Valesh, "Conditions of Labor in Europe. I—Cannes, France," 25.

14. Valesh, "Conditions of Labor in Europe. I—Cannes, France," 25.

15. Eva McDonald Valesh, "Conditions of Labor in Europe. III—Malta, Italy," *American Federationist* 3 (June 1896): 64–66.

16. Valesh, "Conditions of Labor in Europe. III—Malta, Italy."

17. Ibid, 66.

18. Ibid; Valesh, "Conditions of Labor in Europe. II—Marseilles, France," 43.

19. Eva McDonald Valesh, "Conditions of Labor in Europe. IV—Austria," *American Federationist* 3 (July 1896): 83.

20. Eva McDonald Valesh, "Conditions of Labor in Europe. V—Austria," *American Federationist* 3 (August 1896): 112.

21. Ibid., 111–13; Valesh, "Conditions of Labor in Europe. IV—Austria," 84.

22. Eva McDonald Valesh, "Conditions of Labor in Europe. VI—Germany," *American Federationist* 3 (October 1896): 155–56.

23. Ibid.

24. *Reminiscences*, 32.

25. Samuel Gompers to Eva McDonald Valesh, 13 July 1896, reel 9, vol. 15, pp. 566–67; Gompers to Valesh, 31 July 1896, reel 9, vol. 15, pp. 637–38, Gompers Letterbooks, LC.

26. Gompers to Valesh, 24 December 1896, reel 10, vol. 17, p. 252; Gompers to Valesh, 1 March 1897, reel 11, vol. 18, p. 246, Gompers Letterbooks, LC.

27. Samuel Gompers to Eva McDonald Valesh, 28 September 1894, in *Samuel Gompers Papers*, vol. 3, *Unrest and Depression, 1891–94*, ed. Stuart B. Kaufman and Peter J. Albert (Urbana, Ill. 1989), 591–93.

28. Gompers to Valesh, 22 September 1896, reel 10, vol. 16, pp. 293–94, Gompers Letterbooks, LC.

29. Gompers to Valesh, 30 April 1896, reel 9, vol. 15, pp. 93–95; Gompers to Valesh, 1 March 1897, reel 11, vol. 18, p. 246, Gompers Letterbooks, LC.

30. Gompers to Valesh, 24 December 1896, reel 10, vol. 17, p. 252, Gompers Letterbooks, LC.

31. Samuel Gompers to Eva Valesh, 22 September 1896, reel 10, vol. 16, pp. 293–94, Gompers Letterbooks, LC.

32. Samuel Gompers to Samuel Ross, 20 January 1898, reel 14, vol. 22, pp. 403–405; Gompers to Eva Valesh, 24 December 1896, reel 11, vol. 17, p. 252, Gompers Letterbooks, LC.

33. Eva McDonald Valesh to Albert Dollenmayer, 23 March 1892, Box 2, Dollenmayer Papers, MHS.

34. Samuel Gompers to Eva Valesh, 1 March 1897, reel 11, vol. 18, p. 246, Gompers Letterbooks, LC.

35. Divorce Papers, copy 4 and 5 048, "Summons and Complaint," State of Minnesota, Hennepin County District Court, 4th Judicial District, Eva Valesh Plaintiff, Frank Valesh Defendant, 26 November 1906, Eva McDonald Valesh Papers, MHS; "Death of Frank Valesh," *Graceville Enterprise*, 10 November 1916; "Loss Keenly Felt," *Graceville Enterprise*, 17 November 1916.

36. Samuel Gompers to Eva Valesh, 4 September 1897, reel 12, vol. 21, p. 112, Gompers Letterbooks, LC.

37. *Reminiscences*, 49.

38. Ibid., 50–51.

39. See George Juergens, *News from the White House: The Presidential-Press Relationship in the Progressive Era* (Chicago, 1981), 15ff, on interviewing the president. One article declared Valesh was "the only reporter of either sex to achieve the distinction"; see "Mrs. E. M. Valesh," *Boston Record*, n.d. (January 1898), clipping, Scrapbook of clippings concerning the 1898 Textile Strike at New Bedford (hereafter cited in notes as NBTSS Scrapbook), 4 vols., collected by the former editor of the *New Bedford Evening Standard*, Widener Library, Harvard University.

40. *Reminiscences*, 51.

41. The *New York Journal* had at least three name changes—*New York Journal, New York Journal and Advertiser, New York Journal American*, and *New York American*, all of which were owned by Hearst.

42. *Reminiscences*, 51.

43. Arthur J. Russell, *Good-bye, Newspaper Row: Incidents of Fifty Years on the Paper* (Excelsior, Minn., 1943), 1.

44. Willis J. Abbot, *Watching the World Go By* (Boston, 1933), 148.

45. Ibid., 137.

46. Ishbel Ross, *Ladies of the Press* (New York, 1936), quoted in Marion Marzolf, *Up from the Footnote: A History of Women Journalists* (New York, 1977), 33.

47. Abbot, *Watching the World Go By*, 145. For biographies of Hearst, see W. A. Swanberg, *Citizen Hearst* (New York, 1961); Roy Everett Littlefield III, *William Randolph Hearst: His Role in American Progressivism* (Lantham, Md., 1980).

48. *Reminiscences*, 52–53.

49. Ibid., 54.

50. Ibid., 55–56.

51. In her oral history, the young woman is called Mary McGuire.

52. "Girl Victim of a Suicide Club," *New York Journal*, September 2, 1897.

53. Ibid.

54. *Reminiscences*, 57–58.

55. Samuel Gompers to Eva Valesh, 1 March 1897, reel 12, vol. 18, p. 246; Gompers to Valesh, 4 September 1897, reel 13, vol. 21, p. 112, Gompers Letterbooks, LC.

56. *Reminiscences*, 58.

57. On the strike, see Henry F. Bedford, *Socialism and the Worker in Massachusetts, 1886–1912* (Amherst, 1966), 78–82; Mary Blewett, *Constant Turmoil: The Politics of Industrial Life in Nineteenth Century New England* (Amherst, Mass., 2000), chapter 10.

58. Eva McDonald Valesh, "Journal Woman with Strikers," *New York Journal*, 19 January 1898.

59. *Reminiscences*, 62.

60. Eva McDonald Valesh, "Strike Inquiry Now Assured," *New York Journal*, 20 January 1898; Valesh, "*Journal* Strike Inquiry Ordered," *New York Journal*, 28 January 1898; Valesh, "Bay State Adopts Journal's Plan," *New York Journal*, 3 February 1898; "New Bedford Strike to Be Investigated," *Boston Post*, n.d. All in NBTSS Scrapbook.

61. "New Bedford Had Its First Introduction," *Fall River Globe*, 22 January 1898; "They Want Sensation," *Fall River Herald*, n.d., both in NBTSS Scrapbook.

62. Eva McDonald Valesh, "McKinley Talks to the *Journal* about the Great Strike," *New York Journal*, 22 January 1898; Valesh, "Dingley Calls the Strike a Sectional Necessity," *New York Journal*, 25 January 1898; Valesh, "*Journal* Strike Inquiry Ordered," *New York Journal*, 28 January 1898; Valesh, "*Journal*'s Bill for the Weavers," *New York Journal*, 29 January 1898; Valesh, "Bay State Adopts *Journal*'s Plan," *New York Journal*, 3 February 1898. All in NBTSS Scrapbook.

63. The *Journal* took up the case of Jane Gallagher, who sued a textile manufacturer for the fines imposed on her. Other newspapers also took up the cause of both the fine system and employer blacklist. See, for example, "Weavers to Fight against Unjust Fines," *New York World*, 21 January 1898; Anne O'Hagan, "All New England May Be Involved in Mill Strike," *New York Journal*, 22 January 1898; "System of Fining Women," *New York Journal*, 25 January 1898; "Black List a Weapon of Mill Men," *New York World*, 25 January 1898; "Mill Owners' War on Women," *New York Journal*, 25 January 1898; Anne O'Hagan, "Strike Keynote Is Fine System," *New York Journal*, 26 January 1898. All in NBTSS Scrapbook.

64. Eva McDonald Valesh, "State Listens to a *Journal* Woman," *New York Journal*, 9 February 1898, NBTSS Scrapbook.

65. For Valesh's coverage of the hearings, see "State Listens to a *Journal* Woman"; "Mill Men Fight *Journal*'s Bill," *New York Journal*, 19 February 1898; "Mill Men Will Meet Weavers," *New York Journal*, 11 February 1898; "Arkwright Club Is Worried," *New York Journal*, 13 February 1898. All in NBTSS Scrapbook.

66. "Arkwright Club Is Worried," *New York Journal*, 13 February 1898, NBTSS Scrapbook.

67. Eva McDonald Valesh, "Mill Men Will Meet Weavers," *New York Journal*, 11 February 1898; Valesh, "Arkwright Club Is Worried," NBTSS Scrapbook.

68. Untitled article, "Yellow Journalism Has Received the Attention," n.d.; "The McKinley Interview," n.p., 24 January 1898; "They Want Sensation," *Fall River Herald*, n.d. All in NBTSS Scrapbook.

69. "They Want Sensation," *Fall River Herald*, n.d.; "Worried Labor Men," *Fall River Herald*, 10 February 1898, both in NBTSS Scrapbook.

70. "Worried Labor Men," *Fall River Herald*, 10 February 1898; "State Listens to a *Journal* Woman," *New York Journal*, 9 February 1898, NBTSS Scrapbook.

71. *Reminiscences*, 65.

72. Abbot, *Watching the World Go By*, 223.

73. *New York Journal*, 28 January 1899, quoted in Frank Mott, *American Journalism: A History of Newspapers in the United States through 260 Years, 1690–1950*, rev. ed (New York, 1950), 523.

74. For the new journalism and the war with Spain, see Charles H. Brown, *The Correspondent's War: Journalists in the Spanish American War* (New York, 1967); Mott, *American Journalism*, 514–45; Michael Schudson, *Discovering the News: A Social History of Newspapers in America* (New York, 1978), 61ff; Abbot, *Watching the World Go By*, 207–26; Marcus Wilkerson, *Public Opinion and the Spanish American War: A Study in War Propaganda* (Baton Rouge, 1932); Joseph Wisan, *The Cuban Crisis as Reflected in the New York Press, 1895–1898*, Studies in History, Economics, and Public Law, no. 43 (New York, 1934).

75. For the history of the Cuban crisis and the Spanish-American War, see David F. Trask, *The War with Spain in 1898* (New York, 1981); Gerald F. Linderman, *The Mirror of War: American Society and the Spanish-American War* (Ann Arbor, 1974).

76. "The *Journal's* War Fleet, Correspondents and Artists," *New York Journal*, 24 February 1898; "Our Fleet at Key West," *New York Journal*, 1 March 1898; "Congressional Commission to Visit Cuba," *New York Journal*, 2 March 1898; "*Journal* Commission Off for Cuba," *New York Journal*, 3 March 1898; "*Journal* Commission Speeding to Cuba," *New York Journal*, 4 March 1898.

77. *Reminiscences*, 66–68.

78. "*Journal's* Commission Had a Rough Experience," *New York Journal*, 5 March 1898; Herbert Javrin Browne, "Brave Congressmen Face Death in Cuba," *New York Journal*, 6 March 1898.

79. Eva McDonald Valesh, "*Journal's* Envoys in Havana Today," *New York Journal*, 9 March 1898.

80. "*Journal* Legislative Commission Reaches Havana Today," *New York Journal*, 9 March 1898; Herbert Javrin Browne, "*Journal's* Commission in Havana," *New York Journal*, 11 March 1898; William E. Lewis, "*Journal* Envoys in Matanzas," *New York Journal*, 13 March 1898; "Journal Presents First Report of Commission," *New York Journal*, 14 March 1898; Herbert Javrin Browne, "Journal Envoys See Fields Ablaze," *New York Journal*, 16 March 1898; "Amos Cummings Looks into an Inferno," *New York Journal*, 17 March 1898; "*Journal* Envoys Speak on Cuba," *New York Journal*, 21 March 1898; "*Journal's* Commission Declares," *New York Journal*, 21–22 March 1898; "Senator Gallinger in Senate," *New York Journal*, 24 March 1898; Brown, *The Correspondents' War*, 130, 139–40.

81. Eva McDonald Valesh, "*Journal* Envoys in Havana Today," *New York Journal*, 9 March 1898; "*Journal's* Commission in Havana," *New York Journal*, 11 March 1898; Valesh, "*Journals* Envoys among the Starving," *New York Journal*, 12 March 1898.

82. Eva McDonald Valesh, "*Journal* Envoys among the Starving," *New York Journal*, 12 March 1898.

83. Herbert Javrin Browne, "*Journal's* Commission in Havana," *New York Journal*, 11 March 1898; Jacob Gallinger, "Chapter of Blood and Death," *New York Journal*, 13 March 1898; "*Journal* Presents First Report of Commission," *New York Journal*, 14 March 1898; Cummings, "Amos Cummings Looks into an Inferno," *New York Journal*, 17 March 1898.

84. Harry S. Fulton, "Mrs. Thurston Dies in Cuba," *New York Journal*, 15 March 1898; Harry S. Fulton, "Mrs. Thurston Dies Pitying Cuba," *New York Journal*, 16 March 1898; "Report of *Journal's* Work Stirs Washington, Thurston's Eloquence at the Command of Silent Lips," *New York Journal*, 25 March 25, 1898.

85. "Mrs. Thurston's Appeal to American Mothers," *New York Journal*, 13 March 1898.

86. *Reminiscences*, 71–72.

87. On the syndicated newsletter, see *Reminiscences*, 72–73, 75–76. On the press gallery, see *Reminiscences*, 76.

88. See Samuel Gompers to August Gansser, 12 March 1901, *Samuel Gompers Papers*, vol. 5, *An Expanding Movement at the Turn of the Century, 1898–1902*, ed. Stuart B. Kaufman, Peter J. Albert, and Grace Palladino (Urbana, Ill., 1996), 329–30. For other references to the syndicated newsletter, see Ada Patterson, "Eva McDonald Valesh, Joan of Arc of the Women of the Working Classes," *Human Life* (December 1908); Helen Marot to Eva McDonald Valesh, 22 April 1910, transcript in National Executive Board Minutes, 20 May 1910; Valesh to Marot, 28 April 1910, transcript in National Executive Board Minutes, 20 May 1910, both in National Women's Trade Union League Papers, LC.

89. *Reminiscences*, 74.

90. Ibid., 75.

91. Ibid.

92. Ibid., 78.

93. Ibid., 82.

94. Ibid., 83.

95. Ibid., 83–84.

96. See Philip Ethington, *The Public City: The Political Construction of Urban Life in San Francisco, 1850–1900* (Cambridge, 1994), 308ff; Leonard, *The Power of the Press*.

97. American Federation of Labor, *Proceedings of the Twentieth Annual Convention*, Louisville, Ky., 6–15 December 1900 (Washington, D.C., 1901), 85; Samuel Gompers to Thomas Tracy, 14 May 1901, *Samuel Gompers Papers*, 5: 356.

Chapter 7. Samuel Gompers's "Right-Hand Man"

1. Edward O'Donnell, "Women as Bread Winners—the Error of the Age," *American Federationist* 4:8 (1897) 186–87.

2. James Kenneally, *Women and American Trade Unions* (St. Albans, Vt., 1978), 23; American Federation of Labor, *Proceedings of the Twentieth Annual Convention*, Louisville, Ky., 6–15 December 1900 (Washington, D.C., 1901), 85. On the date of her hire, see the financial statement for May 1901, *American Federationist* 8 (July 1901): 285. It lists her salary for the first time on staff.

3. Samuel Gompers, *Seventy Years of Life and Labor*, rpt. ed., vol. 1 (New York, 1967), 229–30, 270–72, 329, 375; Bernard Mandel, *Samuel Gompers: A Biography* (Yellow Springs, Ohio, 1963), 89–90, 171.

4. First notice of Eva Valesh's salary ($69.50 for four weeks) in the financial statement, *American Federationist* 8 (July 1901): 285. Financial statements list increasing but variable salary payments. In May 1903, her salary was $125 for five weeks (*American Federationist* 10 [May 1903]: 615). In 1908, it was $30 a week (*American Federationist* 15 [December 1908]: 1103).

5. For example, Samuel Gompers to Eva McDonald Valesh, 17 December 1901, reel 37, vol. 49, p. 167, Rosa Lee Guard to Valesh, 9 November 1903, reel 68, vol. 80, p. 834; Gompers to Valesh, 13 June 1905, reel 89, vol. 101, p. 464. All in Gompers Letterbooks, LC.

6. *Reminiscences of Eva McDonald Valesh* (1952), p. 87, in the Columbia University Oral History Research Office Collection (hereafter cited in the notes as *Reminiscences*).

7. Gertrude Beeks to Eva McDonald Valesh, 21 December 1907, "The Correspondence of Eva McDonald Valesh," microfilm, National Civic Federation Records, Manuscripts and Archives Division, New York Public Library, Astor, Lenox and Tilden Foundations (hereafter cited in notes as NCF Records, NYPL).

8. *Reminiscences*, 125–26.

9. Ibid., 125.

10. Ibid., 137–38.

11. Ibid., 90.

12. Ibid., 102.

13. Ibid., 86.

14. Ibid., 87.

15. Mandel, *Samuel Gompers*, 89–90.

16. *Reminiscences*, 85–86.

17. Eva McDonald Valesh, "Wage-Working Women," *American Federationist* 13 (1906): 963–67; Samuel Gompers, "Should the Wife Help to Support the Family?" *American Federationist* 13 (1906): 36. For articles on women in unions, see, among others, Esther Taber, "Women in Unions," *American Federationist* 12 (1905): 927–28; Sophie Yudelsohn, "Women in Unions," *American Federationist* 13 (1906): 19–21; John R. Commons, "Women in Unions," *American Federationist* 13 (1906): 382–83.

18. See Eva McDonald Valesh, "Three Notable Lines of Labor Work," *American Federationist* 8 (1901): 454–62; Irene Ashby-McFadden, "Abolish Child Labor," *American Federationist* 9 (1902): 19–20, and "Child Life vs. Dividends," *American Federationist* 9 (1902): 215–23; "Child Labor Symposium," *American Federationist* 10 (1903): 339–60; "Child Labor Laws," excerpt of Florence Kelley's report to the National Consumers' League, *American Federationist* 12 (1905): 391, 467–68, 536; Eva McDonald Valesh, "Child Labor," *American Federationist* 14 (1907): 157–72; Eva McDonald Valesh, "Child Labor Legislation," *American Federationist* 16 (1909): 675.

19. Eva Valesh would emulate the style of the *American Federationist* down to columns on organizational work and financial statements when she later established her own journal.

20. On the AFL in the 1906 campaign, see Julie Greene, *Pure and Simple Politics: The American Federation of Labor and Political Activism, 1881–1917* (Cambridge, 1998), 105–14; Philip S. Foner, *The History of the Labor Movement in the United States*, vol. 3, *The Policies and Practices of the American Federation of Labor, 1900–1909* (New York, 1964), 308–34.

21. Greene, *Pure and Simple Politics*, 166–67; Foner, *The History of the Labor Movement in the United States*, 3: 335–66.

22. Eva McDonald Valesh to Gertrude Beeks, 20 September (1906?); Valesh to Beeks, 11 November 1908, NCF Records, NYPL.

2. Lawrence Glickman, *A Living Wage: American Workers and the Making of Consumer Society* (Ithaca, N.Y., 1998).

24. See Samuel Gompers, "Attitudes of Labor toward Government Regulation of Industry," *Annals of American Academy of Political and Social Science* 32 (July 1908): 75–81. Also note Michael Rogin, "Voluntarism: The Political Uses of an Anti-Political Doctrine," *Industrial and Labor Relations Review* 15 (July 1962): 521–35; George Gilmary Higgins, *Voluntarism in Organized Labor in the United States, 1930–1940* (1944; New York,

1969); Eugene T. Sweeney, "The AFL's Good Citizen, 1920–1940," *Labor History* 13 (Spring 1972): 200–216.

25. Foner, *The History of the Labor Movement in the United States*, 3: 32–110.

26. Andrew Edward Neather, "Popular Republicanism, Americanism, and the Roots of Anti-Communism, 1890–1925," Ph.D. diss. (Duke University, 1994), is the best analysis of craft-union republicanism, esp. 31–223. See also Linda Schneider's insightful study, "American Nationality and Workers' Consciousness in Industrial Conflict, 1870–1920: Three Case Studies," Ph.D. diss. (Columbia University, 1975), and "The Citizen Striker: Workers' Ideology in the Homestead Strike of 1892," *Labor History* 23 (Winter 1982): 47–66.

27. The idea of the citizen worker first emerged in the Progressive Era among social scientists who argued for the shifting of the basis of citizenship away from residence to wage-earner status. See Kirk Porter, *A History of Suffrage in the United States* (Chicago, 1918), for one of the first expressions of this argument.

28. Tom Arter, Macon, Georgia, letter to *Monthly Journal of the International Association of Machinists* 3:8 (September 1891), 246, quoted in Neather, "Popular Republicanism," 152.

29. Patricia A. Cooper, *Once a Cigar Maker: Men, Women, and Work Culture in American Cigar Factories, 1900–1919* (Urbana, Ill., 1987), 4. The literature on masculinity in the skilled trades has become prolific. See David Montgomery, *Workers' Control in America: Studies in the History of Work, Technology, and Labor Struggles* (Cambridge, 1979); Anne Phillips and Barbara Taylor, "Sex and Skill: Notes toward a Feminist Economics," *Feminist Review* 6 (October 1980): 79–88; Mary Blewett, "Manhood and the Market: The Politics of Gender and Class among the Textile Workers of Fall River, Massachusetts,, 1870–1880," in *Work Engendered: Toward a New History of American Labor*, ed. Ava Baron (Ithaca, N.Y., 1992), 92–113; Nancy A. Hewitt, " 'The Voice of Virile Labor': Labor Militancy, Community Solidarity, and Gender Identity among Tampa's Latin Workers, 1880–1921," in *Work Engendered: Toward a New History of American Labor*, 142–67; Alice Kessler-Harris, "Treating the Male as 'Other': Re-defining the Parameters of Labor History," *Labor History* 34 (Spring–Summer 1993): 190–204; Ileen DeVault, " 'To Sit among Men,': Skill, Gender, and Craft Unionism in the Early American Federation of Labor," in *Labor Histories: Class, Politics and the Working-Class Experience*, ed. Eric Arnesen, Julie Greene, and Bruce Laurie (Urbana, Ill., 1998), 259–83.

30. *American Federationist* (April 1911), excerpted in Samuel Gompers, *Labor and the Employer*, comp. and ed. Hayes Robbins (New York, 1920), 141–42.

31. Gompers, *Seventy Years of Life and Labor*, 156–57; Mandel, *Samuel Gompers*, 27–28.

32. Gompers, *Seventy Years of Life and Labor*, 1: 8–9, 494.

33. "Labor," *Tribune*, 12 August 1894.

34. Testimony before the Industrial Commission, Washington, D.C., 18 April 1899, in Gompers, *Labor and the Employer*, 134.

35. George McNeill, testimony, U.S. Industrial Commission, *Report on the Relations of Labor and Capital Employed in Manufactures and General Business*, vol. 1 (Washington, D.C., 1901), 118, quoted in Neather, "Popular Republicanism," 161.

36. Eva McDonald Valesh, "Woman and Labor," *American Federationist* 2 (February 1896): 223.

37. Eva McDonald, "The Factory's White Slave," *Journal of United Labor* 9 (18 April 1889).

38. Eva Gay, "Working in the Wet," *St. Paul Globe*, 15 April 1888.

39. "Woman and Labor," which reprinted the speech Valesh made at the 1891 convention. See American Federation of Labor, *Proceedings of the Eleventh Annual Convention*, Birmingham, Ala., 14–19 December 1891, 26–27.

40. Valesh, "Woman and Labor."

41. American Federation of Labor, *Proceedings of the Eleventh Annual Convention*, 36; Alice Henry, *The Trade Union Woman* (New York, 1915), 37.

42. Foner, *Women and the American Labor Movement*, 1: 220–22, 226, 229, 234; Kenneally, *Women and American Trade Unions*, 20, 23; Alice Kessler-Harris, "Where Are the Organized Women Workers?" *Feminist Studies* 3 (1975): 99.

43. Valesh, "Wage-Working Women." The article was reprinted by other labor newspapers; see, for example, *Labor Clarion* (San Francisco), 7 December 1906, citation courtesy of Rebecca Mead.

44. Gompers, "Should the Wife Help to Support the Family?"

45. Valesh, "Wage-Working Women," 965.

46. Ibid.

47. Eva McDonald Valesh, "The Ethics of the Labor Movement," *Trades and Labor Directory of Minneapolis and St. Paul* (Minneapolis, 1892), 85, 88–89.

48. Valesh, "Child Labor."

49. Annual Report to the AFL Convention, Cincinnati, Ohio, December 1896, in Samuel Gompers, *Labor and the Common Welfare*, comp. and ed. Hayes Robbins (New York, 1919), 5–6.

50. Annual Report to the AFL Convention, St. Louis, Missouri, December 1888, in Gompers, *Labor and the Employer*, 118–19.

51. Valesh, "Child Labor," 172.

52. Annual Report to the AFL Convention, Detroit, December 1890, in Gompers, *Labor and the Employer*, 119–20.

53. *American Federationist* (January 1914), in Gompers, *Labor and the Employer*, 127.

54. Annual Report to the AFL Convention, Scranton, Pa., December 1901, in Gompers, *Labor and the Employer*, 121.

55. Eva McDonald Valesh, "Labor Unions and Good Citizenship," *American Federationist* 16:10 (October 1909): 871.

56. From the circular "Labor Omnia Vincit" to "All Wage-Workers of America" (1894), excerpted in Gompers, *Labor and the Employer*, 4. Compare the argument that "trade unions were 'clogging the wheels by 'strikes' and 'waging war against natural law,' and legislation in this area would lead only to unrest and hard times." Sidney Fine, *Laissez Faire and the General Welfare State: A Study of Conflict in American Ideas, 1865–1900* (Ann Arbor, 1956), 44, 62.

57. "Labor," *Tribune*, 28 April 1895. See also Frank Valesh, "Alleged Anti-Trust Laws," *American Federationist* 4:2 (1897), 25–26.

58. *American Federationist* (April 1916), in Gompers, *Labor and the Employer*, 149, and *Labor and the Common Welfare*, 54, 51; Mollie Ray Carroll, *Labor and Politics: The Attitude of the American Federation of Labor toward Legislation and Politics* (New York, 1923).

59. *American Federationist* (January 1917), in Gompers, *Labor and the Employer*, 153.

60. See Carroll, *Labor and Politics*, 75ff.

61. This was an era of pauper disenfranchisement, poll taxes, and restriction of suffrage; the fear that dependency might lead to the loss of political rights was certainly a reasonable one.

62. *American Federationist* (January 1914), in Gompers, *Labor and the Common Welfare*, 127.

63. Philip Foner, *History of the Labor Movement in the United States*, vol. 3, *The Policies and Practices of the American Federation of Labor, 1900–1909* (New York, 1964), 336ff.

64. Catherine Collomp, "Unions, Civics, and National Identity: Labor's Reaction to Immigration, 1881–1897," *Labor History* 29 (1988): 450–74.

65. Eva McDonald Valesh, "The Right to Quit," *American Federationist* 16 (September 1909): 770–78, and "Labor Unions and Good Citizenship." On the end of the strike, see Eva McDonald Valesh, "Problems to Be Solved," *American Federationist* 16 (October 1909): 871–76.

66. Valesh, "Labor Unions and Good Citizenship."

67. See John Commons, *Races and Immigrants in America* (New York, 1907), 222, for the restriction of craft-union membership to those who have applied for naturalization papers or who are already naturalized or born citizens of the United States.

68. Jeff Hearn, *The Gender of Oppression: Men, Masculinity, and the Critique of Marxism* (London, 1988), 76.

69. Washington, D.C., city directories. Valesh resided at 1407 F Street, next to the office, in 1900–1901; at the Plaza at 2214 Pennsylvania Avenue in 1903; and at 815 Connecticut Avenue in 1907.

70. Dolores Lautman to the author, 3 September 1994.

71. The photograph of Eva and her son appears in Ada Patterson, "Eva McDonald Valesh, Joan of Arc of the Women of the Laboring Classes," *Human Life* (December 1908), 21ff. The other photograph is in the family collection of Dolores Valesh Lautman.

72. In a letter to Gertrude Beeks of the NCF she wrote, "I am seldom visible before 10:30 in the morning, unless there is something special on hand" (Valesh to Beeks, 20 November 1903, NCF Records, NYPL).

73. *Reminiscences*, 103.

74. Samuel Gompers to Eva McDonald Valesh, 20 January 1898, Gompers Letterbooks, reel 14, vol. 22, p. 413.

75. Reminiscences of Blanche MacDonald, 1956, quoted in Rhoda R. Gilman, "Eva McDonald Valesh, Minnesota Populist," in *Women of Minnesota*, ed. Barbara Stuhler and Gretchen Kreuter (St. Paul, 1977), 55.

76. Samuel Gompers to Eva McDonald Valesh, wire, 2 July 1902, reel 45, vol. 58, p. 921; Gompers to Valesh, 4 August 1902, reel 45, vol. 58, pp. 743–45; Gompers to Frank Morrison, 4 August 1902, reel 45, vol. 58, pp. 746–47, all in Gompers Letterbooks; *Reminiscences*, 6–7. Patterson (in "Eva McDonald Valesh") has a photograph of Eva Valesh and Blanche McDonald with British trade unionist John Burns.

77. Eva Valesh to Gertrude Beeks, 27 January 1909, on having charged a hotel bill to Beeks's account: "I'm truly one of those thriftless people we were talking of at lunch." A series of letters followed, in which Ralph Easley, the head of the NCF, was involved. Beeks to Valesh, 29 January 1909; Valesh to Beeks, 30 January 1909; Easley to Valesh, 2 February 1909; Beeks to Valesh, 3(?) February 1909; Easley to Valesh, 3 February 1909. All in NCF Records, NYPL.

78. On her second European trip, see Eva McDonald Valesh to Gertrude Beeks, n.d. (1906?); Valesh to Beeks, 8 January 1909, NCF Records, NYPL; *Reminiscences*, 141ff. She asked each of her friends for a hundred dollars, rather than taking a loan from the bank.

79. Divorce Papers, copy 4 and 5 048, "Summons and Complaint," State of Minnesota, Hennepin County District Court, 4th Judicial District, Eva Valesh Plaintiff, Frank Valesh Defendant, 26 November 1906, Case 100056, State of Minnesota, 4th Judicial District, *Valesh v. Valesh*, Judgment Roll, 7 March 1907, final divorce decree, Eva McDonald Valesh Papers, MHS; W. J. Murphy to Frank Valesh, Graceville, Minnesota, 11 July 1907, Lautman Papers, Dolores Lautman to the author, 27 January 1993.

Chapter 8. *"Joan of Arc of the Women of the Laboring Classes"*

1. *Reminiscences of Eva McDonald Valesh* (1952), pp. 9–10, in the Columbia University Oral History Research Office Collection (hereafter cited in the notes as *Reminiscences)*.

2. "I ask you to keep your eyes open for the occasional talented girl among the workers" (Eva McDonald Valesh, "Women in Welfare Work," *American Federationist* 15 [April 1908[: 282–84).

3. In effect, her days as a working stiff lie in front of her, as Valesh would spend the last twenty-five years of her life as a proofreader for the *New York Times*.

4. *Reminiscences*, 117.

5. Valesh, "Women and Welfare Work."

6. For the use of terms like *experience* and *authenticity*, see Joan W. Scott, "The Evidence of Experience," *Critical Inquiry* 17 (Summer 1991): 773–97.

7. Debs quoted in Marguerite Green, *National Civic Federation and the American Labor Movement* (Washington, D.C., 1956), 242.

8. See Julie Greene, *Pure and Simple Politics: The American Federation of Labor and Political Activism, 1881–1917* (Cambridge, 1998).

9. On the Chicago Civic Federation, see Richard Schneirov, *Labor and Urban Politics: Class Conflict and the Origins of Modern Liberalism in Chicago, 1864–97* (Urbana, Ill., 1998), 329–63.

10. The best work on the connections between the NCF and the AFL is Green, *The National Civic Federation and the American Labor Movement*. See also James Weinstein, *The Corporate Ideal in the Liberal State, 1900–1918* (Boston, 1968); Gerald Kurland, *Seth Low: The Reformer in an Urban Industrial Age* (New York, 1971).

11. It is interesting to note in this regard that the legal council for Gompers and Mitchell in the *Buck's Stove* case was Wall Street lawyer Alton B. Parker, later president of the NCF; Andrew Carnegie was a major contributor to the defense fund. See Weinstein, *Corporate Ideal in Liberal America*, 16.

12. Eva McDonald Valesh to Gertrude Beeks, n.d. (1906?), 20 September 1906, 21 December 1907; Beeks to Valesh, 22 September 1906. All in "The Correspondence of Eva McDonald Valesh," NCF Records, NYPL.

13. Valesh to Beeks, n.d. (1906?), 27 January 1909, NCF Records, NYPL.

14. The characterization of women's reform efforts in the Women's Municipal Club in New York by Elizabeth Ann Payne, *Reform, Labor, and Feminism: Margaret Dreier Robins and the Women's Trade Union League* (Urbana, Ill., 1988), 24.

15. On this social world, see Elisabeth Marbury, *My Crystal Ball: Reminiscences* (London, 1924); May King Van Rensselaer with Frederick Van de Water, *The Social Ladder* (New York, 1924); Florence Jaffray (Mrs. J. Borden) Harriman, *From Pinafores to Politics* (New York, 1923); Peter Geidel, "Alva E. Belmont, a Forgotten Feminist," Ph.D.

diss. (Columbia University, 1993); Alfred Allan Lewis, *Ladies and Not-So-Gentle Women* (New York, 2000).

16. Harriman, *From Pinafores to Politics*, 75ff; Elsie de Wolfe, *After All* (New York, 1935), 55–66; Jane S. Smith, *Elsie de Wolfe: A Life in High Style* (New York, 1982), 102–12, quotation from p. 103.

17. Eva Valesh to Gertrude Beeks, 11 May 1908, on the wage statement on women artisans; Eva McDonald Valesh, "The Wages of Women Workers: They Should Be Equal to That of Men for the Same Class of Work," MSS enclosed in letter, NCF Records, NYPL.

18. Mary Kingsley Simkhovitch, "Friendship and Politics," *Political Science Quarterly* 17 (June 1902): 189–205; Jane Addams, *Democracy and Social Ethics*, ed. Anne Firor Scott (Cambridge, 1964).

19. Gertrude Beeks to Eva Valesh, 1 March 1908 and 2 March 1908; Valesh to Beeks, 2 March 1908, NCF Records, NYPL.

20. *Reminiscences*, 120.

21. Mary Tolford Wilson, "Anne Tracy Morgan," *Notable American Women: The Modern Period*, ed. Barbara Sicherman and Carol Hurd Green with Ilene Kantrov and Harriette Walker (Cambridge, 1980), 498–99; Henry Hope Reed, "Elisabeth Marbury," *Notable American Women: A Biographical Dictionary*, vol. 2, ed. Edward T. James, Janet Wilson James, and Paul S. Boyer (Cambridge, 1971), 493–95; Marbury, *My Crystal Ball*; Susan Ware, "Florence Jaffray Hurst Harriman," *Notable American Women*, 2: 314–15; Harriman, *From Pinafores to Politics*; Kristie Miller, *Ruth Hanna McCormick: A Life in Politics* (Albuquerque, N.M., 1992).

22. *Reminiscences*, 119.

23. Gertrude Beeks to Eva Valesh, 3 March 1908 and 4 March 1908, NCF Records, NYPL.

24. See Ellen Du Bois, "Working Women, Class Relations, and Suffrage Militance: Harriot Stanton Blatch and the New York Woman Suffrage Movement, 1894–1909," *Journal of American History* 74 (June 1987): 34–58; see also Du Bois's *Harriot Stanton Blatch and the Winning of Woman Suffrage* (New Haven, Conn., 1997).

25. Eva Valesh to Gertrude Beeks, 11 March 1908, NCF Records, NYPL.

26. "Mrs. Taft to Aid Workers," *Washington Post*, 16 March 1909.

27. "Will Feed Workmen," *Washington Post*, 16 March 1909; "Plans to Aid Women," *Washington Post*, 28 March 1909; "What Miss Morgan's Visit Did," *Washington Post*, 28 March 1909; "Street Car Crews at Tea," *Washington Post*, 13 April 1909; "Jeers Turned to Cheers," *Washington Post*, 19 June 1909; "Lunchroom for Brooklyn Navy Yard Mechanics," *National Civic Federation Review* 3 (July 1909): 16–18; "Industrial and Government Phases of Occupation," *National Civic Federation Review* 3 (July 1909): 22–24.

28. Gompers to R. L. Jordan, president, National Retail Liquor Dealers Association, 8 July 1904, Gompers Letterbooks, reel 78, vol. 90, p. 834, LC.

29. "Girls Favor a Union," *Washington Post*, 21 March 1909; "Plan a Fair Invasion," *Washington Post*, 26 March 1909; "Unions to Aid Girls," *Washington Post*, 5 April 1909.

30. *Reminiscences*, 122.

31. Ibid., 123.

32. "Plan a Fair Invasion," *Washington Post*, 26 March 1909; "Meet as Sisters," *Washington Post*, 20 March 1909.

33. "To Speak for Women," *Washington Post,* 19 March 1909; "Meet as Sisters," *Washington Post,* 20 March 1909. The speech was published as Elisabeth Marbury, "Organization the Remedy," *American Federationist* 16 (May 1909): 433–36.

34. "Meet as Sisters," *Washington Post,* 20 March 1909.

35. "Unions to Aid Girls," *Washington Post,* 5 April 1909.

36. "Women Ask More Pay," *Washington Post,* 23 March 1909; "Plans to Aid Women," *Washington Post,* 28 March 1909.

37. "Women Ask More Pay," *Washington Post,* 23 March 1909; "Plan a Fair Invasion," *Washington Post,* 26 March 1909; "Girls Appeal to Congress," *Washington Post,* 3 April 1909; "Unions to Aid Girls," *Washington Post,* 5 April 1909.

38. "Statistician Takes Poison," *Washington Post,* 24 March 1909; "C. A. Hall Asks Divorce," *Washington Post,* 3 April 1909; "Union to Get Charter," *Washington Post,* 24 March 1909.

39. "Meet as Sisters," *Washington Post,* 20 March 1909.

40. "Plans to Aid Women," *Washington Post,* 28 March 1909; "Will Aid Bureau Women," *Washington Post,* 16 April 1909; "Seek a Moral Uplift," *Washington Post,* 17 April 1909.

41. "Seek a Moral Uplift," *Washington Post,* 17 April 1909; "Angered by Dispatch," *Washington Post* 18 April 1909; George P. Foster, chairman, Executive Board, Washington Plate Printers' Union, No. 2, "Marriage as Proof," *Washington Post,* 18 April 1909; "They Need No Inquiry," *Washington Post,* 19 April 1909.

42. Ralph Easley to Eva McDonald Valesh, 21 April 1909, on letter sent to Mrs. Grace Brock, referring to "Washington Flurry"; see also Easley to Grace Brock, 21 April 1909; Valesh to Easley, 22 April 1909, NCF Records, NYPL.

43. See *Reminiscences,* 129–30, 151, on resigning from the AFL. The timing is not clear. Both she and WTUL members asserted she was an official AFL representative. See Eva McDonald Valesh to Mary Dreier, 17 February 1910; Valesh to Dreier, 16 April 1910, letter of resignation, both transcribed in National Executive Board Minutes, 20 May 1910, National Women's Trade Union League Papers, Library of Congress (hereafter cited in notes as NWTUL Papers, LC); Mary Dreier to Gretchen (Margaret Dreier Robins), 12 April 1910, Robins Papers, reel 21, fr. 0581, Women's Trade Union League Papers, microfilm edition (hereafter cited in notes as WTUL Papers); New York Women's Trade Union League, Special Executive Board Minutes, 28 January 1910, Collection 4, microfilm reel 1, fr. 0532, WTUL Papers.

44. Standard accounts of the strike are, among others, Helen Marot, "A Woman's Strike—an Appreciation of the Shirtwaist Makers of New York," *Proceedings of the Academy of Political Science of the City of New York* (New York, 1910), 119–28; Lawrence Levine, *The Ladies Garment Workers: A History of the International Ladies Garment Workers Union* (New York, 1924), 144–67; Nancy Schrom Dye, *As Equals and as Sisters: Feminism, the Labor Movement and the Women's Trade Union League of New York* (Columbia, Mo., 1980), 88–121; Meredith Tax, *The Rising of the Women* (New York, 1980), 205–40. For a provocative rereading, see Nan Enstad, *Ladies of Labor, Girls of Adventure: Working Women, Popular Culture, and Labor Politics at the Turn of the Twentieth Century* (New York, 1999), 84–160.

45. Dye, *As Equals and as Sisters,* 88–90. As Enstad argues in *Ladies of Labor,* beneath the official list of grievances there lie unexplored the issue of sexual harassment of working women.

46. National Executive Board Minutes, 20 May 1910, NWTUL Papers, LC.

47. "Autos for Workers in Shirtwaist War," *New York Times*, 21 December 1909; "Waist Strike Pickets Parade through Shop Districts in Autos," *New York Call*, 22 December 1909; National Executive Board Minutes, Friday morning session, 20 May 1910, NWTUL Papers, LC.

48. "Mrs. Belmont on Girls' Bond," *New York Times*, 20 December 1909; "Autos for Strikes in Shirtwaist War," *New York Times*, 21 December 1909; "More Aid for Girl Strikers," *New York Times*, 29 December 1909.

49. Colette Hyman, "Labor Organization and Female Institution-Building: The Chicago Women's Trade Union League, 1904–1924,"in *Women, Work, and Protest: A Century of U.S. Women's Labor History*, ed. Ruth Milkman (Boston, 1984), 22–41; Karen M. Mason, " 'Feeling the Pinch': The Kalamazoo Corset Makers Strike of 1912," in *"To Toil the Livelong Day": America's Women at Work, 1780–1980*, ed. Carol Groneman and Mary Beth Norton (Ithaca, N.Y., 1987), 141–60.

50. Margaret Dreier Robins, 1916, quoted in Diane Kirkby, *Alice Henry: The Power of Pen and Voice. The Life of an Australian American Labor Reformer* (Cambridge, 1991), 73.

51. Marot, "A Woman's Strike," 121.

52. Enstad, *Ladies of Leisure*, 93–101, 129–30.

53. "Autos for Strikers in Shirtwaist War," *New York Times*, 21 December 1909; "Hope to End Strike by New Year," *New York Times*, 24 December 1909; "Facing Starvation to Keep Up Strike," *New York Times*, 25 December 1909; "Strike End Near, Both Sides Assert," *New York Times*, 27 December 1909; "Invade Wall Street in Strikers' Behalf," *New York Times*, 30 December 1909; "Strikers Vote Down Peace Plan," *New York Times*, 31 December 1909; "State Arbitrators in Girls' Strike," *New York Times*, 4 January 1909; "Strike Funds Low," *New York Times*, 5 January 1909; "New Trade Union," *New York Tribune*, 22 January 1909.

54. Françoise Basch, introduction to Theresa Serber Malkiel, *The Diary of a Shirtwaist Striker* (New York, 1910), 50–51; Sally M. Miller, "From Sweatshop Worker to Labor Leader: Theresa Malkiel, a Case Study," *American Jewish History* 68 (December 1978): 189–205.

55. "Strike Near End, Both Sides Assert," *New York Times*, 27 December 1909; "Invade Wall Street," *New York Times*, 30 December 1909; "Strikers Vote Down Peace Plan," *New York Times*, 31 December 1910; "State Arbitration in Girls' Strike," *New York Times*, 4 January 1910; "Strike Funds Low," *New York Times*, 5 January 1910.

56. "New Trade Union," *New York Tribune*, 22 January 1910. It is on this meeting, Malkiel's *Diary*, and subsequent discussions in the WTUL that most historians base their scant knowledge of Valesh's labor politics. See, for example, Dye, *As Equals and as Sisters*, 102; Tax, *The Rising of the Women*, 231–34; Mari Jo Buhle, *Women and American Socialism, 1880–1920* (Urbana, Ill., 1981), 200; Du Bois, *Harriot Stanton Blatch*, 117–18; Enstad, *Ladies of Leisure*, 108, 150.

57. Mary Dreier to Eva McDonald Valesh, 25 February 1910, transcript, NWTUL Executive Board Minutes, 20 May 1910; Valesh to Helen Marot, 25 January 1910, Executive Board Minutes, both in NWTUL Papers, LC. Margaret Dreier Robins quoted in New York WTUL, Executive Board, Special Meeting, Minutes, 28 January 1910, Collection 4, microfilm reel 1, fr. 0530, WTUL Papers; Samuel Gompers to Anne Morgan, 27 January 1910, Gompers Letterbooks, microfilmed, vol. 152, reel 140, pp. 995–96, LC; "To Unite Women's Unions," *New York Times*, 30 January 1910.

58. Raymond Robins to Margaret Dreier Robins, 3 February and 5 February 1910, both in cited in Tax, *The Rising of the Women*, 239–40; Mary Dreier to Gretchen (Margaret Dreier Robins), 17 February 1910, Margaret Dreier Robins Papers, reel 21, fr. 0537, WTUL Papers.

59. Malkiel, *Diary of a Shirt Waist Striker*, 45, 68–69.

60. Eva McDonald Valesh to Gertrude Beeks, 13 March 1908, NCF Records, NYPL.

61. Eva McDonald Valesh to Helen Marot, 28 April 1910, transcript in National Executive Board Minutes, 20 May 1910, NWTUL Papers, LC.

62. Eva McDonald Valesh to Mary Dreier, 26 February 1910; Dreier to Valesh, 1 March 1910; Valesh to Dreier, 8 March 1910, transcripts in NWTUL Executive Board Minutes, 20 May 1910, NWTUL Papers, LC; New York Women's Trade Union League Executive Board, Special Meeting, 23 March 1910, Minutes, microfilm, Collection 4, reel 1, fr. 0556, WTUL Papers.

63. Mary Dreier to Gretchen (Margaret Dreier Robins), 12 April 1910, Margaret Dreier Robins Papers, microfilm reel 21, fr. 0580, WTUL Papers; Eva McDonald Valesh to Mary Dreier, 16 April 1910, letter of resignation; Helen Marot to Valesh, 22 April 1910; Valesh to Marot, 28 April 1910. All transcripts and hearing records in National Executive Board Minutes, 20 May 1910, NWTUL Papers, LC; New York Women's Trade Union League, Special Executive Board Meeting, 30 April 1910, Minutes, Collection 4, microfilm reel 1, fr. 0572, WTUL Papers.

64. Van Rensselaer, *The Social Ladder*, 35.

65. Marbury, *My Crystal Ball*, 40.

66. Ibid., 219.

67. Du Bois, "Working Women, Class Relations, and Suffrage Militance"; Nancy F. Cott, *The Grounding of Modern Feminism* (New Haven, Conn., 1987), 33; Marbury, "Organization the Remedy."

68. Marbury, *My Crystal Ball*, 34.

69. Marbury's touching tribute to de Wolfe is one of the richest passages of *My Crystal Ball*: "I think I can truthfully state that the great secret of our happiness has lain in the fact that neither of us ever attempted to dominate the individuality of the other" (284).

70. See Du Bois, "Working Women"; Richard Jensen, "Family, Career, and Reform: Women Leaders in the Progressive Era," in *The American Family in Social-Historical Perspective*, ed. Michael Anderson (New York, 1973), 267–80.

Conclusion. Proofing the Truth

1. "Mrs. Valesh's Latest," *Minneapolis Labor Review*, 11 November 1910.

2. *Reminiscences of Eva McDonald Valesh* (1952), pp. 153–54, in the Columbia University Oral History Research Office Collection (hereafter cited in the notes as *Reminiscences*).

3. Ibid., 154.

4. Ibid., 155.

5. Ada Patterson, "Eva McDonald Valesh, Joan of Arc of the Women of the Laboring Classes," *Human Work* (December 1908), clipping in the *New York Journal American* morgue file, Center for American History, University of Texas at Austin.

6. On Valesh joining Alva Belmont's Political Equality League, see "Eva McDonald Valesh," in *A Woman's Who's Who of America*, ed. John Leonard (New York, 1914), 833.

7. Eva McDonald Valesh to Ralph Easley, 24 December 1911, "The Correspondence of Eva McDonald Valesh," microfilm, NCF Records, NYPL. The first number of *American Club Woman* bears the date of December 1911.

8. "Editorially Speaking," *American Club Woman* 1 (December 1911): 1.

9. *Reminiscences*, 155.

10. N. W. Ayer and Son, *American Newspaper Annual and Directory* (Philadelphia, 1916, 1918), gives the subscription list as 151,000 in 1916 and 154,000 in 1918.

11. *Reminiscences*, 182.

12. See, for example, "War Children's Christmas Fund," *American Club Woman* 8 (November 1914): 74; "War Children's Christmas Fund," *American Club Woman* 8 (December 1914): 98; "War Children's Christmas Fund," *American Club Woman* 9 (January 1915): 7–8; "Statement of Finances," *American Club Woman* 9 (January 1915): 10; "From the Little Children," *American Club Woman* 13 (January 1917): 7–8.

13. Mary Ellen Zuckerman, *A History of Popular Women's Magazines in the United States, 1792–1995* (Westport, Conn., 1998), 1–101.

14. *Reminiscences*, 181–82.

15. Ibid., 184.

16. "Crosspatch Farm Scene of Jolity Despite Rain on Labor Day," *Kingston Freeman* (1920); "Halloween at Crosspatch," *Kingston Freeman*, 4 November 1920; "Community House Opened," *Kingston Freeman* (December 1920); "Christmas at Crosspatch," *Kingston Freeman*, 14 December 1920; "For Polish Relief; Mrs. B. Franklin Cross Collects $3,600 for Madame Paderewski," *Kingston Freeman*, 7 February 1921; "Santa Is Coming to Crosspatch," *Kingston Freeman*, 11 December 1922; "Community Christmas at Crosspatch Center," *Kingston Freeman*, 8 December 1924; "Coming Dance at Crosspatch," *Kingston Freeman*, August (192?); "Last Dance at Crosspatch," *Kingston Freeman*, 30 August 1927.

17. *Reminiscences*, 225.

18. Evelyn Cross, "Europe on Your Own," *Kingston Freeman*, 10, 11, and 13 September 1937.

19. *Reminiscences*, 226–27.

20. Ibid., 228.

21. Ibid., 226.

22. See Eva McDonald Valesh Cross to Alice Valesh, 22 February 1914, Valesh Papers, MHS; Benjamin Franklin Cross to Frank Valesh, 5 February 1917, 13 March 1917, Dolores Lautman Papers; Dolores Lautman to the author, 27 January 1993, 27 March 1993.

23. Dolores Lautman to the author, 26 and 30 July 2000; "Eva Valesh, 90, dies; Aide to Gompers," obituary, *New York Times*, 9 November 1956.

24. *Reminiscences*, 227.

25. Dolores Lautman to the author, 27 January 1993.

26. See Eva Valesh Cross to "little daughter Alice," Washington's Birthday (1918?), Eva McDonald Valesh papers, MHS; interviews with Dolores Lautman, Valesh's granddaughter, 25 and 29 July 1993.

27. Carolyn Kay Steedman, *Landscape for a Good Woman: The Story of Two Lives* (New Brunswick, N.J., 1987), 24, 38; Nan Enstad, *Ladies of Labor, Girls of Adventure: Working Women, Popular Culture, and Labor Politics at the Turn of the Twentieth Century* (New York, 1999). See also Cheri Register, *Packinghouse Daughter* (St. Paul, 2000).

Essay on Sources

Writing this biography has been an almost archaeological labor. Tracking down and sifting through a mountain of fragments and piecing them together constituted the vast majority of the work. I have a file bulging with letters from sympathetic librarians and archivists telling me that their indexes revealed nothing of interest or aid. A dozen sent back photocopied newspaper clippings, pointed to new directions for research, or found a listing in a city directory. Late in the game I realized that while this study fit comfortably in cultural history with its attention to language, it was my training in social history that had served me best. For more than three decades, a generation of historians has been working to uncover the history of the working and popular classes by the method of "thick description" (with nods to anthropologist Clifford Geertz). Interpreting city directories, photographs, the backs of envelopes on which notes were written, the clues in letterhead stationery, census data, the back pages of newspapers, and fragmentary manuscripts, they uncovered a history that had missed most of their predecessors. In writing this book, I found that I needed every piece I could find. Social history methodology made possible writing the cultural, intellectual, and political history of Eva McDonald Valesh, the reformers and journalists who inhabited her world, and the working people for whom she served as advocate.

As a journalist and speaker, Eva McDonald Valesh was well-known to her contemporaries, and her activities and opinions were publicized widely at the time. Reading the historical record, however, is somewhat more hit and miss. Valesh appears in the women's history literature both as a promising young populist and as a self-serving middle-aged red-baiter. There is no standard biography, and many of the historical studies in which she makes a fleeting appearance have, thus, made mistakes about who she was and what she was doing. The errors are not surprising. As a journalist, Valesh only occasionally turned her attention to the "lights and shadows" of the past. It has occurred to me she might have preferred life that way.

Eva McDonald Valesh left behind limited sources on her personal and professional life. The single best source is the interview she gave in 1952, four years before her death, to the Columbia Oral History Project, the transcript of which is available on microfiche from Columbia University. The Minnesota Historical Society has the complete interview on microfilm and a portion in typescript. The interview itself is largely factual about her public life, despite some shadings and imaginative retellings. When I doubted, I looked for evidence and sometimes found it, which made me trust her opinions more. It also made me realize that the lapses were largely due to her own memory. That is not to say that Eva Valesh wasn't self-serving. There are some blatant untruths about her first and second husbands. She stated that her husbands died, which was true only in the sense they were dead at the time of the interview. She was twice divorced, not twice widowed. There are minor problems with telescoping of time. And, yes, she lied about her age. She did that more than half her life, so it is with great consistency and with the excuse that she did look younger than her age.

Valesh was, from what I gather, an avid and frequent letter writer. She used her personal correspondence to do her publicity work, keep friends informed, blurt out small confessions, apologize for rudeness, and beg for information. She wanted people on her side, and her rhetoric in letters may be as important as her public rhetoric. Nonetheless, of the thousands of letters that she wrote and received and in which she was mentioned, fewer than two hundred survive, and some of those are not particularly useful. There are reasons for why the bulk have disappeared. In November of 1893, Eva McDonald Valesh wrote Sarah Christie Stevens that she had destroyed "a whole bushel of correspondence" when she moved. Stevens, who kept every scrap of paper about her career, must have been appalled. The warehouse fire that Valesh noted in her oral history interview must have destroyed even more. The pattern of her life, though, was to keep moving and not look back. She, like most of the vast majority of men and women, had little conception of herself as historical.

What remains? The Letterpress Copybooks of Samuel Gompers, stored at the Library of Congress, are on microfilm and contain about forty letters written to Eva Valesh between 1891 and 1914, about ten that make reference to her, and fifteen written to Frank Valesh, most of which are short business letters. The AFL Papers include just three memos. In his research on the AFL, Philip Foner used the papers while they still were housed at the AFL building in Washington, D.C. As researchers have known for some time, the collection was donated to the State Historical Society of Wisconsin and evidently vetted before shipped. Why Eva Valesh's letters, so long after Gompers's death, would have disappeared is unclear; but in the 1950s, Foner read at least four of them, as his footnotes from Vol. 2 reveal. Gompers did not even mention Eva Valesh in his two-volume autobiography, although they worked together in the same office for nine years. He did, however, mention Frank Valesh. It must have been those boxes of Christmas cigars.

The National Civic Federation's Records, housed in the New York Public Library's Rare Books and Manuscript Division, contain the personal and organizational correspondence of Ralph Easley, Gertrude Beeks (Easley), and the NCF's various departments. A search through the NCF Records came up with some one hundred documents, which were microfilmed and now available on the reel, National Civic Federation, the Papers of Eva McDonald Valesh. The bulk of the letters come from boxes 75 and 90 of the collection, which contain the papers of the welfare and woman's departments. The National Women's Trade Union League Papers from the Schlessinger Library at Radcliffe College and the Library of Congress both had manuscript letters and hearings relating to the shirtwaist-makers strike of 1909–10 and Valesh's role. The Schlessinger Library has a small file of materials on Valesh, mostly newspaper clippings relating to her and the play that was performed about her at the North American History Theater in St. Paul in 1984.

The Minnesota Historical Society has several collections about Eva McDonald Valesh. In the Albert Dollenmayer and Family Papers are the fourteen letters from Valesh to Dollenmayer and a letterbook with four of his letters to her. They are wonderful letters, filled with detail and revealing in their intimacy. The James C. Christie Family Papers hold the six letters that Eva McDonald wrote to Sarah Christie Stevens, a Populist candidate for school superintendent. John P. McGaughey's Papers largely refer to his life, including a few interesting letters of reference and a deteriorating scrapbook, but they also hold one of the few copies of the District Assembly #79 Knights of Labor Proceedings (three exist on microfilm in the Powderly Papers). Populist politician and writer Ignatius Donnelly left behind a large manuscript collection that is available on microfilm. His references to Valesh in his writing, clippings, and diary entries are precious. There is as well a small file of Eva McDonald Valesh letters, containing marriage and divorce papers and a wonderful letter she wrote to her daughter-in-law, Alice. Dolores Valesh Lautman of Seattle has a small collection of her father Frank Valesh's papers, to which she gave me access, as well as some family photographs.

Much of Eva Valesh's public writing appeared as newspaper articles, both signed and unsigned, and as speeches, some of which were transcribed or published in article form. It constituted a large body of work, and yet only a small proportion of her journalism can be identified or has survived. The only complete run of the *New York Journal* is in the Humanities Research Center Library of the University of Texas at Austin. The morgue file of that newspaper yielded few articles; I picked up the rest from microfilm and in the scrapbooks on the New Bedford textile strike at the Widener Library of Harvard University.

Valesh, however, worked for over a decade as a reporter for the *St. Paul Globe*, the *Minneapolis Tribune*, and the *New York Journal* and worked as assistant editor for the *American Federationist* for nearly a decade afterwards. Much of her writing and editing went unsigned. Valesh's political letters, syndicated articles for Bacheller and Johnson and the labor press, ghostwritten articles, and occasional pieces for the reform press were next to impossible to track down. The good will of historians who knew I had an interest in Valesh brought me some of what is listed below. Perhaps, once this book is published, more will surface.

There are only a few published primary or secondary biographical sketches of Eva McDonald Valesh. Rhoda R. Gilman, "Eva McDonald Valesh, Minnesota Populist," in *Women of Minnesota*, ed. Barbara Stuhler and Gretchen Kreuter (St. Paul: Minnesota Historical Society Press, 1977), 55–76, is the only scholarly study of any length. Contemporary accounts include Annie L. Diggs, "The Women in the Alliance Movement," *Arena* 6 (1892), 590–604; Albert Dollenmeyer (unsigned), "Eva McDonald Valesh," in *A Woman of the Century*, ed. Frances E. Willard and Mary A. Livermore (New York: Mast, Crowell & Livingston, 1897), 729–30; Ada Patterson, "Eva McDonald Valesh, Joan of Arc of the Women of the Laboring Classes," *Human Life* (December 1908), clipping, morgue file for the *New York Journal American*, Center for American History, University of Texas at Austin; "Eva McDonald Valesh," in *Woman's Who's Who of America*, ed. John W. Leonard (New York: American Commonwealth Co., 1914), 833. Recent biographical entries include Mary Jo Wagner, "Eva McDonald Valesh," *Handbook of American Women's History*, ed. Angela Howard Zophy (New York: Garland, 1990), 633; Elizabeth Faue, "Eva McDonald Valesh," *American National Biography*, vol. 22, (New York: Oxford University Press, 1999), 141–42.

The primary sources I used, both in manuscript and as published, are listed below, including a short bibliography of the writings of Eva McDonald Valesh (aka Eva Gay) and the newspapers read, which exist mostly in microfilm format. After all my work, I know without a doubt that there are articles I missed, letters squirreled in collections that are unindexed, and materials hidden away in some attic. History tells us we will never find it all. It has either been destroyed or mislaid, but some day some enterprising researcher will find more. Send me copies.

Primary Sources

Manuscript Collections

American Federation of Labor Records: The Samuel Gompers Era. State Historical Society of Wisconsin. Microfilm edition.

Christie, James C. and Family. Papers. Minnesota Historical Society.

Dollenmayer, Albert and Family. Papers. Minnesota Historical Society.

Donnelly, Ignatius. Papers. Microfilm edition. Minnesota Historical Society.

Folwell, William. Papers. Minnesota Historical Society.

Gompers, Samuel. *The Letterpress Copybooks of Samuel Gompers*. Library of Congress. Microfilm edition.

Lautman, Dolores V. Private papers. Seattle, Washington.

McGaughey, John P. Papers. Minnesota Historical Society.

Minneapolis Historical Collection. Minneapolis Public Library.

Minnesota Federal Writers' Project. Annals of Minnesota. Subject Files. Microfilm edition. Minnesota Historical Society.

Mitchell, John. Papers. Catholic University. Washington, D.C.

National Civic Federation Records, Manuscript and Archives Division. New York Public Library, Astor, Lenox, and Tilden Foundations.

National Women's Trade Union League. Papers. Schlessinger Library, Radcliffe College. Microfilm edition.

National Women's Trade Union League. Papers. Library of Congress.

New York Journal American morgue. Humanities Research Center Library, University of Texas at Austin.

Powderly, Terence Vincent. Papers. Catholic University. Washington, D.C. Microfilm edition.

Robins, Raymond. Papers. State Historical Society of Wisconsin.

Scrapbook of Clippings Concerning the 1898 Textile Strike at New Bedford. 4 vols. Collected by the former editor of the *New Bedford Evening Standard*. Widener Library, Harvard University.

Valesh, Eva McDonald. The Correspondence of Eva McDonald Valesh. National Civic
 Federation Records. Manuscripts and Archives Division, New York Public Library.
 Astor, Lenox, and Tilden Foundations. Microfilm.
Valesh, Eva McDonald. Papers. Minnesota Historical Society.
Valesh, Eva McDonald. Papers. Schlesinger Library, Radcliffe College.
Valesh, Eva McDonald. *Reminiscences.* Columbia Oral History Project interview. Tran-
 script. Minnesota Historical Society.

Newspapers and Journals

American Club Woman (New York)
American Federationist
Chicago Tribune
Chicago Times
Farm, Stock and Home (Minneapolis)
Farmer's Wife (Topeka)
Great West (St. Paul)
Illinois State Journal (Springfield)
Industrial Age (Duluth)
Interocean (Chicago)
Irish Standard (St. Paul)
Journal of the Knights of Labor
Journal of United Labor
Kingston Freeman (Kingston, N.Y.)
Labor (Duluth)
Labor Echo (St. Paul)
Life and Labor (Chicago)
Minneapolis Daily Tribune
Minneapolis Journal
Minneapolis Labor Review
Minneapolis Star
National Civic Federation Review
National Economist
New York Call
New York Daily Tribune
New York Journal
New York Times
New York World
Northwestern Chronicle (St. Paul)
Northwestern Labor Union (Minneapolis)
Progressive Age (Minneapolis)
Railway Times
St. Paul Daily Globe
St. Paul Pioneer Press
St. Paul Trades and Labor Bulletin
Washington Post
Washington Times

Interviews

Alice Finnerty, phone interview with the author, 7 March 1993.
Dolores Valesh Lautman, interviews with the author, 25 and 29 July 1993, Seattle, Washington.

Published Writings of Eva McDonald Valesh

Cross, Evelyn. "Europe on Your Own." *Kingston Freeman*, 10, 11, and 13 September 1937.
Gay, Eva. " 'Mong Girls Who Toil." *St. Paul Globe*, 25 March 1888.
——. "And So She Flunked." *St. Paul Globe*, 24 February 1889.
——. "Behind the Scenes." *St. Paul Globe*, 22 July 1888.
——. "Can Work the Wires." *St. Paul Globe*, 26 August 1888.
——. "Catches the Ladies." *St. Paul Globe*, 19 March 1889.
——. "A Chapter on Pugs." *St. Paul Globe*, 3 February 1889.
——. "A Curious Class." *St. Paul Globe*, 11 November 1888.
——. "Diamonds . . . Despair." *St. Paul Globe*, 30 September 1888.
——. "Didn't Fill the Bill." *St. Paul Globe*, 2 December 1888.
——. "Dress Reform Craze." *St. Paul Globe*, 17 February 1889.
——. "Eva at a Gymnasium." *St. Paul Globe*, 10 February 1889.
——. "Eva Takes a Bath." *St. Paul Globe*, 4 August 1989.
——. "Eva Gay's Inquiries." *St. Paul Globe*, 20 January 1889.
——. "Eva Gay's Searching." *St. Paul Globe*, 7 October 1888.
——. "Eva Gay's Travels." *St. Paul Globe*, 22 April 1888.
——. "Eva Gay's Travels." *St. Paul Globe*, 6 May 1888.
——. "Girls in Politics." *St. Paul Globe*, 19 August 1888.
——. "Girls Make Boxes." *St. Paul Globe*, 3 June 1888.
——. "Girls Make Cigars." *St. Paul Globe*, 27 May 1888.
——. "Girls Make Money." *St. Paul Globe*, 13 May 1888.
——. "The Girls Rejoice." *St. Paul Globe*, 1 July 1888.
——. "How Girls Clerk." *St. Paul Globe*, 17 June 1888.
——. "In Cap and Apron." *St. Paul Globe*, 15 July 1888.
——. "Life of a Fair One." *St. Paul Globe*, 13 January 1889.
——. "Like Birds of Prey." *St. Paul Globe*, 3 March 1889.
——. "Looking for a Place." *St. Paul Globe*, 9 September 1888.
——. "Makes Girls Blind." *St. Paul Globe*, 25 December 1888.
——. "My Lady's Chamber." *St. Paul Globe*, 27 January 1889.
——. "Not the Sole Aim." *St. Paul Globe*, 18 November 1888.
——. "On the Bright Side." *St. Paul Globe*, 24 June 1888.
——. "Only One Objection." *St. Paul Globe*, 29 July 1888.
——. "Search for Homes." *St. Paul Globe*, 5 August 1888.
——. "The Sewing Girls." *St. Paul Globe*, 10 June 1888.
——. "Shorthand Fever." *St. Paul Globe*, 23 September 1888.
——. "Song of the Shirt." *St. Paul Globe*, 8 April 1888.
——. "Striking Maidens." *St. Paul Globe*, 29 April 1888.
——. *A Tale of the Twin Cities: Lights and Shadows of the Street Car Strike in Minneapolis and St. Paul, Minnesota*. Minneapolis: Thomas Clark Co., 1889.

——. "That You, Central?" *St. Paul Globe*, 12 August 1888.

——. "Their Sunday Out." *St. Paul Globe*, 14 October 1888.

——. "The Toiling Women." *St. Paul Globe*, 1 April 1888.

——. "Up in the World." *St. Paul Globe*, 16 September 1888.

——. "The White Cross." *St. Paul Globe*, 8 July 1888.

——. "Who Keep the Cash." *St. Paul Globe*, 2 September 1888.

——. "Workers in Wool." *St. Paul Globe*, 20 May 1888.

——. "Working in the Wet." *St. Paul Globe*, 15 April 1888.

——. "Yes, You Know Her." *St. Paul Globe*, 4 November 1888.

McDonald, Eva. "The Factory's White Slave." *Journal of United Labor*, 18 April 1889, 1ff.

——. "Far Worse than Slavery." *Journal of United Labor*, 23 August 1888, 1ff.

——. "What Will the Girls Do?" *Journal of United Labor*, 28 February 1889, 1ff.

——. "The Women's Organization." *Journal of United Labor*, 12 July 1888, 1ff.

Valesh, Eva McDonald, ed.. *American Club Woman*, 1914–20.

——. "Au Revoir to Samuel Gompers." *American Federationist* 16 (July 1909): 606.

——. "Arkwright Club Is Worried." *New York Journal*, 12 February 1898.

——. "Bay State Adopts *Journal*'s Plan." *New York Journal*, 3 February 1898.

——. "Changes in Our Governmental System." *National Economist* 7 (3 September 1892): 395.

——. "Child Labor." *American Federationist* 14 (March 1907): 157–73.

——. "Child Labor Legislation." *American Federationist* 16 (August 1909), 672–75.

——. "Conditions of Labor in Europe." *American Federationist* 3 (April 1896): 23–26; (May 1896): 41–43; (June 1896): 64–66; (July 1896): 83–85; (August 1896): 111–13, and (October 1896): 155–56.

——. "Coquetting with the Fire Fiend." *Good Housekeeping* 56 (February 1913): 275–79.

——. "Dingley Calls Strike a Sectional Necessity." *New York Journal*, 25 January 1898.

——. "Education in the Labor Movement." *Railway Times*, 2 September 1895.

——. "The Ethics of the Labor Movement." In *Trades and Labor Directory of Minneapolis and St. Paul*. Minneapolis: Trades and Labor Assembly, 1892. 81–89.

——. "A Historic Conference." *American Federationist* 9 (November 1902): 793–800.

——. "An Instructive Exhibit." *American Federationist* 14 (September 1907): 681–89.

——. "*Journal* Envoys in Havana Today." *New York Journal*, 9 March 1898.

——. "*Journal* Envoys among the Starving." *New York Journal*, 14 March 1898.

——. "*Journal* Plan to End Strike Gladly Accepted." *New York Journal*, 19 January 1898.

——. "*Journal* Strike Inquiry Ordered." *New York Journal*, 28 January 1898.

——. "*Journal* Woman with Strikers." *New York Journal*, 17 January 1898.

——. "*Journal*'s Bill for the Weavers." *New York Journal*, 29 January 1898.

——. "Labor" (Sunday column). *Minneapolis Tribune*, 5 March 1893–December 1896.

——. "Labor Unions and Good Citizenship." *American Federationist* 16 (October 1909): 866–71.

——. "Machinists Win Nine-Hour Day." *American Federationist* 8 (June 1901): 199–201.

——. "McKinley Talks to the *Journal* about the Great Strike." *New York Journal*, 22 January 1898.

——. "Mill Men Fight *Journal*'s Bill." *New York Journal*, 9 February 1898.

——. "Mill Men Will Fight Weavers." *New York Journal*, 11 February 1898.

——. "More Leisure for Women." *Farmer's Wife* (Topeka) (September 1891).

——. "The New Political Economy." *Great West* (February–April 1891).

——. "The People's Movement." *National Economist*, 9 April 1892, 51.

——. "Problems to Be Solved." *American Federationist* 16 (October 1909): 871–76.

——. "A Review of Current Economics." *American Federationist* 8 (August 1901): 301–302.

——. "The Right to Quit." *American Federationist* 16 (September 1909): 770–78.

——. "A Score of A. F. of L. Conventions." *American Federationist* 8 (December 1901): 517–20.

——. "Settled by Arbitration." *American Federationist* 1 (July 1894): 97.

——. "State Listens to a *Journal* Woman; Labor's Champion." *New York Journal*, 9 February 1898.

——. "Strengths and Weaknesses of the People's Movement." *Arena* 6 (1892): 727–31.

——. "Strike Inquiry Now Assured." *New York Journal*, 20 January 1898.

——. "The Tenement House Problem." *Arena* 7 (1893): 580–86.

——. "Three Notable Lines of Labor Work." *American Federationist*. 3 (November 1901): 454–62.

——. "Wage Working Women." *American Federationist* 13 (December 1906): 463–67.

——. "Women and Labor." *American Federationist* 2 (February 1896): 221–23.

——. "Women in Welfare Work." *American Federationist* 15 (April 1908): 282–84.

INDEX